THEMES IN IGWEBUIKE PHILOSOPHY AND THEOLOGY

Ikechukwu Anthony KANU

authorHOUSE®

AuthorHouse™ UK
1663 Liberty Drive
Bloomington, IN 47403 USA
www.authorhouse.co.uk
Phone: UK TFN: 0800 0148641 (Toll Free inside the UK)
       UK Local: (02) 0369 56322 (+44 20 3695 6322 from outside the UK)

Published by AuthorHouse 06/23/2022

ISBN: 978-1-6655-9967-2 (sc)
ISBN: 978-1-6655-9966-5 (e)

In Memory
of
Sir Emmanuel Nwafor Kanu, KSJI
An Igwebuike Philosopher

CONTENTS

INTRODUCTION

The concept *Igwebuike* began first as a methodology and philosophy. Gradually, its philosophical elements began to have serious implications for theological discourse, especially with the increasing need to do theology that arises from the philosophy of the African people. Such a theology would always have an inescapable element of philosophy, speaking to people in their own native context, because it is expressed in categories of thought that arises out of the philosophy of the African people. This affirms the reality of the link between philosophy and theology, especially regarding the links between the great philosophical questions and the mysteries of salvation which are studied in theology under the guidance of the higher light of faith. In *Igwebuike* theology, theology takes on the form of a bridge that connects the human person who lives within the context of a changing culture to God who is beyond the law of change.

The first paper in this collection of essays, focuses on *Igwebuike* theology of *Ikwa Ogwe* which attempts at building a bridge between two conflicting inheritances or worldviews of the African Christian: the Western heritage and the heritage of his/her ancestors. This is followed by *Igwebuike* theology of *Omenani* and *Udi* in relation to the understanding of culture as the seed of the Word of God, which already pre-existed in Africa even before the emergence of the Western missionaries. There is also a focus on *Igwebuike* as a traditional mode of communication.

Igwebuike as a complementary and holistic method of inquiry is also employed in the study of the relationship between the 1883 Code of Canon Law and the Second Vatican Council. This method is employed in the study of the Canon Law and the Holy Bible and the relationship between the Code of Canon Law and the Catechism of the Catholic Church. Focusing on the Scripture, the Ninevites' reaction to Jonah's preaching of doom (Jonah 3:1-10) and the message of unity and harmony in Psalm 133 are studied in relation to *Igwebuike* philosophy.

This piece remains a major contribution to the corpus of literature on *Igwebuike* theology. I, therefore, introduce this piece to all lovers of African theology, culture and philosophy.

IGWEBUIKE THEOLOGY OF IKWA OGWE AND THE CROSS-CULTURAL CONFLICTS OF THE MISSIONARY ERA

Ikechukwu Anthony KANU
Department of Philosophy and Religious Studies
Tansian University Umunya, Anambra State
ikee_mario@yahoo.com

ABSTRACT

This piece on Igwebuike theology of Ikwa Ogwe has attempted at building a bridge between two conflicting inheritances or worldviews of the African Christian: the Western heritage and the heritage of his/her ancestors. The researcher attempted doing this with maturity and creativity, and without destabilizing the wholeness of the African Christian. It defined Igwebuike theology contextually, and the Igwebuike concept of culture as a preparation for the gospel, basing this on Clement of Alexandria's Stromata. This created a basis for an Igwebuike theology of Ikwa Ogwe. It argued that until this bridge is built, the Word of God cannot be effectively communicated-in such a way that the people hearing the Word understand who they are and who others are. It observed that communicating the gospel without building a bridge would rather take people away from themselves, thus, creating a problem of identity. It discovered that the major task of the gospel message, which is the transformation of worldviews and conceptual systems, would not be adequately achieved without Ikwa Ogwe. Igwebuike theology of Ikwa Ogwe, therefore, emphasizes identifying with the people and communicating the message through their categories. The purpose of this study is to make a contribution to the ongoing efforts at resolving the cross-cultural conflicts of the missionary era. The theoretical framework employed is the Igwebuike holistic and complementary understanding of evangelization and culture, which focuses on the bigger picture of reality and believes that all parts of reality are interconnected.

Keywords: *Igwebuike*, Theology, *Ikwa Ogwe*, Missionary Enterprise, Culture, Conflicts

INTRODUCTION

In the 20th century, with the movements towards political changes leading to independence in many African colonial territories, the quest for theological independence became unavoidable.

In the contention of Parratt (2001), "It seemed incongruous to African Christians that while African nations were becoming independent politically, the church in Africa should remain essentially controlled by European missionaries" (p. 2). The late Harold MacMillan, one time British Prime Minister (cited in Mbefo 1989), remarked about the events of the time thus:

> We have seen the awakening of national consciousness in people who have for centuries lived in dependence of some other power… In different places it takes different forms, but it is happening everywhere. A wind of change is blowing through this continent, whether we like it or not (p.11).

The echoing of the quest for freedom within the walls of the Church, as though the struggle for political independence was also a demand for an independent African Church, was unavoidable, since the Church cannot be spoken of in isolation of the world, for the questions that the Church grapples with are the questions raised by and in the world.

Interestingly, around the same period and within the same context of the search for independence, there was a positive appreciation of African traditional beliefs and customs among Africans, together with a marked sense of their cultural identity. There was a great impetus from the literary movement in French-speaking Africa, popularly known as Negritude, which emerged through the study of human sciences, like social or cultural anthropology and sociology, and through the monographs of trained anthropologists and the surveys of scholars such as Geoffrey Parrinder, among others.

The factors that led to a positive appreciation of African traditional beliefs and cultures and the emergence of African theology were not only from within, several external factors also made it possible. Such factors include the contribution of some Western missionaries who observed a problem with the current method of evangelization and, thus, saw the need for a different approach. These include great African missionaries, like Father Placid Tempels, a Belgian priest posted to Belgium DRC Congo where he worked for 29 years, and as a result of his great experience among the Congo nation, he developed the Bantu philosophy, which was rich and systematic in its presentation. Later, missionaries, like Bishop Sundkler and Harold Tuner, promoted the study of African Christian theology by editing several works done by African theologians (Barga, 2012). A second impetus from outside of Africa was the Second Vatican Council which has a positive appreciation of local cultures and called for the need for adaptation in all spheres of Church life, including theology.

The development of *Igwebuike* theology may be considered a third stage in the development of African theology. It is not primarily concerned about the failings of the missionary approach to evangelization, even though it not totality cut off from it. It is not focused on emphasizing the need for an African theology, even though it is a product of that struggle. It rather focuses on attending to the conflicts between the African and Western religious cultures in Christianity for the purpose of making the Christian faith more at home in Africa. This study is important as the African church still lives with the consequences of an unresolved religio-cultural conflict emerging from the encounter between the Missionaries and African culture. To ensure the resolution of the above-established conflict, this piece, therefore, proposes *Ikwa Ogwe* (bridge building) as a method in *Igwebuike* theology for the resolving of this conflict so that the gospel brought to Africa can become culture, and culture becomes the gospel.

THE CONCEPT 'IGWEBUIKE THEOLOGY'

Igwebuike theology is an attempt to make theology more contextual, and as an African theology, it aims at making the African to understand and enter more deeply into the community where they have been placed by God, and to discern and respond to His presence and action in such a manner that greater witness is born. This is contrary to the model that first kicks off by introducing the African into the world of the evangelizer, that through the world of the evangelizer, the African may discern and respond to God's presence and action- this approach leads to conflicts and stunts understanding and appreciation of the faith.

Igwebuike theology is structured on the Incarnate Word who became man at a particular place and time. It is contextual and biblical: the Bible is made up of various books, written to various people from particular places, and such books are shaped by the particularity and peculiarity of the place, and sometimes requiring the knowledge of the particular place and culture to understand the particular text. This is the spirit that animates *Igwebuike* theology. It takes into cognizance the African worldview and the basic elements of the Christian message in African theological discourse.

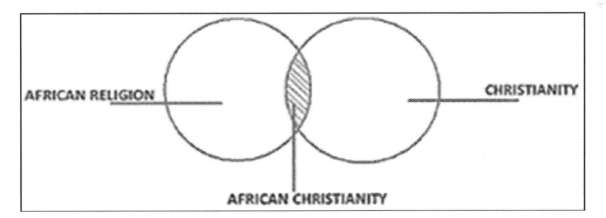

Figure 1- Source: Mndende, M. (2013)

The diagram above from Mndende (2013) describes in a pictorial way what evangelization should have done, and if followed, what evangelization in Africa should have brought about. Evangelization should have taken into cognizance the African culture and religion, which should not only have served as a vehicle for the communication of the Christian message, but would have enriched the Christian message. If this was taken into consideration in most parts of the missionary engagements with African culture and religion, such an engagement should have given birth to an African Christianity.

In defining *Igwebuike* theology, it is worthwhile to mention that *Igwebuike* as a concept began as a methodology and philosophy. However, its philosophical elements are beginning to have serious implications for theological discourse, especially with the increasing need to do theology that arises from the philosophy of the African people. Such a theology would always have an inescapable element of philosophy, speaking to people in their own native context, because it is expressed in categories of thought that arise out of the philosophy of the African people. Thus, the value that the concept *Igwebuike* brings into theology is that it creates a context for theological discussion or reflection, a context that is the African complementary worldview.

This notwithstanding, the expression, *Igwebuike* is a combination of three Igbo words. It can be understood as a word or a sentence: as a word, it is written as *Igwebuike*, and as a sentence, it is written as, *Igwe bu ike,* with the component words enjoying some independence in terms of space. Literally, *Igwe* is a noun which means 'number' or 'multitude', usually a large number or population. The number or population in perspective are entities with ontological identities and significances; however, part of an existential order in which every entity is in relation to the other. *Bu* is a verb, which means *is*. *Ike* is a noun, which means *strength* or *power* (Kanu, 2016a&b). *Igwe, bu* and *Ike* put together, means 'number is strength' or 'number is power' (Kanu, 2017f). However, beyond the literal sense of *Igwebuike,* it means *otu obi* (one heart and one soul) – *cor unum et anima una*. It is used within the Igbo linguistic setting to refer to relational engagement in the world, accomplished in solidarity and complementarity, and the powerful and insurmountable force therein (Kanu, 2017g). The closest words to it in English are complementarity, solidarity and harmony. In this way, *Igwebuike* conceptualizes or captures the nature of the African universe.

What *Igwebuike* does is that it captures the nature of the African universe and uses it as a framework for discussions within theology or philosophy. The value that it brings to the table of theological discussions is its emphasis on the African worldview as an indispensable element in any successful African theological discussion. The purpose or relevance of this framework in philosophical or theological discussions is that it makes such a discussion relevant to the African and his/her environment. As such, *Igwebuike* theology would mean the quest to arrive at a unique understanding of faith in Christ in such a way that it captures the African worldview and the life circumstances of the African people. Only thus will evangelization respond to the inadequacies of the missionary enterprise, give birth to a new African personality, address contextual issues and be in accord with the legitimate aspiration of the African people. The fact of *Igwebuike* theology does not in any way imply a change in the Church's theology- it is the same theology, a systematic and scientific discourse on God, presented in such a way that it fits into the African religious, social, anthropological and philosophical realities, mentality and needs. The focus on Christ, the Scripture and tradition is not altered in any way. They remain the inevitable revelatory agents.

This notwithstanding, *Igwebuike theological* approaches include: understanding theology as contextual, that is, a theology of life and culture that is accountable to the context in which the African people live; understanding reality as complementary and interconnected; understanding African traditional religion and culture as a preparation for the gospel message; understanding theology as an enterprise that provides answers to the African person's innermost and deepest longings, that is, the search for happiness (God). Its sources include: the Bible, Church tradition, African philosophy, religion and culture, African anthropology, and African experiences.

THEORETICAL FRAMEWORK

The theoretical framework employed in this research is the *Igwebuike* holistic and complementary understanding of evangelization and culture. *Igwebuike* as a thought current focuses on the bigger picture of reality and believes that all parts of reality are interconnected. How will this approach affect this study? There are two dimensions to this framework that are relevant to discourses in African theology:

1. *Igwebuike* understands culture as an incomplete enterprise that continues to evolve as long as the human person continues to adapt himself/herself to the environment. When this approach speaks of culture as incomplete, it means that even the Christian culture that was brought by the missionaries was not complete and thus needed the African incomplete culture for its completeness. For the grounding of Christianity in Africa, therefore, the African culture becomes the missing link. While the African culture finds completeness in the Christian culture, the Christian culture would reach its full potential in the African culture, especially as the African people are involved. The incompleteness of the Christian culture here referred to does not speak of the core of the Christian faith; it rather refers to the cultural garment in which it was clothed and brought to the African people.

2. Within the context of the *Igwebuike* framework which is complementary (Kanu 2017), the African culture is understood as not only completing the Christian message that has been brought to Africa, but makes the Christian message richer and more meaningful to the African people than it came. In this sense, the encounter between both cultures has a way of sharpening the different cultural perspectives; that is, if both cultures maintain connection with the resources that are outside of them. In terms of this openness to the other, Torrance (1970) writes that: "One becomes human by making use of the energy available from outer sources to become a better integrated personality, to interact at a deeper level with the environment, and to achieve greater fulfillment of his potentialities" (p. 10). One loses his/her humanness when he/she is

estranged, isolated, rejected, and cut off from other sources of information, inspiration and spiritual strength. This also happens each time a culture denigrates the other rather than allowing the other to enrich her.

This framework will provide the need for understanding culture as a preparation for the gospel message and the basis for the *Igwebuike* theology of *Ikwa Ogwe,* that is, building a bridge between the African culture and the Christian message.

IGWEBUIKE CONCEPT OF CULTURE AS A PREPARATION FOR THE GOSPEL

A major problem with the missionary enterprise is the clear gulf that was created between the African religion and culture and the Christian message, and the stories created around each that made the possibility of their relationship look like the impossibility of heaven and hell meeting together. Rather than understand culture as a disjointed element in relation to the gospel message, *Igwebuike* theology understands it as a preparation for the gospel. The concept of culture as a preparation for the gospel message was analyzed by Clement of Alexandria at a time and in a culture where philosophy was considered worthless and dangerous for Christianity. The African culture was also thought in the same way in relation to Christianity.

In his work, *Stromata,* Clement of Alexandria addressed the issue of the relationship between Greek philosophy and Christianity. This was necessary at a time when Christianity had moved into the Greek world where Neoplatonism was the dominant idea. He argued that pagan philosophy contained seeds of the *Logos* and was given to the Greeks by God to prepare them for the coming of Christ, just as the Law was given to the Hebrews for the same purpose (Mirus 2015). He writes thus:

> Accordingly, before the advent of the Lord, philosophy was necessary to the Greeks for righteousness. And now it becomes conducive to piety; being a kind of preparatory training to those who attain to faith through demonstration. "For thy foot," it is said, "will not stumble, if thou refer what is good, whether belonging to the Greeks or to us, to Providence." For God is the cause of all good things; but of some primarily, as of the Old and the New Testament; and of others by consequence, as philosophy. Perchance, too, philosophy was given to the Greeks directly and primarily, till the Lord should call the Greeks. For this was a schoolmaster to bring "the Hellenic mind," as the law, the Hebrews, "to Christ." Philosophy, therefore, was a preparation, paving the way for him who is perfected in Christ. (*Strom.* 1, 5)

His own interpretation of Greek philosophy is that it was not only necessary for the Greeks as an intellectual enterprise, but very useful in preparing Christians to accept the faith, as well as helping them to understand it better and defend it against error. His idea becomes clearer when we understand that the early Christian thinkers used Neoplatonic concepts to clarify the Christian message, thus, using philosophy as a vehicle for conveying the Christian message.

To give a divine origin to his perspective, Clement traced Greek philosophy to the prophecy of the Old Testament. He took his time to show that, through a comparative study, Plato learned much from the books of Moses. In this, he proved that all wisdom, whether of the Jews or the Greeks, has a common origin: God.

The African culture and religion belong to this category. Thus, *Igwebuike* theology of African culture and religion as a preparation for the gospel message points to the fact that African religion and culture, if appreciated, could contribute to the understanding of the Christian message to the African, as it would deliver the message within categories that the African would understand. It understands African culture and religion as a gift given to the African people from God. Imperfect as it was, it contained great wisdom that kept the African in the path of goodness. This, therefore, creates a basis for the theology of *Ikwa Ogwe* (building a bridge) across the chasm created between African culture and religion, on the one hand, and the Gospel message, on the other hand.

IGWEBUIKE THEOLOGY OF IKWA OGWE

Ikwa Ogwe is taken from the Igbo language, and it means to 'build a bridge'. The *Igwebuike* theology of *Ikwa Ogwe* is based on the complementary relatedness of the African reality and thought which works by building systems and thoughts as a pre-condition for the attainment of true knowledge and gaining insight into reality. It is within this context that Igbo traditional thinkers would say: *onye kwa ogwe amara uche ya* (when a person builds bridges then you know his/her mind). This means that it is only by establishing connections that you come to understand the reality that is being communicated. Understanding reality without recourse to the aspects that make its whole leads to inadequate and dangerous knowledge. The missionary enterprise would have been greater, with less conflict, if such bridges were built across religious cultures.

The idea of *Igwa Ogwe* brings with it a new reality: the understanding of the search for knowledge as a scientific and systematic, as it involves a system that ensures building knowledge from a solid foundation and then making the connections and strengthening what is known. This cannot be understood better with the modern understanding of building bridges. In Igbo traditional societies, bridges were built with bamboo sticks and ropes. This involved standing the bamboo from the ground and connecting different bamboos, taking into cognizance the different angles needed and how the bamboos matched with one another, and then tying them together with rope. It was more of weaving together than just building a bridge. It is this process of making bridges, which follows one step after another (*ime ihe na usoro na usoro*), that makes *Igwebuike* theology a science.

However, according to Asouzu (2007): "No matter the way the master-builder builds the bridge, what makes his art useful is its relevance to all users of the bridge and this he does taking cognizance of the multidimensional composition of all bridge users and not in consideration of the exclusive rights of some individuals" (p. 125). This has great implications for evangelization among a 'local' people and the development of theology. It has to be a theology that is relevant to her users. The missionaries built a theology that was relevant to them while they served as missionaries. However, with the emergence of African theologians, there is the need for the reconstruction of the bridge in such a way that it serves the interest of the African people. The theology of the missionaries lacked the science of weaving together - that which is African and that which is Christian; and the consequence is that it was not very meaningful to the African people.

To refuse to reconstruct the bridge is to await the danger of the collapse of the bridge and everyone would run the risk of being submerged, that is, the collapse of Christianity. It is important at this juncture to make reference to the Christianity in Ethiopia and the Christianity in North Africa. The major reason why Ethiopia remained a Christian nation after the attacks of Muslim Jihadists was because it was a Christianity that had taken home in Africa: there was a weaving together of basisc elements of the Ethiopian religion and culture with the Christian faith for the realization of an Ethiopian Christianity - the context of the Ethiopian people was put into consideration to the point that it has become their religion and not the white man's religion. In the case of North Africa, which produced some of the finest of the Church Fathers, Christianity collapsed, not just because of the Muslim Jihadists attacks, but because it was an opportunity for the people to revolt against the Romans, a Church that taught them in Latin rather than in their local language. It was rather a Roman Church in North Africa.

This systematic framework of bridge building, beginning first from the foundation of understanding the human person who is involved, makes the mission to have a head and a tale (*ihe nwere isi na odu*), that is, that which is complete. It is difficult, if not impossible, to administer a message to the people that you do not know. If you do not know a people, how would you then deliver the message through what Okonkwo (1998 and 2000) refers to as the press of the people? The missionaries built the bridge in such a way that it was so tight that it could not allow for multidimensionality or recognition of the multifarious nature of the bridge users. The consequence is that it has led to chaos in its usage, and in fact this chaos was the basis for the agitation for an African theology and the reconstruction of the missionary approach. This kind of bridge succeeded in blocking communication and stiffening the African church.

CONCLUSION

Africans, as a result of the relationship of centuries that they have had with the West, and the relationship they continue to have with the west through the instrumentality of globalization, have now become a people of two heritages, a kind of a cultural hybrid, the one foreign and the other indigenous. However, our wholeness depends on our ability to handle these inheritances with maturity and creativity. This piece on the *Igwebuike* theology of *Ikwa Ogwe* is an attempt at building a bridge between the two conflicting inheritances or worldviews. It is regarded as a conflict because of the clash of the two worldviews involved in this historical encounter. Such a bridge is possible only when there is a better understanding and appreciation of both religious cultures. To appreciate one and not appreciate the other is the basis of the conflict.

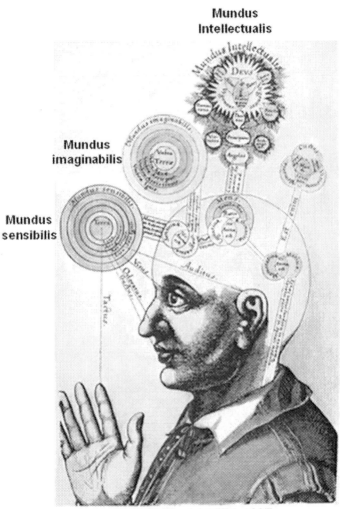

Mundus
Intellectualis

Mundus
imaginabilis

Mundus
sensibilis

Robert Fludd 1574-1637

Figure 2: source- Agnati, et al (2013)

Until this bridge is built, the Word of God cannot be effectively communicated in such a way that the people hearing the Word understand who they are and who others are. Communicating the gospel, without building a bridge, would rather take people away from themselves, thus, creating a problem of identity. The major task of the gospel message, which is the transformation of a people's worldview and their conceptual system, would not be adequately achieved. *Igwebuike* theology of *Ikwa Ogwe*, therefore, emphasizes identifying with the people and communicating the message through the press of the people or the media of the people, using the language imbued with the people's 'mundus sensibilis' (perceived world) which is indicative of their 'locus intellectus' (context for understanding), and putting into consideration the people's pastoral geography and social physics as the Incarnate Christ did. The act of building a bridge between both religious cultures is to ensure that the gospel becomes culture and the culture becomes gospel; thus, the gospel message becomes culturally situated, and tongue-dependent.

REFERENCES

Agnati, F. L. et al (2013). The Neurobiology of Imagination: Possible role of interaction –dominant dynamics and default mode dynamics. *Frontiers in Psychology. Vol. 4. Art. 296.* pp. 1-17.

Asouzu, I. (2007). Ibuanyidanda. New complementary ontology. Beyond world-immanentism, ethnocentric reduction and impositions. Germany: LIT.

Barga, Timothy. *A Pastoral Approach to African Christian Theology.* Jos: Fab Anieh, 2012

Clement of Alexandria, *Stromata.* Fathers of the Church- New Advent. Translated by William Wilson. Edited by Alexander Roberts, James Donaldson, and A. Cleveland Coxe. Buffalo, NY: Christian Literature Publishing Co., 1885

Engineering Discoveries (2018). Why bamboo is more stronger than steel re-enforcement? Retrieved from https://engineeringdiscoveries.com/wp-content/uploads/2019/11/4d31d a0d459a75fc75c62e71fc07243b.jpg

Kanu, A. I. (2017c). *Igwebuike* as an Igbo-African philosophy of inclusive leadership. *Igwebuike: An African Journal of Arts and Humanities.* Vol. 3 No 7. pp. 165-183.

Kanu, A. I. (2017d). *Igwebuike* philosophy and the issue of national development. *Igwebuike: An African Journal of Arts and Humanities.* Vol. 3 No 6. pp. 16-50.

Kanu, I. A. (2016a). *Igwebuike* as an Igbo-African Hermeneutics of Globalisation. *IGWEBUIKE: An African Journal of Arts and Humanities,* Vol. 2 No.1. pp. 61-66.

Kanu, I. A. (2016a). *Igwebuike* as the consummate foundation of African Bioethical principles. *An African journal of Arts and Humanities* Vol.2 No1 June, pp.23-40.

Kanu, I. A. (2016b) *Igwebuike* as an Expressive Modality of Being in African ontology. *Journal of Environmental and Construction Management. 6. 3.* pp.12-21.

Kanu, I. A. (2017). *Igwebuike* as an Igbo-African Philosophy for Christian-Muslim Relations in Northern Nigeria. In Mahmoud Misaeli (Ed.). *Spirituality and Global Ethics* (pp. 300-310). United Kingdom: Cambridge Scholars.

Kanu, I. A. (2017g). *Igwebuike* and the logic (Nka) of African philosophy. *Igwebuike: An African Journal of Arts and Humanities.* 3. 1. pp. 1-13.

Kanu, I. A. (2019). A Hermeneutics of the Igbo-African Kola-Nut as a "Type" of Holy Communion. Nnadiebube Journal of Philosophy Vol. 3. No. 2. pp. 27-40.

Kanu, I. A. (2014a). Igbo proverbs as *depositum* of Igbo-African philosophy. *International Journal of Humanities and Social Sciences. Vol. 4. No. 1.* pp. 164-168.

Kanu, I. A. (2014a). Suicide in Igbo-African ontology. *Developing Countries Studies.* Vol. 4. No. 5. USA. pp. 27-38.

Kanu, I. A. (2014b). Suffering in Igbo-African Ontology. *Research on Humanities and Social Sciences.* Vol. 4. No. 5. pp. 8-13.

Kanu, I. A. (2014b). The place of Igbo myths in Igbo-African philosophy. *American Journal of Contemporary Research. Vol. 4. No. 2.* pp. 98-102.

Kanu, I. A. (2015). African traditional democracy with particular reference to the Yoruba and Igbo political systems. *International Journal of Philosophy and Public Affairs. Vol. 2. No. 3.* pp. 147-160.

Kanu, I. A. (2015). *Personal identity and punishment in John Locke* (A Dissertation for the Award of Master of Arts Degree in Philosophy- Metaphysics), University of Nigeria, Nsukka, Enugu State.

Kanu, I. A. (2015a). *African philosophy: An ontologico-existential hermeneutic approach to classical and contemporary issues.* Nigeria: Augustinian Publications.

Kanu, I. A. (Ed.) (2016a). *Complementary ontology: Provocative essays on Innocent Asouzu's African philosophy of integration for progressive transformation.* Germany: Lambert Academic Publishing.

Kanu, I. A. (Ed.) (2016b). *Ibuanyidanda: A complementary systematic inquiry. Reflections on Innocent Asouzu's African philosophy.* Germany: Lambert Academic Publishing.

Kanu, I. A. (2016). *Igbo-African Christology: A cultural Christological construct in Post-Missionary Africa.* Germany: Lambert Publications.

Kanu, I. A. (2016a). African traditional folk songs as dialogue between education and entertainment. *Cambridge International Journal of Contemporary Education Research.* *6. 6.* pp. 53-64.

Mbefo, L. N. (1989). *Towards a mature African Christianity.* Enugu: Spiritan Publications.

Mirus, Thomas V. (2015). Church Fathers: Clement of Alexandria, Part I. Catholiic Cultuture. org.https://www.catholicculture.org/commentary/articles.cfm?id=655

Mndende, M. (2013). Law and Religion in South Africa: An African Traditional Perspective. *NGTT Journal. Vol. 54. No. 4*

Okonkwo, J. I. (1998). Folks-Media and the New Era of Evangelisation: The Igbo Perspective, In: *Communication Socialis: International Zeitschrift fur Kommunication in Religion, Kirche und Gesselschaft,* Salzburg

Okonkwo, J. I. (1998). Oramedia-Traditions and the Igbo Question in Nigeria: A Philosophy of Identity, In Gehlaar, S. (Ed.), *Prima Philosophia,* Cuxhaven-Dartford

Okonkwo, J. I. (2000). Language and Evangelisation: The Challenges of the Igbo Pastor, In Okonkwo, J. (Ed). *Pastoral Language and Evangelisation.* Enugu, Fourth Dimension Publishers

Parratt John (2001). A Reader in African Christian Theology. New Edition. Great Britain: SPCK

Spanneut, M (2004). Clement of Alexandria. Encyclopedia.com. https://www.encyclopedia.com/people/philosophy-and-religion/roman-catholic-and-orthodox-churches-general-biographies/clement-alexandria

Torrance E. P. (1970). What it means to become human. In Scoby M and Graham G. (Eds.). *To nurture humanness* (pp. 3-13). Washington, Association for Supervision and Curriculum Development.

IGWEBUIKE THEOLOGY OF OMENANI AND THE CRISIS OF THE MISSIONARY BIFURCATION OF HORIZONS

Ikechukwu Anthony KANU
Department of Philosophy and Religious Studies
Tansian University Umunya, Anambra State
ikee_mario@yahoo.com

ABSTRACT

African theology points to the fact that every particular situation or context calls for a particular theological reflection, that is, if the theological reflection is to make meaning within that unique circumstance. It is within this context that the Igwebuike theology of Omenani emerges in relation to the understanding of culture as the seed of the Word of God, which already pre-existed in Africa even before the emergence of the Western missionaries. The purpose of adopting this idea of culture as the seed of the Word of God is to enhance the reconciliation between the African and Christian/Western 'worldhoods'. This piece presented the African culture as an important element in evangelization in Africa, as it is the spirit that animates the African people. It further emphasized the indispensability of integrating the African worldview in the communication of the gospel to the people of African. It, therefore, located the seed of the Word of God in the Omenani (the law of the land) of the African people through which they were able to achieve holiness, even before the advent of the gospel. It observed that the failures of the missionary enterprise were majorly because of missionaries' lack of openness to the African religion and culture. The identification of Omenani as the seed of the Word of God showed that culture is not an enemy of the gospel, but an instrument for its transmission.. The purpose of this study is to bridge the bifurcation created by the missionaries between the Christian and African 'worldhoods'. The theoretical framework employed in this research is the Igwebuike sympathetic and non-derogatory framework, which emphasizes evangelization with a sense of understanding. It is a polite and humane approach, and excludes the influences of bias in the process of knowing and relationship.

Keywords: *Omenani, Logos Spermatikos,* Culture, African, Igbo, Evangelization, *Igwebuike*

INTRODUCTION

African theologians are agreed that the religious invasions in Africa, among other experiences, have made the African homeless at home. Even the theologians, who had the privilege of going to Europe to study theology at the feet of European theologians during the missionary era, have discovered that to make a distinctive meditation upon faith in Christ in such a way that it does justice to the life circumstances of the African Christian would not be possible without executing a dismantling and an appropriate reconstruction; in this way, making theology fit into the African reality and Christianity at home in Africa. This notwithstanding, the question looming at the horizon is: how can the Church be more and more at home in Africa and Africa more and more at home in the Church? Pope Paul VI (cited in Mbefo 1989) asks:

> Does the church in Africa retain a certain Christian religious form that was brought in from outside and which makes her, as it were, a stranger and pilgrim among her people? Should new and more suitable means be sought in theology and in pastoral practice? (p. 9)

These questions, among others, led to the emergence of African theology in the twentieth century. As it is with the emergence of new concepts, with the introduction of the concept "African theology", there arose the question of the limits of its content and meaning. The need for conceptualization was necessary, not because of the need to give the rightful place to African culture and worldview, but to what extent this should be included in relation to the substance of the faith. In the midst of these discussions, Dickson (1984) defines African theology thus:

> The expression 'African theology' is not a slogan of vindication and whatever its popular use might connote, it is not meant to be simply an amalgamation of Christian and traditional belief elements; the aim of those involved in the quest is to arrive at a distinctive meditation upon faith in Christ that does justice to the life circumstances of the African (p. 122).

This concept of African theology points to the fact that every particular situation or context calls for a particular theological reflection, that is, if the theological reflection is to make meaning within that unique circumstance or environment. It is within this context that the *Igwebuike* theology of *Omenani* emerges, in relation to the understanding of culture as the seed of the Word of God, which already pre-existed in Africa, even before the emergence of Western missionaries. The purpose of adopting this idea of culture as the seed of the Word of God is to enhance the reconciliation between the African and the Western perspectives. It presents the African culture as an important element in evangelization in Africa, as it is the spirit that animates the African. It emphasizes the indispensability of integrating the African worldview in the communication of the gospel to the African people. This paper further locates the seed of the Word of God in the *Omenani* (the law of the land) of the African people through which they were able to achieve holiness, even before the advent of the gospel.

DEFINING *IGWEBUIKE* THEOLOGY

The concept, *Igwebuike,* began first as a methodology and philosophy. Gradually, its philosophical elements began to have serious implications for theological discourse, especially with the increasing need to do theology that arises from the philosophy of the African people. Such a theology would always have an inescapable element of philosophy, speaking to people in their own native context, because it is expressed in categories of thought that arise out of the philosophy of the African people. This affirms the reality of the link between philosophy and theology, especially regarding the links between the great philosophical questions and the mysteries of salvation which are studied in theology under the guidance of the higher light of faith (Kanu, 2010). Pope Lee XIII makes a connection between philosophy and theology:

> Philosophy if rightly made use of by the wise, in a certain way tends to smooth and fortify the road to true faith, and to prepare the souls of its disciples for the fit reception of revelation; for which reason is well called by ancient writers sometimes a stepping stone to the Christian faith; sometimes the help and prelude of Christianity, sometimes the Gospel teacher (p. 1).

In *Igwebuike* theology, theology takes on the form of a bridge that connects the human person who lives within the context of a changing culture to God, who is beyond the law of change. While this bridge is the message, for it to reach the human person, it requires the agency of revelation and culture. Revelation without culture would be a message that is not understood. Culture is the symbolic network of meanings through which the human person interprets the world. As such, any message from God must come through cultural symbols. Theology, therefore, becomes a dialogue between revelation and culture; the level of this dialogue would determine the level of absorption of the Christian message. Below is a bridge illustration of theology to help convey this point.

The Bridge of Theology

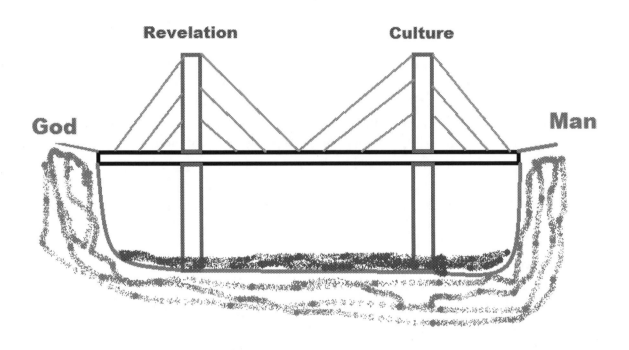

Figure 1- Source: Missionmusings (2017)

This notwithstanding, *Igwebuike* is a combination of three Igbo words. It can be understood as a word or a sentence: as a word, it is written as *Igwebuike*, and as a sentence, it is written as, *Igwe bu ike,* with the component words enjoying some independence in terms of space. Literally, *Igwe* is a noun, which means 'number' or 'multitude', usually a large number or population. The number or population in perspective are entities with ontological identities and significances; however, part of an existential order in which every entity is in relation to the other. *Bu* is a verb, which means *is*. *Ike* is a noun, which means *strength* or *power* (Kanu, 2016a&b). *Igwe, bu* and *Ike* put together, means 'number is strength' or 'number is power' (Kanu, 2017f). However, beyond the literal sense of *Igwebuike,* it means *otu obi* (one heart and one soul) – *cor unum et anima una*. It refers to the relational engagement in the world, accomplished in solidarity and complementarity, and the powerful and insurmountable force therein (Kanu, 2017g). The closest words to it in English are complementarity, solidarity and harmony. In this way, *Igwebuike* conceptualizes or captures the nature of the African universe.

Thus, what *Igwebuike* does is that it captures the nature of the African universe and uses it as a framework for discussions within the enterprise of theology. The value that it brings to the table of theological discussions is its emphasis on the African worldview as an indispensable element in any successful African theological discussion and missionary enterprise. This makes theological discussions relevant to the African and his/her environment.

Igwebuike theology is a quest to arrive at a unique understanding of faith in Christ in such a way that it captures the African worldview and the African's life circumstances. Only thus will evangelization respond to the inadequacies of the missionary enterprise, give birth to a new African personality and be in accord with the legitimate aspirations and concerns of the African people. *Igwebuike* theology does not in any way imply a change in the Church's theology- it is the same theology, a systematic and scientific discourse on God, presented in such a way that it fits into the African religious, social, anthropological and philosophical realities, mentality and needs. The focus on Christ, the Scripture and tradition is not altered in any way. They remain the inevitable revelatory agents.

As a result of the uniqueness of *Igwebuike* theology, it has peculiar approaches, which include: understanding theology as contextual, that is, a theology of life and culture that is accountable to the context in which the African people live; understanding reality as complementary and interconnected; understanding African traditional religion and culture as preparation for the gospel message; understanding theology as an enterprise that provides answers to the African person's innermost and deepest longings, that is, the search for happiness (God). Its sources include: the Bible, Church tradition, African philosophy, religion and culture, African anthropology and African experiences.

THEORETICAL FRAMEWORK

The theoretical framework employed in this research is the *Igwebuike* sympathetic and non-derogatory framework in evangelization. It emphasizes evangelization with a sense of understanding. It is polite and humane, and excludes the influences of bias in the process of knowing. It is sympathetic and non-derogatory to that which is within the circumference of the other. Okonkwo (1998 & 2019), taking from the encounter between Paul and the Athenians in Acts of the Apostles, describes the sympathetic and non-derogatory approach.

Paul, the missionary per excellence, though he was so exasperated at the sight of Athens, an idol-ridden pantheistic city and people, did not, *prima facie*, condemn neither the idols nor the people. Rather, he adopted a secular wisdom and intellection and called the 'idol-ridden-pantheistic Athenians' - "a God-fearing and extremely scrupulous people in religious matters" (Act, 17:23). Paul did not gloss-over their religious and cultural values; rather, he showered understanding on them. St. Paul, after his polite and humane method of meeting with foreigners – the Gentiles, he still was vehement and firm in his solemn proclamations in the condemnation of false gods and idolatry.

This same sympathetic and non-derogatory approach we find in Jesus, the apostles and the Church fathers. In sowing the seed of the gospel, they had respect for other peoples' cultures. Jesus and His apostles came from the Jewish background whose religiosity, prayers and practices of worship were well-defined. However, Jesus' attitudes toward the Jewish cult were represented in two categories: fidelity and autonomy. In fidelity, Jesus had respect for the traditions of his time. He came not to abolish the law and the prophets but to fulfill them (Matthew 5:17). He was faithful in observing the offering of sacrifices in the temple (Matthew 21:12), the service of words in the synagogue (Matthew 6:6), observing the day of the Sabbath, the feasts of Passover, Tabernacle, and Dedication (Matthew 26:17-19). However, his fidelity did not lie in passivity, but represented that of a "critical yes", a reforming fidelity that placed a demand of purification on the worship of its time. His autonomy found expression in His challenge to fellow Jews to spiritualize and interiorize the Jewish religion, and in this process, He was giving birth to the era of Christian worship.

When Jesus preached the gospel, he used categories familiar to his audience. We hear of absentee Lords and Tenant revolts (Matthew 21:31-45), small family-run farms (Matthew 21:28-30), debts and debtors (Matthew 18:25-35), extortion and corruption (Luke 16:1-9), uncaring rich (Luke 12:18), day labourers paid merely subsistent wages (Matthew 20:1-6). These graphically reflect the detail of the picture of Palestinian countryside during His time. St Paul wrote, "To the Jews I became a Jew, in other to win Jews... I have become all things to all men that I might by all means save some" (Philippians 9:20 & 22). In the opinion of Metuh (1996), St Paul was talking about missiology, and at the same time using the language of contextual theology in which lies the theology of inculturation: bringing the Christian experience into the culture of the people, a process that makes alive the dynamic and eternal motion of the incarnation. Freyne (1980) observes how St Paul criss-crossed the Mediterranean world on sea and land with the Good News of Christ vying for the souls of the masses with religious leaders and philosophers. Any contemporary missionary will testify to the value of Paul's acquaintance with the language of the people and his ability to share many of their assumptions with them.

After Jesus, Dulles (1983) observes that His Apostles continued to employ the same model in their attempt to bring the Good News to the peoples of their time. With the conversion and subsequent mission of St Paul to the Gentiles, so many of them were converted to Christianity and there now arose the question as to whether to allow the Gentiles to become Christians without imposing on them the law of circumcision held in high esteem by the Jews. This called for the Council of Jerusalem between 49- 50AD. The Judaizers held that circumcision, as contained in the Old Testament, was necessary for salvation, while St Paul and his followers maintained that all that was needed for salvation was faith in Jesus and baptism in His name (Acts 15). According to Schineller (1991),

> Peter's position which agreed with Paul's, prevailed, and it was decided not to lay extra burdens on the Gentile converts. Because of this liberating decision,

the mission of Paul continued with great success, and the Church expanded far beyond the borders of Palestine. One did not first have to become Jewish before becoming a Christian. (p. 30).

This sympathetic and non-derogatory approach points to the importance of beginning from where the people are and what they know to where they need to be or need to know. Jesus began with worshipping the Jewish way, and taught the people within the contexts of the Jewish categories. He did not begin with condemnation or looking down on the people. In the same way, Saint Paul began with addressing the Athenians as religious people. In relation to the missionary enterprise in Africa, this framework would advocate the missionary first discovering the seed of the Word of God within a particular culture, rather than condemnation of the culture of the people.

AFRICAN CULTURE AS THE SEED OF GOD'S WORD

During the 2nd century, Christianity had moved beyond the walls of Jerusalem to the Greek and Roman territories, with the challenge of Christianity coming face to face with other religious and cultural traditions outside of Judaism. This required a more dynamic method of evangelisation that does not in any way compromise the gospel message. Rather than a radical rejection of Greek culture, they indulged in a great appreciation and partial acceptance of the Greek culture as a starting point for their sowing of the seed of the gospel. Although they were primarily Christian theologians, they employed Greek culture and philosophy for the service of the gospel. They found philosophical themes and concepts useful for developing and clarifying the Christian message.

At the time that these Christian thinkers brought the message to the Greeks, Neo-Platonism, a revival of Platonic philosophy, was at its peak. These Christian thinkers found Neo-Platonism a useful tool for the explanation of Christian doctrines. Prominent among these Christian writers were: Justine Martyr, Clement of Alexandria, Gregory of Nyssa, Origen, Augustine, among others. According to Omoregbe (1997):

> These men Christianized Neoplatonism by giving Christian interpretation to certain theme and concepts in Neoplatonic philosophy, such as Logos, the divine mind, creation, the soul, the problem of evil, the problem of the universal and the particular, the problem of man's freedom and God's foreknowledge, etc. (p. 93)

They were, therefore, the first, outside of the apostles, to raise the problem of the relationship between the doctrinal tradition of the Church and other cultures outside of Jerusalem. However, more interesting is the position taken by Justine Martyr on this matter, when he tried to engraft Stoic concept of the logos into Christian revelation. Justine, in his analysis of natural law, linked it to his concept of man. He saw man as composed of three distinct parts: body (σῶμα, *soma*), soul (ψυχή, psyche), and spirit (πνεῦμα, pneuma). He used the term ζωτικόν πνεῦμα (*zotikon pneuma*), in Latin (*spiritus vitalis*) to describe the spiritual dimension of the human person. The ζωτικόν πνεῦμα, he understands as the divine principle in human beings, the distinguishing feature of his nature, his unique dignity and as a participation in the very life of the *Logos*, and so he calls it the "seed of the word" or "reason in man", in Greek, the σπερματικός λόγος (*spermaticos logos)* and in Latin, the *ratio seminalis.*

Through the σπερματικός λόγος, the divine principle in the human person, humanity was able to govern itself and pursued virtue, even before the coming of Christianity. This divine principle, he argues, has an intimate connection with the Divine *Logos*, the Word of God. In every human being, St. Justin Martyr believed, "there is a divine particle, his reason, which at least before Christ's coming was human person's best guide in life" (*Ap. II* 10.8). This created a burden in human beings to live in accordance with reason and not against or without reason. By this, the human person participated in divine reason, which formed his fundamental law. Through this reason, human beings, without express faith in Christ, already experienced Christ the *Logos* at work in them (Lex Christianorum 2010). He writes:

> We have been taught that Christ is the First-born of God, and we have declared . . . that He is the Word of whom every race of men were partaken, and those who lived reasonable are Christians, even though they have been thought atheists." (*Apol. I,* 46.1-4)

He writes further that:

> All right principles that philosophers and lawgivers have discovered and expressed, they owe to whatever of the Word they have found and contemplated in part. The reason why they have contradicted each other is that they have not known the entire Word, which is Christ. (*Apol. II,* 10.1-3)

In his use of the concept 'Logos', St. Justin Martyr was certainly not viewing these *Logoi Spermatokoi*, these divine sparks in human beings, as being of the same substance (*homoousios*), as the divine *Logos* itself, though they clearly share in His mind, in some insubstantial, created, and relatively distant sense, in the divinity of the *Logos* (*homoiousious*).

An image which scholars have used to explain St. Justin Martyr's concept of *Logos Sparmatikos* is Plato's chariot allegory of the soul. In his dialogue, *Phaedrus* (sections 246a - 254e), Plato uses the allegory of a chariot to explain his view of the human soul. Plato describes the inner workings of the human being as a charioteer governing a chariot pulled by two horses, one white and one black. The white horse is long-necked, well-bred, well-behaved, and runs without a whip. The black horse is short-necked, poorly bred, and undisciplined, requiring constant guidance. St. Justin Martyr would make his *Logos Spermatikos* the charioteer charged with the task of using intellect and reason, that is, *logos*, to guide the white horse of the soul (*psyche*), and its rational moral impulses, and the black horse of the body (*soma*), with is irrational and concupiscent nature, to the true and the good.

To St. Justin, the governing principle in us, the *spermatikos logos* or *zotikon pneuma*, is the source of the faculty of the natural moral law, the law that God has placed in the heart of every human being and which distinguishes him/her from beasts. It is what makes him/her a child of the one only God, and makes him/her brother and sister with all those of his/her . It is the ruler, the pilot, of the lesser natures, part rebellious, part docile (Lex Christianorum 2010).

IGWEBUIKE THEOLOGY OF *OMENANI* AS THE SEED OF GOD'S WORD

Justin the Martyr holds that different cultures were inspired by God and should be appropriate for His service. He saw culture as a prefiguration of Christ: a *Logos Spermatikos* (seed bearing word). He taught that the *Spermatic Logos* has been implanted in the heart of every human culture, since all things were created through Christ, with Him and for Him. Thus, Christ was already present in local cultures in an imperfect way, even before the Word of God was preached to these cultures. This understanding he connects with the scriptural parable of the sower (Mtt 13:3-9), as grace sowed already in the hearts of men, or in terms of creation, where men, even before the coming of Christ, were already created in the image and likeness of God (Gen 1:26-27).

This work, within the context of Justin the Martyr's argument, situates the prefiguration of the seed of the Word of God in African culture in the *Omenani* of the African people. *Omenani*, also called *omenala* (translated as the tradition of the land), is the system of unwritten moral principles or rules of conduct taught by *Chukwu* to the first Igbo ancestor and handed down from one ancestor to another, which includes provisions, prohibitions, traditional beliefs and practices, that guide the day-to-day life of the Igbo-African, with a view to preserving order and maintaining the community bond. After *Chukwu* created the human person, as it is in the book of Genesis, there was need for a moral standard that would guide the relationship between human persons and *Chukwu,* and just as God gave Adam and Eve the command to eat only of the fruit of a particular tree, Igbo traditional religious thought has it that *Chukwu* also gave laws to humanity.

Traditionally, the goddess *Ala* or *Ani* is considered the custodian of Igbo morality. *Ala* is a merciful mother and no deity takes action against the Igbo without first asking her to warn her children. However, if she decides to strike, no deity can stop her. As the custodian of Igbo morality, when the law is broken, it is called *nso-ala*, that is 'Taboo', she takes action to save the community, and thus, its individuals.

The connection that *Omenani* has with *Chukwu, Ala* deity and the college of the ancestors, is what makes the community to hold these laws in high esteem, and to see them as a way of preserving the community, maintaining solidarity with *Chukwu*, the deities, the living dead and preserving their individual destinies. It is by keeping these laws and regulations that individual members of the community are able to arrive at the world of the ancestors. Examples of *omenani* include:

a. Prohibition of claim of equality with God and the spirits
b. Prohibition of homicide
c. Prohibition of suicide
d. Prohibition of a man marrying another man
e. Prohibition of incest
f. Prohibition of adultery
g. Prohibition of fornication
h. Prohibition of theft
i. Prohibition of the alteration of land boundaries

The coloring that *omenani* brings to the table in theological discussions, regarding African culture and evangelization, is that it points to the fact that:

1. The laws in question are from God
2. The laws are the laws of the land that has been in existence from the first ancestor(s) created by God

The fact that the *Omenani* came from God, transmitted from one generation to another, makes African culture a preparation for the gospel. Its divine origin is what made it possible for the Igbo to attain salvation through it, even though it did not contain the fullness of revelation. As imperfect as it was, it pointed to the fullness of revelation in Christ. Below is a table showing the relationship between *Omenani* and Christian morality, and that the African moral principles already contained the Christian morality, even before the advent of the gospel.

TABLE 1: *A TABLE SHOWING THE RELATIONSHIP BETWEEN OMENANI AND CHRISTIAN MORALITY*

No.	*Omenani*	**Christian Morality and Belief**
1.	An Igbo man's ancestral heritage, called "Ana Obi," is not sellable, elders will not permit this. If this is somehow done due to the influence of the West, the person is considered a fool and is ostracized by the community.	**1 King 21:3:** When Ahab asked Naboth for his vineyard, he said to him: "I inherited this vineyard from my ancestors, and the Lord forbid that I should sell it, said Naboth".

2.   In Igbo land, it's a tradition that the male children are circumcised on the 8th day.

Leviticus 12:3: Scripture says: "On the eighth day, the child shall be circumcised"

3.   The seventh commandment (v. 14) treats the family as a sacred social unit, and thus sees adultery as a desecration of the marriage bond.

Adultery has never been tolerated among African people. Both the elders of the land and the gods forbid it.

4.   Among the Igbo, the spilling of blood is something that is avoided under normal circumstance, except during warfare. Once you spill blood, it was believed that the blood would go into the land as a testimony and Ala deity will avenge such a death.

The sixth commandment (v.13) is concerned with the protection of human life within the community of Israel, against destruction by fellow Israelites.

The fact of this possible connection between *omenani* and Christian morality shows that, in spite of the fact that it was not a Christian era, it carried within it the seed of the Word of God awaiting full revelation in the New Testament. The missionaries would have made more impact if they began from what they people knew to what they did not know. Discarding as evil or condemning the African culture, religion and morality outright by most missionaries was a move in the wrong direction, and the basis for crisis in the Christian faith in Africa.

CONCLUSION

Christianity came into existence in a Greco-Roman world, with Judaism as its first encounter. These two worlds played significant parts in shaping its character and influencing its history, in the sense that Greek philosophy and culture shaped early Christian theological formulations, and the Roman world, with its rich organizational structures, shaped the organizational and practical dimensions of the life of the Christian church, and its religious impulses from the rich Jewish tradition. As Christianity moved to the shores of Africa, its encounter with African traditional religion and culture, its sympathetic, non-derogatory and non-dominant touch was not felt in relation to its encounter with the Greek, Roman and Jewish cultures. There was a smugness toward African traditional religion and culture, which generated barrage of names like primitive, pagan, heathen, magic, ancestor worshippers, juju, animists, fetish, animism, etc (Kanu, 2015a).

This smugness towards the African religion and culture shaped the missionaries' conception of the African religion and culture and limited the African personality (Kanu, 2019). The early missionaries, therefore, saw the African culture in the negative light. The first strategy employed was that of disassemblage. They made no appraisal of African languages enriched with traditions of centuries or the African parables, many of them the quintessence of family and national histories; the African modes of thought, influenced more or less by local circumstances our poetry which reveals the profundity of African literary wizardry. The drums were banned from sounding in most churches. African names for baptism were rejected, and as a replacement, they encouraged the adoption of not only Christian names, but also European family names like De Santos (Kanu, 2015b).

It is from this background that this piece, beginning with the understanding of *Igwebuike* theology, and adopting the *Igwebuike* theoretical framework of the sympathetic and non-derogatory approach, interpreted culture as the seed of the Word of God, using *Omenani* as a context. It argued that the failures of the missionary enterprise were majorly because of their lack of openness to the African religion and culture. The understanding of *Omenani* of the Igbo-African people as the seed of the Word of God, even before the advent of the missionaries to the African soil, shows that culture is not an enemy of the gospel, but could be employed as an instrument for the transmission of the gospel message.

REFERENCES

Dickson Kwesi (1984). Theology in Africa. Orbis Books: Maryknoll.

Dulles, A. (1983). An ecclesial model for theological reflection. In J. Hug (Ed.).

Freyne, S. (1980). *The world of the New Testament*. Delaware: Michael Glazier.

Justin the Martyr (1885). *The Second Apology.* Translated by Marcus Dods and George Reith. From Ante-Nicene Fathers, Vol. 1. Edited by Alexander Roberts, James Donaldson, and A. Cleveland Coxe. Buffalo, NY: Christian Literature Publishing Co.

Kanu, I. A. (2010). A Discourse on the Romance between Philosophy and Christian Theology. *International Journal of Theology and Reformed Tradition*, Vol. 2. pp. 185-198.

Kanu, I. A. (2015). *A hermeneutic approach to the study of African traditional religion, theology and philosophy.* Augustinian publications, Nigeria

Kanu, I. A. (2015). *An Ontologico-Existential Hermeneutic approach to classical and contemporary issues.* Augustinian publications, Nigeria

Kanu, I. A. (2016a). *Igwebuike* as an Igbo-African Hermeneutics of Globalisation. *IGWEBUIKE: An African Journal of Arts and Humanities*, Vol. 2 No.1. pp. 61-66.

Kanu, I. A. (2016a). *Igwebuike* as the consummate foundation of African Bioethical principles. *An African journal of Arts and Humanities* Vol.2 No1 June, pp.23-40.

Kanu, I. A. (2016b) *Igwebuike* as an Expressive Modality of Being in African ontology. *Journal of Environmental and Construction Management. 6. 3.* pp.12-21.

Kanu, I. A. (2017). *Igwebuike* as an Igbo-African Philosophy for Christian-Muslim Relations in Northern Nigeria. In Mahmoud Misaeli (Ed.). *Spirituality and Global Ethics* (pp. 300-310). United Kingdom: Cambridge Scholars.

Kanu, I. A. (2017g). *Igwebuike* and the logic (Nka) of African philosophy. *Igwebuike: An African Journal of Arts and Humanities. 3. 1.* pp. 1-13.

Kanu, I. A. (2019). A Hermeneutics of Amadioha as a Prefiguration of Christ in Igbo Traditional Religion. *Nnadiebube Journal of Philosophy* Vol. 3. No. 2. pp. 1-13.

Kanu, I. A. (2019a). Collaboration within the Ecology of Mission: An African Cultural Perspective. *The Catholic Voyage.* Vol. 15. pp. 125-149.

Kanu, I. A. (2014a). Igbo proverbs as *depositum* of Igbo-African philosophy. *International Journal of Humanities and Social Sciences. Vol. 4. No. 1.* pp. 164-168.

Kanu, I. A. (2014a). Suicide in Igbo-African ontology. *Developing Countries Studies.* Vol. 4. No. 5. USA. pp. 27-38.

Kanu, I. A. (2014b). Suffering in Igbo-African Ontology. *Research on Humanities and Social Sciences.* Vol. 4. No. 5. pp. 8-13.

Kanu, I. A. (2014b). The place of Igbo myths in Igbo-African philosophy. *American Journal of Contemporary Research. Vol. 4. No. 2.* pp. 98-102.

Kanu, I. A. (2015). African traditional democracy with particular reference to the Yoruba and Igbo political systems. *International Journal of Philosophy and Public Affairs.* Vol. 2. No. 3. pp. 147-160.

Kanu, I. A. (2015). *Personal identity and punishment in John Locke* (A Dissertation for the Award of Master of Arts Degree in Philosophy- Metaphysics), University of Nigeria, Nsukka, Enugu State.

Kanu, I. A. (2015a). *African philosophy: An ontologico-existential hermeneutic approach to classical and contemporary issues.* Nigeria: Augustinian Publications.

Kanu, I. A. (Ed.) (2016a). *Complementary ontology: Provocative essays on Innocent Asouzu's African philosophy of integration for progressive transformation.* Germany: Lambert Academic Publishing.

Kanu, I. A. (Ed.) (2016b). *Ibuanyidanda: A complementary systematic inquiry. Reflections on Innocent Asouzu's African philosophy.* Germany: Lambert Academic Publishing.

Kanu, I. A. (2016). *Igbo-African Christology: A cultural Christological construct in Post-Missionary Africa.* Germany: Lambert Publications.

Kanu, I. A. (2016a). African traditional folk songs as dialogue between education and entertainment. *Cambridge International Journal of Contemporary Education Research.* 6. 6. pp. 53-64.

Leo XIII, *The Restoration of Christian Philosophy*, 1, 879. Retrieved 20th. http://search.sweetim. com/search.asp?src=2&q=On+the+restoration+of+philosophy%2C+Leo+XIII

Lex Christianorum (2010). *St. Justin Martyr: The Spermatikos Logos and the Natural Law. lexchristianorum.blogspot.com/2010/03/st-justin-martyr-spermatikos-logos-and.html*

Mbefo, L. N. (1989). *Towards a mature African Christianity.* Enugu: Spiritan Publications.

Metuh, I. E. (1991). *African religions in western conceptual schemes: The problem of interpretation.* Jos: Imico.

Missionmusings (2017). Contextua Evangelical Theology. Retrieved from https:// munsonmissions.org/2015/02/24/contextual-evangelical-theology

Okonkwo, J. I. (1998). Folks-Media and the New Era of Evangelisation: The Igbo Perspective, In: *Communication Socialis: International Zeitschrift fur Kommunication in Religion, Kirche und Gesselschaft*, Salzburg: pp, 246-270.

Okonkwo, J. I. (2019). Chi And Christ: The Search For The Universal Essence Of God In Igbo And Christian Thoughts. In M. R, Duru (Ed.). *Amarachi: A Festschrift in Honour of Amarachi Anthony, J. V. Obinna on the Event of His Arch-Episcopal Silver Jubilee* (pp. 221-238). Owerr: Divine Favour Digital Concepts.

Omoregbe, J. I. (1997). A simplified history of Western philosophy: Ancient and Medieval Philosophy. Joja Educational Research and Publishers Limited

Schineller, P. (1990). *A handbook on inculturation.* New York: Paulist.*Tracing the Spirit* (pp. 218-241). New York: Paulist.

IGWEBUIKE THEOLOGY OF UDI: RECONCILING GOD'S UNCHANGING REVELATION WITH MAN'S CHANGING CULTURE

Ikechukwu Anthony KANU
Department of Philosophy and Religious Studies
Tansian University Umunya, Anambra State
ikee_mario@yahoo.com

ABSTRACT

The questions that have been looming at the thoughts of many African theologians for years have been: How can the Christian faith be made to be at home in Africa, in such a way that it harmonizes with African beliefs and practices, thus becoming the religion of the African people? What is the relationship between African traditional religion and culture with the Christian faith? Does being a Christian mean that I should distance myself from my traditional religious and cultural heritages? It is from this background that Igwebuike theology emerges as an African theology, posting that effort towards evangelization must begin from the understanding of the African worldview and the incorporation of such in the processes of the communication and learning of the Christian faith. This work presented the theology of African typology (udi, meaning type, kind or nature) within the context of Igwebuike theology, with a view to creating a balance in the midst of the conflicts between Christianity and African religion and culture by connecting the events of the New Testament to events and persons in African traditional religion and culture. This connection is such that the events, persons, realities, etc., in African traditional religion and culture find meaning and fulfillment in the New Testament Scriptures. The Igwebuike theology of udi has created an aperture for further dialogue of culture with faith. It provided a deeper meaning and wider capacity for the application of the concept, 'typology'. It has contributed to the continuous search for better ways of making the Christian faith feel at home in Africa, and also making it possible for the redemption of the African culture through its interaction with faith. For the purpose of this study, the Igwebuike theoretical framework, which emphasizes beginning from and valuing what is known, and using what is already known as a stepping stone to get to the unknown, was adopted.

Keywords: *Igwebuike*, Theology, *Udi*, Faith, Revelation, Culture, Missionaries

IKECHUKWU ANTHONY KANU

INTRODUCTION

The missionary enterprise in Africa, aimed at converting 'pagans' and establishing the Church, was not without a methodology. First, they employed the methodology of imposition of the Christian message; the second was the translation of the Christian message which was mostly in English to the local languages of the African people, and third, the adaptation of the Christian message into the African religious culture. Through imposition, doctrines, religious customs, morals and ways of acting and praying taken from foreign cultures were forced on the African people. While this might seem like a clear option left to the missionaries, they disregarded and belittled the culture of the African people in the process; the consequence is that the faith has no root and thus, the message remains strange to those who host it. The idea of imposition was based on a wrong conception of Christianity as a finished product rather than a faith that reaches its full potential through dialogue with the local cultures of host communities.

This might have worked with the early missionaries; however, with Africans being part of evangelization, disenchantment began to emerge as regards the missionaries' spiteful attitude to African culture and tradition (Bujo, 1992) and her highhanded approach to the African reality (Dickson, 1984). It was from this background that the need for an African theology emerged; a theology that would put into consideration the African reality in its approaches. The concept of *Igwebuike* theology flows from this background, however, putting into cognizance and giving a special place to the rich African heritage. It is, therefore, from the principles of *Igwebuike* that the idea of an African typology would be generated and discussed for the purpose of creating a balance in the midst of the conflicts between Christianity and African religion and culture. The African theology of *udi* (type or image), an Igbo-African concept of typology, would be employed to connect the events of the New Testament to events and persons in African traditional religion and culture. These connections would be made in a way such that the events, persons, realities, etc., in African traditional religion and culture would find meaning and fulfillment in the New Testament Scriptures.

UNDERSTANDING *IGWEBUIKE* THEOLOGY

The questions looming at the thoughts of many African theologians for years have been: How can the Christian faith be made to be at home in Africa, in such a way that it harmonizes with African beliefs and practices? What is the relationship between African traditional religion and culture with the Christian faith? Does being a Christian mean that I cannot be part of the traditional activities of my people? Why must I change my name to a foreign name before I can become a Christian? It is from this background that *Igwebuike* theology emerges as an African theology that strongly believes that effort towards evangelization must begin from the understanding of the African worldview and the incorporation of such in the processes of the communication and learning of the Christian faith. For theology to be at home in Africa, *Igwebuike* theology argues that it must be contextual rather than hang on an ivory tower; and by being contextual, the looming questions begin to get their answers.

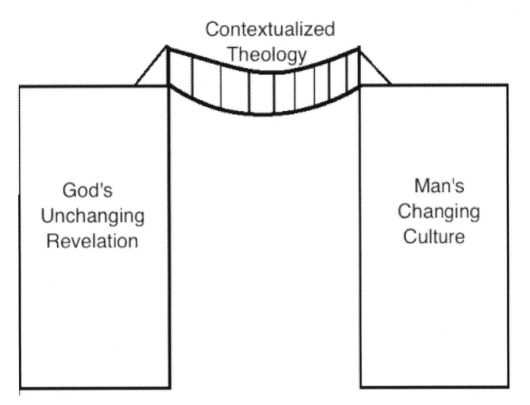

Figure 1- Source: Missionmusings (2017)

The basis for contextualization is the change that is possible within the permanence of the Christian faith. God's revelation and the cultural context of the respondent are two different realities, however, forming the bridge for communication. While God's revelation is unchanging, comprising the Christ, Holy Bible, tradition, the culture of the human is dynamic and more varied. The faith would be irrelevant unless it is understood and valued by the recipients in their respective cultures. What theology does is to create a forum for dialogue of faith and culture in such a way that it is understood and appreciated by peoples of all cultures. Thus, *Igwebuike* theology as a contextualized enterprise creates a bridge between God's unchanging revelation and the human person's changing culture.

The concept *Igwebuike* began first as a methodology and philosophy. Gradually, its philosophical element began to have implications for theological discourse, especially with the increasing need to do theology that arises from the philosophy of the African people. Such a theology would always have an inescapable element of philosophy, speaking to people in their own native context, because it is expressed in categories of thought that arises out of the philosophy of the African people. However, the expression, *Igwebuike,* is an Igbo word which means 'number is strength' or 'number is power' (Kanu, 2017f). However, beyond the literal sense of *Igwebuike,* it means *otu obi* (one heart and one soul) – *cor unum et anima una.* In a metaphoric sense, it is used within the Igbo linguistic setting to refer to relational engagement in the world, accomplished in solidarity and complementarity, and the powerful and insurmountable force therein (Kanu, 2017g). The closest words to it in English are complementarity, solidarity and harmony. In this way, *Igwebuike* conceptualizes or captures the nature of the African universe.

What *Igwebuike* does is that it captures the nature of the African universe and uses it as a framework for discussions within theology. The value that it brings to the table of theological discussions is its emphasis on the African worldview as an indispensable element in any successful African theological discussion, that such a discussion might be relevant to the African. Thus, *Igwebuike* theology would mean the quest to arrive at a unique understanding of faith in Christ in such a way that it captures the African worldview and his/her life circumstances. Only thus will evangelization respond to the inadequacies of the missionary enterprise, give birth to a new African personality and be in accord with the legitimate aspiration of the African people. *Igwebuike* theology does not in any way imply a change in the Church's theology- it is the same theology, a systematic and scientific discourse on God, presented in such a way that it fits into the African religious, social, anthropological and philosophical realities, mentality and needs. The focus on Christ, the Scripture and tradition is not altered in any way. They remain the inevitable revelatory agents.

This notwithstanding, *Igwebuike* theology is based on the following fundamental lines:

a. It understands theology as contextual, that is, a theology of life and culture that is accountable to the context in which the African people live.
b. It understands reality as complementary and interconnected.
c. It understands African traditional religion and culture as a preparation for the gospel message.
d. It understands theology as an enterprise that provides answers to the human person's innermost and deepest longings, that is, the search for happiness (God).
e. Its sources include the Bible, African philosophy, religion and culture, African anthropology, and African experiences.

THEORETICAL FRAMEWORK

This research is based on the *Igwebuike* theory of beginning from and valuing what is known as a first step, and then using what is already known as a stepping stone to get to the unknown. It uses the known as a stepping stone to get to the unknown reality. This approach is based on the very nature of learning itself. The first step of learning is observation (Kanu, 2019). What children observe become "known" to them, and it is by comparing what they already know with some other thing unknown to them that they learn new realities.

In relation to evangelization, you begin from the culture of the people, which is the known and from there you take the people to what they do not know. To disregard the culture of a people and then begin to tell them about what they do not know would not only affect their disposition but would create a missing link. What missing links does is that it distorts the complementary whole of reality. In this context, the African culture serves as a missing link in the process of evangelization, and giving it its rightful place helps evangelization to have 'a head and a tail' (*nwe isi na odu*). There is the need for mutual service in complementarity between the African culture and the Christian faith. Thus, Asouzu (2007) avers that: "… any mode in which being finds expression has an intrinsic moment of dynamic mutual service in Complementarity" (p. 266). Outside the circumference of the understanding of culture as a missing link in evangelization, evangelization ends in chaos and conflicts.

This understanding of culture as a missing link within the framework of evangelization is anchored on the cultural realism that holds that no culture is inherently superior or inferior to the other. The thought of inferiority of superiority kills regard for the other, which is an indispensable part of the whole. The reason for the position that no culture is superior or inferior to the other is because cultures are distinct, and there is no common standard for the judging of culture. The standard for the evaluation of one culture might not be the standard for the evaluation of the other culture. Most missionaries were ethnocentric, in the sense that they judged African culture, believing that its standards and values were inferior to the Western or Christian culture.

TOWARDS AN AFRICAN TYPOLOGY (*UDI*)

An interesting aspect of biblical studies is the area of typology. Bullinger (1968) defines typology as "a figure or ensample of something future and more or less prophetic, called the 'Antitype'" (p. 768). Muenscher (cited by Terry, 1890) understands typology as a study of "the preordained representative relation which certain persons, events, and institutions of the Old Testament bear to corresponding persons, events, and institutions in the New" (Terry, 1890, 246). In the contention of Broomall (1960): "A type is a shadow cast on the pages of Old Testament history by a truth whose full embodiment or antitype is found in the New Testament revelation" (p. 533). As a theological concept and method of investigation, there are several words in the New Testament scripture that form its scriptural basis.

Paul uses the Greek word *Tupos* in Romans 5:14 (which means a 'type of' in English), to speak of Adam as a type of Christ. A second word is *Skia* in Colossians 2:17 (which means 'shadow'); Paul employs it to speak of the Mosaic system as a shadow of things to come. Related to these is *Hupodeigma* in Hebrews 9:23 (which means 'copy'). *Parabole* in Hebrews 9:9 (which means 'parable') has also been used to speak of the tabernacle of the Old Testament as a figure for the present time. Another word that points to typology is *Antitupon* in Hebrews 9:24 (which means 'figure', 'likeness' or 'pattern'). They were employed to denote the fulfillment of a prophetic picture or a correspondence between things, persons, events, etc., in the Old Testament and the New Testament. Moorehead (1930) brings out the distinctive features of typology thus:

What are the distinctive features of a type? A type, to be such in reality, must possess three well-defined qualities. (1) It must be a true picture of the person or the thing it represents or prefigures. A type is a draft or sketch of some well-defined feature of redemption, and therefore it must in some distinct way resemble its antitype, e.g. Aaron as high priest is a rough figure of Christ the Great High Priest, and the Day of Atonement in Israel (Leviticus 16) must be a true picture of the atoning work of Christ. (2) The type must be of divine appointment. In its institution it is designed to bear a likeness to the antitype. Both type and antitype are preordained as constituent parts of the scheme of redemption. As centuries sometimes lie between the type and its accomplishment in the antitype, of course infinite wisdom alone can ordain the one to be the picture of the other. Only God can make types. (3) A type always prefigures something future (pp. 3029-3030).

Examples of type in the scripture include: the Passover, with its spotless lamb (Exodus 12:5) which was slain "between the two evenings" (12:6), i.e., between three and 3:00 P.M., without any bones being broken (12:46). It was a type of the death of Jesus (cf. 1 Corinthians 5:7), who was without spot or blemish (1 Peter 1:19), who died at about 3:00 P.M. (Matthew 27:46), and who had none of His bones broken (John 19:33ff). The Feast of the First-Fruits (Leviticus 23:10), i.e., Pentecost, was a celebration in which the initial produce of the harvest was offered to God as a token of the full crop to follow. This ritual typified: (1) the early influx of the Jews into the Church of Christ (Romans 11:16); and, (2) the resurrection of the Lord Jesus as God's pledge of the general resurrection to ultimately come (1 Corinthians 15:20, 23). The Feast of the Tabernacles was instituted to commemorate Israel's sojourn in the wilderness (Leviticus 23:43). But it was also designed to remind us that we are but sojourners on this earth (1 Peter 2:11), and that someday we will lay aside this earthly tabernacle (2 Corinthians 5:1; 2 Peter 1:13, 14) for a more permanent abiding place (cf. Hebrews 11:9-13).

On the annual Jewish Day of Atonement, amidst numerous other rituals, the high priest presented two goats before the door of the tabernacle. After the casting of lots upon these animals, one was sacrificed as a "sin-offering" and the other was "set alive before Jehovah" (Leviticus 16:9, 10). The blood of the slain goat was taken into the most holy place where it was sprinkled upon the mercy seat. This, of course, was typical of the sacrificial death of Christ (Hebrews 9:11, 12). The high priest then took the living goat, laid hands upon him and confessed over him all the iniquities of the people. Subsequently, by an appointed servant, the animal was led away into the wilderness (Leviticus 16:21, 22). The two goats were, so to speak, two sides of the same coin. Both constituted the solitary offering of Christ. The one signified His death and the atoning effect of his blood, the other His resurrection (cf. Romans 4:25) and the complete removal of our sins (cf. Isaiah 53:4, 6; John 1:29) (Wayne 2019).

The flood of Noah's day (Genesis 6-8) typified the sudden destruction of the world yet to come at the end (Matthew 24:37-39). The miraculous water from the rock in the wilderness

(Exodus 17:6) was a preview of the life-sustaining water provided by our Lord (John 4:14; 1 Corinthians 10:4). The manna from heaven in the wilderness (Exodus 16:14-16) was a type of that spiritual bread who came down from heaven to nourish humanity (John 6:32). The deliverance of Noah's family from a corrupted world, by means of "water," prefigured our salvation, through baptism, from the power of darkness into the kingdom of Christ (cf. 1 Peter 3:20-21; Colossians 1:13). The brazen serpent, lifted up in the wilderness, through which the people found physical healing (Numbers 21:8), was a type of the lifted-up Christ (John 3:14; 12:32), through whom spiritual healing comes (Isaiah 53:5) (Wayne 2019).

Adam is a type of Christ in that, as the former introduced sin into the world, even so, through the latter, a system of righteousness was made available for mankind (Romans 5:19). Melchizedek, who was both king of Salem and a priest of God—**at the same time** (Genesis 14:18-20)—was a type of Christ. Jesus, at His ascension, began to reign on David's throne and to simultaneously function as our high priest (cf. Psalm 110:4; Zechariah 6:12, 13; Hebrews 5:5-10; 6:20; 7:1-17). This point, incidentally, is disastrous for millennialism. If Christ is not yet king (as premillennialism asserts), then He is not yet a priest, and we are **yet in our sins!** Moses, in his noble role of prophet, leader, and mediator for Jehovah's people, was typical of the Lord Jesus who functions in a similar, though in a more exalted, capacity (cf. Deuteronomy 18:15; Acts 3:22; 1 Corinthians 10:2; Galatians 3:27; 3:19; 1 Timothy 2:5) (Wayne 2019).

From the foregoing, it becomes easier to now understand typology from an African context. It is a little bit different from the biblical concept of it, since it relates the Old Testament events, persons, things, places, etc., to New Testament events, persons, things, places, etc. Typology in its Igbo-African context would be expressed as *udi*, which means 'kind' (a kind of something), 'type' (a type of soemthing) or 'nature' (the nature of something). From this root, African typology may be defined as the preordained representative relation, which certain persons, events, and institutions of the African religious and cultural heritage bear to corresponding persons, events, and institutions in the New Testament scriptures.

In relation to African traditional culture and religion, the base for relationship changes from the Old Testament scripture to the religio-cultural experiences, categories, events or persons in traditional African culture and religion, which may find their fulfillment in the New Testament scripture. This is anchored on the fact that African traditional religion and culture is understood as a gift from God, given in preparation for evangelization. It holds that the events, persons and things in traditional African religion were not so much about the time of their expression, but had the capacity for fulfillment in the future with the fullness of revelation in Christ Jesus. These patterns often have their greatest manifestations in the life of Christ or in the eschaton, but there may be one or more other fulfillments elsewhere in human history, especially in the immediate historical context. An example of an African theology of *udi* is the kola nut as *udi* Holy Communion in the New Testament scripture.

TABLE 1: THE KOLA NUT AS *UDI* HOLY COMMUNION

No	Holy Communion	The Kola Nut
1.	The Holy Communion is made of bread, which was a common meal among the Jewish people.	The kola nut among the Igbo is a common meal.
2.	The bread is held with reverence.	When the kola nut is treated with great reverence.
3.	It is the product of the human effort at cultivating the earth.	It is the product of the human effort at cultivating the earth.
4.	The Holy Communion is Life (**John 6:25-59 and John 25:56**).	The kola nut is a symbol of life.
5.	The Holy Communion is a sign of unity.	The kola nut symbolizes mutual respect and community.
6.	Jesus chose from among His followers who would continue to offer this sacrifice.	The kola nut is only blessed by men in Igbo traditional society.
8.	After consecration, the priest breaks the bread and hands it over to worshippers.	After the kola nut has been consecrated, it is broken and shared to those present.
9.	The priest calls on the Saints and asks for their intercession.	During the consecration of the kola nut, the ancestors are invoked.
10.	During the consecration of bread, wine is also offered.	During the consecration of the kola nut, liquor is also offered.
11.	At the end of the Eucharistic celebration, the people are blessed.	The people present at the consecration of the kola nut are blessed as well.
12.	The Holy Communion is a sacrament, which speaks of an earthly sign with inward grace.	The kola nut acknowledges the archetypal patterns of the gods and ancestors in *illo tempore*.
13	The priests preside at the Mass.	The most elderly person present presides at the consecration of the kola nut. In the Greek society, it is *presbyteros*, meaning elder.
14	Only those who are not in the state of sin are allowed to partake of the Eucharistic meal.	Those who have evil in their heart do not share in the kola nut.
15	The Eucharist is the centre and summit of the Church's life and prayer.	The kola nut is the centre and life of Igbo traditional celebrations.

CONCLUSION

Scripture scholars generally agree that the book of Genesis was written during the exile to counter the Babylonian myths of the origin of the human person. It is in this regard that Gallagher (1997) observes that the narrative of Genesis was an early example of dialogue between faith and culture, "as against the Babylonian stories of wars and chaos, Genesis shows God freely and serenely creating as a gift to humanity, and indeed portraying God as an artist rejoicing in the sheer goodness of the finished work" (p. 105). He further maintains that these texts are much more than the stories of origin. They are rooted in God's continuing relationship with us in our responsibility for one another and human history.

When God tells us to multiply and rule the earth, He gives us the mandate of continuing His work of creation, and this provides a biblical basis for us to see culture as a human response to God's continuing creative gift, since culture is a product of human ingenuity and creativity. And if all that God has made is good, human culture is also good. This does not rule out the proclivity of culture to become sour and lose its beauty; in that case, culture would need redemption. For John Paul II (1995), this is where Christianity has the capacity to transform human cultures, where necessary, so that they follow the logic proper to the mystery of redemption.

What *Igwebuike* theology of *udi* does is that it creates an aperture for further dialogue of culture with faith. It provides a deeper meaning and wider capacity for the application of the concept of 'typology'. The purpose of this development is to contribute to the continuous search for better ways of making the Christian faith feel at home in Africa, and also making it possible for the redemption of the African culture through its interaction or relationship with faith.

REFERENCES

Asouzu, I. (2007). Ibuanyidanda. New complementary ontology. Beyond world-immanentism, ethnocentric reduction and impositions. Germany: LIT.

Benezet Bujo (1992). African theology in the social context. Orbis Books: Maryknoll.

Bullinger, E. W. (1968). *Figures of Speech Used in the Bible*. Grand Rapids, MI: Baker.

Dickson Kwesi (1984). Theology in Africa. Orbis Books: Maryknoll.

Gallagher, M. (1997). *Clashing symbols: An introduction to faith and culture*. New York: Pualist.

John Paul II (1995). *Ecclesia in Africa*. Bangalore: Paulines.

Kanu, I. A. (2012). Inculturation and the quest for an Igbo Christology. Masters Thesis, Department of Religion and Human Relations, Nnamdi Azikiwe University, Awka.

Kanu, I. A. (2016a). *Igwebuike* as an Igbo-African Hermeneutics of Globalisation. *IGWEBUIKE: An African Journal of Arts and Humanities*, Vol. 2 No.1. pp. 61-66.

Kanu, I. A. (2016a). *Igwebuike* as the consummate foundation of African Bioethical principles. *An African journal of Arts and Humanities* Vol.2 No1 June, pp.23-40.

Kanu, I. A. (2016b) *Igwebuike* as an Expressive Modality of Being in African ontology. *Journal of Environmental and Construction Management. 6. 3.* pp.12-21.

Kanu, I. A. (2017). *Igwebuike* as an Igbo-African Philosophy for Christian-Muslim Relations in Northern Nigeria. In Mahmoud Misaeli (Ed.). *Spirituality and Global Ethics* (pp. 300-310). United Kingdom: Cambridge Scholars.

Kanu, I. A. (2017g). *Igwebuike* and the logic (Nka) of African philosophy. *Igwebuike: An African Journal of Arts and Humanities. 3. 1.* pp. 1-13.

Kanu, I. A. (2019). A Hermeneutics of the Igbo-African Kola-Nut as a "Type" of Holy Communion. Nnadiebube Journal of Philosophy Vol. 3. No. 2. pp. 27-40.

Kanu, I. A. (2019). *Igwebuike* Research Methodology: A New Trend for Scientific and Wholistic Investigation. *IGWEBUIKE: An African Journal of Arts and Humanities (IAAJAH). 5. 4.* pp. *95-105.*

Kanu, I.A. (2012). Inculturation and Christianity in Africa. *International Journal of Humanities and Social Science.* Vol. 2. No. 17, September, pp. 236-244.

Kanu, I. A. (2014a). Igbo proverbs as *depositum* of Igbo-African philosophy. *International Journal of Humanities and Social Sciences. Vol. 4. No. 1.* pp. 164-168.

Kanu, I. A. (2014a). Suicide in Igbo-African ontology. *Developing Countries Studies.* Vol. 4. No. 5. USA. pp. 27-38.

Kanu, I. A. (2014b). Suffering in Igbo-African Ontology. *Research on Humanities and Social Sciences.* Vol. 4. No. 5. pp. 8-13.

Kanu, I. A. (2014b). The place of Igbo myths in Igbo-African philosophy. *American Journal of Contemporary Research. Vol. 4. No. 2.* pp. 98-102.

Kanu, I. A. (2015). African traditional democracy with particular reference to the Yoruba and Igbo political systems. *International Journal of Philosophy and Public Affairs.* Vol. 2. No. 3. pp. 147-160.

Kanu, I. A. (2015). *Personal identity and punishment in John Locke* (A Dissertation for the Award of Master of Arts Degree in Philosophy- Metaphysics), University of Nigeria, Nsukka, Enugu State.

Kanu, I. A. (2015a). *African philosophy: An ontologico-existential hermeneutic approach to classical and contemporary issues.* Nigeria: Augustinian Publications.

Kanu, I. A. (Ed.) (2016a). *Complementary ontology: Provocative essays on Innocent Asouzu's African philosophy of integration for progressive transformation.* Germany: Lambert Academic Publishing.

Kanu, I. A. (Ed.) (2016b). *Ibuanyidanda: A complementary systematic inquiry. Reflections on Innocent Asouzu's African philosophy.* Germany: Lambert Academic Publishing.

Kanu, I. A. (2016). *Igbo-African Christology: A cultural Christological construct in Post-Missionary Africa.* Germany: Lambert Publications.

Kanu, I. A. (2016a). African traditional folk songs as dialogue between education and entertainment. *Cambridge International Journal of Contemporary Education Research.* 6. 6. pp. 53-64.

Mbefo, L. N. (1989). *Towards a mature African Christianity.* Enugu: Spiritan Publications.

Missionmusings (2017). *Theology as a Contextual Activity. Retrieved from https://munsonmissions.org/2017/03/06/theology-as-a-contextual-activity.*

Terry, M. S. (1890). *Biblical Hermeneutics.* New York, NY: Eaton & Mains.

Wayne, J (2019). "A Study of Biblical Types." *ChristianCourier.com.* Access date: June 22, 2019. https://www.christiancourier.com/articles/126-study-of-biblical-types-a

William G. Moorehead (1930). The typology of scripture. *The International Standard Bible Encyclopedia*, ed. James Orr (Chicago: Howard-Severance Co., 1930), vol. 5, pp. 3029-3030.

A GLANCE AT TRADITIONAL MODES OF COMMUNICATION THROUGH THE LENS OF LITURGICAL INCULTURATION: PERSPECTIVES FROM IGWEBUIKE AND SHIKROT TRADITIONS

Justine John Dyikuk
University of Jos, Plateau State
justinejohndyikuk@gmail.com

ABSTRACT

One of the challenges of pastoral and liturgical communication has been the failure to christen the rich traditional modes of communication for effect worship in an African way. Inspired by the search for genuine liturgical inculturation, the researcher embarked on a qualitative study entitled: "A Glance at Traditional Modes of Communication through the Lens of Liturgical Inculturation: Perspectives from Igwebuike and Shikrot Traditions" to investigate the matter in Igbo and Ngas cultures. It found that music, song and dance, death and funeral rites, baptism and churching, as well as elements of human communication, are traditional modes of communication that are resourceful for liturgical inculturation. With expert-theological insights, such as introducing peoples/cultures into the Church, and enriching the gospel with positive values and cultural diversity, the study recommended rethinking theological content, restoring group/participatory communication and employing signals, signs and symbols as other critical ways of ensuring excellent liturgical inculturation. It concluded that developing an ongoing-evangelization which baptizes the rich values of the cultures under review is crucial for smooth liturgical inculturation.

Keywords: Communication, *Igwebuike*, Inculturation, Liturgical, *Shikrot*, Traditional.

INTRODUCTION

Communication has always been part and parcel of man. Before the advent of colonialism in Africa, people of the continent had their modes and forms of communication. Among various cultures in Africa, different forms of traditional communication, such as idiophones, membranophones, aerophones, symbolography, were effectively employed as traditional modes of communication (Akakuru, Nwokedi & Edi, 2015). Aside from these, the people also saw comedians, town criers, messengers, dancers and musicians as Public Relations' experts who used various forms of human communication to fulfill their role in society. The Igbos of South and Ngas people of North Central Nigeria held traditional modes of communication in high esteem. While the worldview of the Igbos was built around *Igwebuike* (Kanu, 2016 & 2019), that of the Ngas was weaved around *Shikrot*. From birth to death, these philosophies set the parameters for every kind of communication in the society. Since ours is an incarnational faith, part of the history of Christianity has been its encounter with other cultures, being deeply rooted in these cultures (**Udeani**, 2007). Unfortunately, in Africa, the story was different.

As time went by, the arrival of Christian missionaries led to a crisis of faith. Since the early missionaries did not understand the native modes of communication, they framed everything as fetish, thus discarding it. Consequently, they passed the faith to Africans under the cloak of Western culture. For this reason, the message was disdainfully looked upon as one that lacks luster and content which is irrelevant to the daily lives of the people (Umezinwa, 2014). This mentality was, however, met by resistance from emerging local clergy and scholars. There was then agitation to inculturate some aspects of the faith towards harmonizing faith and culture. Reflections of Popes Paul VI and John Paul II, through the Vatican II document, facilitated this. This is because the Church began to teach that, although salvation in Christ is for all peoples, there exists an inclusiveness which reflects on existential religious liberty and pluralism. This is where Igbo traditional religion or *Igwebuike* comes in (Anyanwu, 2019). Umezinwa concurs that "Some efforts - have been made after the Vatican II council to express God's message through culture" (2014,p.199).

Inspired by the dire need for smooth liturgical inculturation in both Igbo and Ngas cultures, amidst a Europeanized-Church in Africa, this study aspires to:

1. Account for the traditional modes of communication in both *Igwebuike* and *Shikrot* traditions;
2. Trace extant sacred objects and cultural values of Igbo and Ngas origins that could be employed for liturgical inculturation;
3. Review extant theological insights of liturgical inculturation *vis-à-vis its* bottlenecks and challenges;
4. Facilitate interreligious dialogue between faith and culture in *Igwebuike* and *Shikrot* traditions, and;
5. Propose valuable recommendations towards revamping liturgical inculturation in *Igwebuike* and *Shikrot* worldviews.

CONCEPTUAL CLARIFICATION

a. **Traditional Modes of Communication**

In this study, traditional modes of communication means the organised system of communication which was in place before the coming of the imperialists to Africa. Also referred to as trado-rural or native media, traditional modes of communication, which were anchored on oramedia, enabled the people to communicate with one another and transmit vital information within the community. In *Igwebuike* and *Shikrot* ontologies, these modes of communication include: directives, news, advertising, public relations, entertainment and education as well as transmission of mores, customs and traditions (Dyikuk, 2019a & Akakuru, Nwokedi, Edi, 2015).

b. **Liturgical Inculturation**

The operational definition of inculturation is the process by which the Church takes up the good values of different cultures (John Paul II, 1995, No 61) and transforms or incarnates them into truths of the gospel. Since every culture has positive values and forms which can enrich the gospel (John Paul II, 2001, No 16), inculturation midwifes the marriage between faith and culture in a new and profound way. It takes into cognizance gestures and signs as well as all other different forms of communication employed by the people of God (Francis, 2013, No 129) in particular churches during liturgical and para-liturgical celebrations.

c. *Igwebuike* **Tradition**

As the lungs or vital organ of Igbo tradition of South Eastern Nigeria, *Igwebuike* philosophy means "number is strength" or "number is power" (Kanu, 2016). It is a worldview which engenders communication and culture through complementarity, harmony and communality. It is also described as a driver for the transmission of values, mores and customs of Igbo people. *Igwebuike* is a mechanism for ensuring unity and the desired synergy for discussion within and outside Igbo land. In this study, *Igwebuike* tradition will be used interchangeably with Igbo tradition, culture, philosophy and worldview (Kanu, 2015, 2017, 2018).

d. *Shikrot* **Tradition**

Shikrot, which translates as "talk of love," encompasses the religious, political and socio-cultural life of the Ngas people of North-Central Nigeria. It covers the ethics and behavioural patterns of the people that are based on charity. The communitarian philosophy further reveals the various forms of communication in the society, even as it showcases the revered culture of the people, such as their mores, customs and traditions (Dyikuk, 2019c). *Shikrot* tradition will be used exchangeably with Ngas culture, tradition, worldview and philosophy.

ARRIVAL OF THE CATHOLIC FAITH IN IGBO AND NGAS LANDS: A HISTORIC APPROACH

Overview of the Faith in Igbo Land

The Igbos of South Eastern Nigeria are said to have originated from the Nri Kingdom. There are other views that Igbo people have ancient Hebrew roots. From whichever perspective one views it, the South-Easterners are said to have settled in cities like Onitsha, Owerri, Nnewi, Okigwe, Aba and Orlu. Their culture and traditions which are displayed through festivals of arts and culture (Obindigbo, 2020) are weaved around *Igwebuike* philosophy, which makes for communalism and shared communication. This philosophy is further expressed in kindred, clan and extended family system. Their patterns of stratification and socialization are also built on a strong sense of fellow-feeling and the need to put the community first.

When the Holy Ghost Fathers evangelized the semi-savannah Northern Igbo land in the 1900s, within the first three decades, the faith was consolidated (Kalu, 1995). Ilogu (1974, pp. 56-62) presents the history of the advent of Catholicism in Igbo land in three phases. The first phase (1885-1900) started with the introduction of missionary policies through contact with the Igbo people, their religion and culture; the second phase (1900-1905) featured a focus on implementing missionary apostolates, like building schools, hospitals and opening new mission churches in major Igbo towns; and the third phase (1931-1967) saw the establishment and growth of the Catholic faith, through consolidation with Catholic schools and hospitals in the area.

Before and within this time, there were a lot of pagan, diabolic, superstitious practices which the early missionaries frowned at. This made the dialogue between faith and culture very difficult. What made matters worse was that the early missionaries simply dismissed African cultural practices as primitive and evil. They frustrated any attempts at inculturation. As time went on, the seeming conflict between faith and culture began to be resolved as local clergy were ordained. This paved way for priests studying up to Doctorate degree levels so as to be experts in various theological disciplines, on the one hand, and to initiate attempts at liturgical inculturation, on the other. From erstwhile heroic witness of Bishop Joseph *Shanahan*, C.S.Sp. (1871–1943), today Catholicism is a nationalreligion for people of the southeast because the region has the highest number of indigenous clergy (including Bishops) and the world's largest Catholic Seminary, Bigard Memorial, located in Enugu (2020 President and Fellows of Harvard College, 2020).

Synopsis of the Faith in Ngas Land

The Ngas people of Plateau State in North Central Nigeria who are now divided into sub-groups in places like Pankshin, Ampang, Amper and Kabwir have Borno as their ancestry (Tolu, 2020). Its people, who are now domiciled in Pankshin and Kanke Local Government

Areas, are driven by *Shikrot* worldview which is a guiding principle for relating to God and humanity. Although Ngas is the most populous language in the two LGA's, its people live amidst diverse cultures with inhabitants who speak many languages, like Mupun, Miship, Fier, Tal, Kadung, Pal and Bijim. Other tribes in Pankshin include: Mupun, Miship, Fier, Tal, Kadung and Pal. There is also the presence of a few Igbos, Yorubas, Idomas, Tivs, etc (Pankshin Local Government Area, 2020). In terms of religion, the Ngas are mostly Christians, with few African Traditional Religionists and Muslims who migrated from Bauchi, Zaria, Katsina Kano and Kebbi.

Like Jos, the Plateau State Capital, the old Pankshin LGA which was split, with Kanke as a new LGA, has been the melting pot of the middle-belt that is blessed with good weather and rich stable food. This made the area an irresistible attraction for Christian missionaries to start new churches (Higazi, 2011). Today, the dominant faiths in Ngas land are Roman Catholic Church, Church of Christ in Nations (COCIN), Anglican Church, Foursquare Gospel Church, Assemblies of God, Redeemed Christian Church of God, Mountain of Fire and Miracles Ministries *(MFM),* to mention just a few.

With the arrival of Society of African Missions (SMA) Catholic Missionaries in Shendam on 12 February 1907, the seed of the faith was planted. One hundred and seven years later, the Catholic Diocese of Pankshin was carved out of the Archdiocese of Jos and Shendam Diocese on March 18, 2014 as the 56th Diocese in Nigeria, with the appointment of Most Rev. Michael Gobal Gokum as its first Bishop. Pankshin Diocese comprises five civil districts of Pankshin, Kanke, Bokkos, Mangu and Kanam, and is a suffragan of Jos Ecclesiastical Province. Holy Cross Pankshin, whose liturgical feast falls on every 14 September, is the Cathedral Church of the new Diocese (Society of African Missions, 2014 & Paulines Publications Africa, 2020). Aside from the substantive Bishop Michael Gokum of Pankshin, it would be recalled that Ngas has had three other bishops: Gabriel Gonsum Ganaka of Jos Archdiocese (24 May 1937 - 11 November 1999), Kevin Aje of Sokoto Diocese (25 April 1934 - 27 May 2019) and Malachy John Goltok of Bauchi (12 July 1965 - 21 March 2015). Today, local clergy are trained in various theological disciplines abroad and locally towards inculturating the faith.

TRADITIONAL MODES OF COMMUNICATION: LITURGICAL INCULTURATION IN IGWEBUIKE AND SHIKROT WORLDVIEWS

Music Song and Dance

Because the Catholic Church in Nigeria opened the way for singing of choruses, playing of local instruments, clapping of hands and dancing her liturgy, the liturgy in Igbo land is saturated with traditional media (Udoette, 2012 & Dyikuk, 2019a, pp.180-181). According to Umezinwa, (2014) the exit of the missionaries in the 1970s saw concrete efforts at using culture to evangelize, like celebrating Holy Mass in vernacular, translation of the Holy Bible and Roman Missal into Igbo language and taking *Exultet* and Passion Narrative of Good Friday, which were hitherto sang in Latin, in Igbo language. It is now common place to find local hymns and instruments accompanied with dance and clapping of hands as features of Igbo liturgical worship.

Anibueze (2018) is of the view that liturgical innovations and renewal in Igbo land started between 1900 and 1977, with the production of Igbo liturgical, biblical and catechetical texts. Praying the Holy Rosary and singing of the Latin hymns like *Lauda Sion* during Eucharistic processions, such as Corpus Christi or Christ the King celebrations, are now celebrated with many traditional modes of communication. Above all, during the celebration of Holy Mass, "The procession is now accompanied with singing of traditional songs and dancing to the rhythm of local instruments" (Umezinwa, 2014,p.209).

The Ngas people use the animal horn flute, which they call *sombi,* for liturgical purposes. During the festival dance of the ancestors, called *fer Nji*, certain rhythms, songs and dance steps are made while the horn flute is blown to appease the ancestors. Women and children could participate in some *fer nji* in these festivals. The songs of the *nji*, ancestors are used during social and festival dances. During emergencies which put the lives of the community at risk, musical instruments like the reed flute, *bel*, the thin corn-stalk flute, *yang I nvelang* or *velang* and the big corn-stalk flute, *kwarak* are used. Small or big drums are used in all festival dances. The small drum *nging* is hung over one shoulder and is beaten by a curved stick, while the free hand hit it. It entails kneeling to control the beat and musical messages communicated. It is used in all social events where two or more drummers perform simultaneously. Because the big drum (kung) is sacred and very big, the drummer has to sit or stand by its side when performing (Habila, & Danfulani, 1996).

Death and Funeral Rites

In Igbo land, "The adoption of traditional religious features into Christian celebrations is very pronounced in funeral rites. Just as in the traditional practice, the funeral mass is often now celebrated in the family compound of the diseased. The burial of the diseased is always in his or her compound and not in the cemetery. This is a hangover from the traditional religion" (Umezinwa, 2014, p.210).

In Ngas land, when someone dies, the person is mourned for three days. The Christian community prays for the person on the third day, with a celebration, to mark the three days Christ spent in the tomb. However, the three days wailing is that of victory over death, since it is believed that somehow the dead are around, and could visit, and death has been defeated. It is held that, psychologically, death is powerless because those who have died are not actually dead but they are *nji* - **living dead which form an extension of the community of the living. Etymologically,** *Nji* **denotes ancestors which derive from the word** *ji,* **which means "come" or "arrival."** *Nji* **could mean "the one who comes back or returns from the dead." Among**

the Chadic-speakers of the Jos-Plateau area, especially the Ngas, there is a strong belief in rebirth. According to Ngas tradition, the dead are buried facing Sara, the east, to facilitate their return to the human world. Sara represents their ancestral home in the east towards the Chad-Borno basin from where the dead are re-borned (Habila, & Danfulani, 1996). This view is now replaced with the hope of union with the resurrected Christ in heaven.

Baptism and Churching

For the Igbos, the Church has adopted some form of inculturation with regard to a child that is born. "After Baptism, the woman goes for churching. This consists of presenting the child formally to the Lord, offering mass of thanksgiving and the eating and drinking that follow soon after the mass. In the traditional religion, sacrifice of thanksgiving was offered to the ancestors generally 28 days after the birth of a child" (Umezinwa, 2014,p.211).

In like manner, Ngas people have the manhood training which was based on a circumcision (Vwang) rite of separation that lasted for about 30 to 60 days. Associated with mysteries of worship, ancestors and the spirit world, this period was aimed at testing to know who is a real man among young men. While those who are brave were called real men, *Gomis,* anyone who died was said to have been eaten by the ancestors: "Won se kora." Women were not part of this ceremony (Ngas cultural festival - Pusdung, 2019 & Dajur cited in Dyikuk, 2019c). Also, there is the *Gwim* rite which is a covenant-making or oath-taking meal, which entails that the people will reach an agreement or take an oath before the spirit realm that they will cease from committing sin and wickedness in the land. This is done when drought is associated with consequences of communal and individual transgression. *Gwim* rite is performed to cleanse or purify the land before a rain maker is begged to invoke rainfall. It is believed that if this rite of oath-taking does not take place, the drought will not abate (Habila, & Danfulani, 1996). Both *Vwang* and *Gwim* are now considered as the sacrament of confirmation.

Elements of Human Communication

Scholars have maintained that various elements of human communication, such as activeness, solidarity and complementarity, ethic of reciprocity and shared philosophy, tradition and religion are rich traditional modes of communication that find expression in *Igwebuike* and *Shikrot* cultures. Describing traditional media as an admixture of beliefs, opinions, systems, models, actions, culture and historical narrative of a given people, they contend that they constitute the oil that greases day-to-day life in rural Africa (Dyikuk, 2019a; DomNwachukwu, 2018; Kanu, 2016 & Kanu, 2017). From active listening during the celebration of Holy Mass, concrete solidarity at Small Christian Communities (SCCs) to shared values, such as the need for saying the truth at all times as well as the place of tradition and religion, these elements of human communication are invaluable assets in liturgical inculturation.

Theology of Liturgical Inculturation: Views and Insights

In attempting to regurgitate or generate a theology of inculturation, it is important to look in the direction of pastoral communication. Perhaps, the best way to initiative is to the Pastoral Instruction on the Means of Social Communication, *Communio Et Progressio*, (CP, No.11) where Christ is described as a Perfect Communicator who related with humanity through His "incarnation." That document further discloses that by totally identifying Himself with those who are expected to receive His communication, He gave His message in words and by the whole manner of His life by preaching the divine message out of the press of His people without fear or compromise. To do that, it continues, He had to adjust to His people's way of life. This epic rendering speaks to the heart of the interplay between faith and culture. Expectedly, the Pontifical *Council for Culture* has demonstrated leadership in framing requisite perspectives for "reading the signs of the time" (Dyikuk, 2017). Without this, there would be no meaningful inculturation.

This study will consider some theological points of view for an important endeavor like liturgical inculturation. From the submissions of the Second Vatican Council to post synodal documents and other papal encyclicals, there is robust support for incarnating the word of God and the liturgy in various cultures. The Church supports liturgical inculturation for the following reasons:

To Introduce Peoples/Cultures into the Church

Just as Jesus was born into Jewish culture, where we are born introduces us to the culture and tradition of our immediate environment. This shows that we all come from different traditions and cultures. As such, the Church "introduces peoples, together with their cultures, into her own community" through inculturation (John Paul II, 1990, No 52 & *Catechesi Tradendae*, 1979, No 53). This it does by making the Christian realize that he is welcome to the faith, without prejudice to where he comes from. In fact, the universality and catholicity of the Church supports this view because, the Church is for people of every tribe, tongue, people and nation.

Enrich the Gospel with Positive Values/Forms

There is no culture that has no positive aspects. For example, the aspect of respect for elders and kneeling in prayer in Igbo and Ngas cultures does not contradict the Catholic faith. Therefore, the Church does not reject those rich aspects of traditional values that can animate the faith. Indeed: "Every culture offers positive values and forms which can enrich the way the Gospel is preached, understood and lived" (John Paul II, 2001, No 16).

Become a Bride Bedecked with Jewels

The analogy of the Church as the bride of Christ lends credence to the theology of liturgical inculturation. This parallel indicates that faith and culture are two sides of a coin. Through using none offensive signs and symbols in liturgical or para-liturgical activities, the Church takes up the values of different cultures and becomes *sponsa ornata monilibus suis*, "the bride bedecked with her jewels" (cf. Is61:10)" (John Paul II, 1995, No 61).

Ensure Cultural Diversity/Unity

In a Church where conservatists, non-conformists and ecclesiastical mavericks think that liturgical inculturation poses a threat to the unity of the Church, the people of God are reminded that "When properly understood, cultural diversity is not a threat to Church unity. The Holy Spirit, sent by the Father and the Son, transforms our hearts and enables us to enter into the perfect communion of the blessed Trinity, where all things find their unity" (Francis, 2013, No 117,p.94). If anything, liturgical inculturation aspires to promote cultural diversity and the unity of the spirit.

Transmit the Faith in Newer Forms

Liturgical inculturation helps to transmit the faith in ever new forms. This is why understanding evangelization as inculturation is key. In trying to undertake inculturation, the culture experiences a rebirth as the people of God in a particular Church are able to translate the gift of God into their life and in consonance with their genius, thus bearing witness to the faith they received. This enriches the faith in a new and eloquent way (Francis, 2013, No 122).

Ensure a Locus Theologicus for New Evangelization

In an era of new evangelization, the people of God are charged to promote and strengthen the faith through continuous inculturation. "Indeed, popular piety, with all its expressions, teaches us to read the signs of time because they are a locus *theologicus* which demands our attention in an era of new evangelization" (Francis, 2013, No 126). Recall that John Paul II employed the term "new evangelisation" in section 33 of his encyclical, *Redemptoris Missio*, to draw the attention of the Church to Mission *ad gentes*, Christian communities and the new evangelisation (Cotter, 2013 & Dyikuk, 2019d).

Create Synthesis with a Particular Culture

Theologians are increasingly looking for avenues where there will be a perfect harmony between faith and culture. Perhaps, that is, Pope Francis warned that the faith should not be predicated on fixed formulations or specific absolute words. He contends that because this communication occurs in different ways, it is not possible to catalogue them all. He surmised thus: "If the Gospel is embedded in a culture, the message is no longer transmitted solely from person to person. In countries where Christianity is a minority, then, along with encouraging each of the baptized to proclaim the Gospel, particular Churches should actively promote at least preliminary forms of inculturation. The ultimate aim should be that the Gospel, as preached in categories proper to each culture, will create a new synthesis with that particular culture" (Francis, 2013, No 129,p.104).

LITURGICAL INCULTURATION: BOTTLENECKS AND CHALLENGES

Doubts and Fears

Most efforts at liturgical inculturation are met with doubt, fear and apprehension. This is because African theologians are sometimes circumspect about which aspect of culture they should push forward and which they should discard. "This is always a slow process and at we can be overly fearful. But if we allow doubts and fears to dampen our courage, instead of being creative we will remain comfortable and make no progress whatsoever. In this case we will not take an active part in historical processes, but become mere onlookers as the Church gradually stagnates" (Francis, 2013, No 129,p.104). Umezinwa, agrees that "There are some people who are not comfortable with the idea of spreading the gospel through the vehicle of culture" (2014,p.213). These unresolved doubts and fears frustrate genuine efforts at inculturating the faith.

Aberrations and Abuses

Various abuses and aberrations have slowed the approval of rites by the Vatican. Some priests experiment liturgical inculturation with changing the structure of Holy Mass. Some even go as far as using another form of bread or other types of unapproved wines for the celebration of the Holy Eucharist. For instance, some traditional beliefs and practices, such as belief in reincarnation, traditional method of healing, libation to the ancestors/spirits and polytheism, which are gradually being adopted into Christian practice in the name of inculturation, are at variance with Christian doctrine and should be opposed (Etuk, 2002). Also, excessive use of incense and wooden utensils which makes purification after Mass difficult is a recurrent decimal in many places. Because Africans love dancing, some priests permit some immodest kinds of dance which are sensual in nature in the name of dancing in an African way. This leaves local ordinaries and major superiors with the burden of sanctioning inculturation attempts with good intention.

Syncretism

For instance, back in the seminary, a novice of Ngas extraction that was taking some courses with the seminarians suggested that dog meat which is a delicacy among the Ngas people should be used for the Eucharist. The rebuttal she got from the seminarians was enough to send home the message that the idea was weird and unacceptable. This is an example of syncretism. It is common to find people in both cultures patronizing dibias or shrines for concoctions and charms which they either use for protection, seeking a lover or to harm a perceived aggressor. This syncretic tendency has the capacity of making people develop a superstitious mentality during liturgical functions so that they see the use of sacraments, such as Holy Water, as having "magical powers." This is a major drawback in developing a theology of liturgical inculturation. Many Africans today declare that are Christians, yet when it comes to matters of inner aspects of their lives, such as passage rites and crises, they turn to their African traditional religions (**Udeani**, 2007). By proposing that the Church needs "to reduce the syncretic practices among its adherents and build up a strong faith that can serve a bulwark in moments of crisis," (Umezinwa, 2014,p.203) this author presupposes that syncretism is a danger that should be expunged.

Lack of Knowing the Culture

The urban/rural migration in Africa in search for a better life and white collar job has forced many people out of their ancestral homes. This has further made them to forget their culture and traditions. Many priests, religious as well as seminarians and novices are products of this cultural dislocation. It becomes very difficult for them to know the deposit of culture. Since they are not in touch with their roots, it becomes very difficult to inculturate the faith. For example, it is over 100 years since Catholic Missionaries came to Pankshin, but Masses are still said in Hausa language in over 95 percent of the parishes across the diocese. Except for the New Testament, *Shikrot Mpwi,* there is no liturgical book, including the sacramentary, in Ngas language. While those who know the culture do not know the faith, those who know the faith do not know the culture – there lies the paradox. Anyanwu (2019) argues that the Church in Igbo land needs to understand the values Igbo people attach to their culture and make use of them for proper inculturation. This is also true for the Ngas people.

Failure to Understand the Deposit of Faith

The African priest is often caught in a dilemma. He learns theology in English and thinks in the local language - Ngas or Igbo. For those who travel to Rome for further studies, the story is worse because they are forced to learn Italian and are taught in that language only to return home and teach in English or struggle to translate what they have learn in the local dialect. As such, the challenge is, thinking in Italian and speaking English, Igbo and Ngas makes it difficult to communicate effectively, let alone talk about inculturating the faith. The point is that the faith often comes in a Westernized form that is difficult to digest. As a result, inculturating becomes some form of randomized trials.

CONCLUSION

From the views of ecclesiastical sources, the study highlighted plausible reasons for liturgical inculturation to include introducing peoples/cultures into the Church, enriching the gospel with positive values/forms, becoming a bride bedecked with jewels, ensuring cultural diversity/unity, transmitting the faith in newer forms, ensuring a locus *theologicus* for new evangelization and creating synthesis with a particular culture. Also, we saw that doubts and fears, aberrations and abuses, syncretism, lack of knowing the culture and failure to understand the deposit of faith are bottlenecks which stand in the way of a robust liturgical inculturation in the African context.

After a careful review of extant literature in both *Igwebuike* and *Shikrot* philosophical points of view, the study highlighted rethinking theological content, employing music and dance, use of signals, signs and symbols, utilizing proverbs and wise sayings, restoring group/participatory communication and debuting inculturation guidelines as doable recommendations. In attempting the romance between faith and culture in Igbo and Ngas traditions, it is important to understand that "A people continuously evangelizes itself" (Puebla Document, 1979, p.450). While evangelisation is a continuum, it must be established that the Holy Spirit is the principal agent of inculturation (Aparecida Document, 2007, p.264).

In conclusion, interreligious dialogue must be employed between the Church and traditional religion (Anyanwu, 2019) in Africa. It is crucial to develop an ongoing kind of evangelization which baptizes the rich values of the cultures under review. Little wonder, one expert opined that: "African inculturation theologians have chiefly re-interpreted western theological traditions of the Church through a retrieval of some traditional African concepts and values" (Ishola, 2012, pp.166-169). Because many Igbos and Ngas people are now Christians, inculturation of the faith has taken roots amongst them (Dyikuk, 2019a). This is why we need more than a glance at the traditional modes of communication through the lenses of liturgical inculturation towards a more concrete empirical research in *Igwebuike* and *Shikrot* traditions which garners support for thinking about God and man's relationship with Him in the way the African thinks and knows best.

RECOMMENDATIONS: TOWARDS LITURGICAL INCULTURATION IN IGWEBUIKE AND SHIKROT WORLDVIEWS

Rethinking Theological Content: Various stakeholders, like theologians, especially lecturers in Nigerian Major Seminaries, the Directorate of Social Communication at the Catholic Secretariat of Nigeria (CSN), the Diocesan and Religious Directors of Social Communications of the Catholic Church in Nigeria, and the Catholic Theological Association of Nigeria (CATHAN), need to rethink the content of theological inculturation. "Religion needs dynamism or growth in order to address the ever changing needs of man. It needs culture contact as well to do the same. The church needs to be dynamic; it needs to grow; it needs to enter into dialogue with Igbo culture in order to be relevant to the people" (Umezinwa, 2014,p.203). What this translates to is that indigenous content of communication, like *Igwebuike* and *Shikrot* philosophies of communication, trado-modern and rural communication, should be included in the curriculum for formation in both philosophy and theology. Future leaders of the Church should be taught on the need to baptize the good aspects of culture towards solving contemporary issues.

Restoring Group/Participatory Communication: The onus lies on the hierarchy of the Church in Nigeria and theologians to make concerted efforts at restoring group and participatory communication in various dioceses. The fertile ground for this is Small Christian Communities (SCCs) where group communication engenders solidarity and fellow feeling. Also, "at the level of interpersonal, group, or trado-rural communication, it behoves all to listen to one another, ask critical questions that affect life as well as the realities of peace and justice so as to drive home wholesome growth in all sectors of life" (Dyikuk, 2018b, p.15).

Employing Music and Dance: Unarguably, music and dance are part and parcel of liturgical celebrations in Africa. Although without official ecclesiastical endorsement, local music and dance have become part and parcel of liturgical celebrations in Nigeria. In Igbo culture, African music and dance have been truly incarnated as genuine aids to the true worship of God (Udoette, 2012 & Dyikuk, 2019a). From Pankshin to Awka, it is common place to find families dancing to the altar, especially during thanksgiving for child dedication. Since this practice has been in place for over two decades now, it is incumbent on the Catholic Bishops of Onitsha and Owerri Provinces (for Igbo) as well as Jos Province, where speakers of Ngas language who are part of Pankshin Diocese are domiciled, to come up with a list of approved instruments for liturgical use, as well as measured kind of liturgical dance that should take place during Eucharistic celebrations. Dyikuk (2018a) stresses that traditional songs and music are used to garnish liturgical celebrations. The African mode of worship, which is dynamic and expressive with bodily movements that express joy, should be incorporated in developing a distinctively Igbo (Anyanwu, 2019) and Ngas liturgy.

Use of Signals, Signs and Symbols: The use of signals, signs and symbols is an indispensable aspect of liturgical inculturation. Since the people of South-Eastern Nigeria often employed signals, namely physical embodiments of a message, such as fire, gunshots, canon shots and wooden or skin drum, to draw the attention of listeners that an important message is about to be passed, it becomes crucial for the Church in the areas under consideration to endorse same. In the two cultures, verbal and non-verbal communication constitutes signs and symbols which affect the behaviour of others in communication contexts and have rich meaning. For instance, the Ngas or Igbo traditional patterns of prayer should be considered for possible inculturation into the Church in these regions to suit the people's cultural context (Anyanwu, 2019). Specifically, Anyanwu (2019) contends that the sacred objects and cultural values of Igbo origin could be used to facilitate an Igbo Church. Dioceses should be encouraged to train people in sign language who would assist the deaf and dumb in various communities to understand the word of God. While these signs are associated with denotative meaning, symbols convey connective meaning. This is why scholars emphasize that symbols need an interpreter to unravel their meaning (Dyikuk, 2019a).

Utilizing Proverbs and Wise Sayings: Because of the importance of proverbs and wise sayings in Igbo and Ngas communities, children were taught how to speak in idioms, proverbs and other figures of speech by elders in society. For example, among the Igbos, it was believed without idioms, proverbs, and figures of speech, conversations would be bland and distasteful (DomNwachukwu, 2018 & Dyikuk, 2019a). Dyikuk (2018a) concurs that the liturgy is often spiced with the use of proverbs and fables which reveal elements of trado-rural communication. Indeed, "Liturgical Inculturation should be taken more seriously in terms of using proverbs for homilies or the use of vernacular in liturgical assemblies" (Dyikuk, 2019b, p.114).

Debuting Inculturation Guidelines: Catholic Bishops should be at the forefront of inculturating the faith (Dyikuk, 2019b). Concerted efforts should be made to incarnate media-use into the Nigerian pastoral context (Dyikuk, 2019b). The journal, *Cultures and Faith,* published by the Pontifical Council for Culture, is a veritable tool for ensuring that the Church gate-keeps her faith while accepting new cultures (Dyikuk, 2017). With these in place, "The synthesis of faith and cultural elements enriches the church and makes it strong" (Umezinwa, 2014, p.203).

REFERENCES

Akakuru, O.C; Nwokedi, C.I & Edi, T.O (2015). Means and forms of traditional communication in Igbo Land in contemporary socio-cultural interactions. Journal of Humanities and Social Science (IOSR-JHSS). Volume 20, Issue 6, Ver. IV, [17-20]. DOI: 10.9790/0837-20641720.

Anibueze, M.R (2018). African Catholicism: The birth of the liturgical vernacular in Igboland. https://churchlifejournal.nd.edu/articles/authors/sr-mary-reginald-anibueze-ddl/. Accessed 5/8/2020.

Anyanwu, U. (2005). Modes of mass communication in traditional Igboland. International Journal of Communication No. 3 [80-85].

Anyanwu, C. (2019). Reshaping the theology and praxis of inculturation through interreligious dialogue between the Catholic Church and African Traditional Religion in Igboland, Nigeria (Doctoral dissertation, Duquesne University). https://dsc.duq.edu/etd/1781. Accessed 5/7/2020.

Aparecida Document (2007). Fifth General Conference of the Latin American and Caribbean Bishops, 29 June.

Apostolic Exhortation *Catechesi Tradendae* (1979). 53: AAS 71 (16 October), 1321.

Dyikuk, J.J (2017). Christianity and the digital age: Sustaining the online Church. International Journal of Journalism and Mass Communication. 3(1): 043-049.

Dyikuk, J.J (2018a). An appraisal of Liturgy as Communication. Igwebuike: An African Journal of Arts and Humanities. Vol. 4 No 5.[62-85].

Dyikuk, J.J (2018b). Communicating the Marshall Plan to Africa: Challenges and responses. Sumerianz Journal of Social Science, 2018, Vol. x, No. x.[11-18].

Dyikuk, J.J (2019a). The intersection of communication in *Igwebuike* and trado-rural media: A critical evaluation. Journal of African Studies and Sustainable Development Vol. 2 No 3, [175-192].

Dyikuk, J.J (2019b). The pros and cons of social communication in the mission of the church in Nigeria. IGWEBUIKE: An African Journal of Arts and Humanities. Vol. 5 No 1 (98-121).

Dyikuk, J.J (2019c). Communication and culture in *Igwebuike* and *Shikrot* philosophies: A critical evaluation. Igwebuike: An African Journal of Arts and Humanities. Vol. 5 No 8 [1-16].

Dyikuk, J.J (2019d). Media and ministry: Examining the role of priests in Nigeria in new evangelisation. Annals of Journalism and Mass Communication. Vol. 1, Is. 2, [15-22].

Etuk, U (2002). Religion and cultural identity. Ibadan: Hope Publications Ltd.

Francis (2013). Apostolic Exhortation *Evangelii Gaudium* of the Holy Father Francis to the bishops, clergy, consecrated persons and the lay faithful on the proclamation of the gospel in today's world.papa-francesco_esortazione-ap_20131124_evangelii-gaudium_en.Accessed 4/30/2020.

Habila, U & Danfulani, D (1996). Rituals as dance and dance as rituals: The drama of Kok Nji and other festivals in the religious experience of the Ngas, Mupun and Mwaghavul in Nigeria. *Scripta Instituti Donneriani Aboensis*.[27-58]. DO - 10.30674/scripta.67222.

Higazi, A (2011). The Jos crisis: A recurrent Nigerian tragedy. Discussion paper. No. 2. Friedrich-Ebert-Stiftung, Abuja, Nigeria.

Ilogu, E (1974). *Christianity and Igbo culture*. New York: NOK Publishers.

Ishola, H.T.K (2012). CRS826 Ecclesiology. National Open University of Nigeria. Victoria Island, Lagos. www.noun.edu.ng. Accessed 4/30/2020.

John Paul II (1990). Encyclical Letter *Redemptoris Missio* (7 December), 52: AAS 83 (1991), 300.

John Paul II (1995). Post-Synodal Apostolic Exhortation Ecclesia in Africa (14 September), 61: AAS 88 (1996), 39.

John Paul II (2001). Post-Synodal Apostolic Exhortation Ecclesia in Oceania (22 November), 16: AAS 94 (2002), 383.

Kalu, O.U (1995). The dilemma of grassroot inculturation of the Gospel: A case study of a modern controversy in Igboland, 1983-1989. *Journal of Religion in Africa*. Vol. 25, Fasc. 1 [48-72]. DOI: 10.2307/1581138.

Kanu, I. A. (2014). *Igwebuikology* as an Igbo-African philosophy for Catholic-Pentecostal relations. *Jos Studies*. 22. pp.87-98.

Kanu, I. A. (2015b). *Igwebuike as an ontological precondition for African ethics*. International Conference of the Society for Research and Academic Excellence. University of Nigeria, Nsukka. 14th -16th September.

Kanu, I. A. (2015c). *Igwebuike as an Igbo-African philosophy of education*. A paper presented at the International Conference on Law, Education and Humanities. 25th -26th November 2015 University of Paris, France.

Kanu, I. A. (2016). Igwebuike as a trend in African philosophy. Igwebuike: An African Journal of Arts and Humanities. Vol.2. No. 1 [97-101].

Kanu, A. I. (2017). Igwebuike as an Igbo-African ethic of reciprocity. Igwebuike: An African Journal of Arts and Humanities. A Publication of Tansian University, Department of Philosophy and Religious Studies. Vol. 3 No 2.[155-160].

Kanu, I. A. (2019). *Igwebuike* research methodology: A new trend for scientific and wholistic investigation. *IGWEBUIKE: An African Journal of Arts and Humanities* (IAAJAH). *5. 4. pp. 95-105.*

Kanu, I. A. (2019). *Igwebuikeconomics*: The Igbo apprenticeship for wealth creation. *IGWEBUIKE: An African Journal of Arts and Humanities* (IAAJAH). *5. 4. pp. 56-70.*

Kanu, I. A. (2019). *Igwebuikecracy*: The Igbo-African participatory cocio-political system of governance. *TOLLE LEGE: An Augustinian Journal of the Philosophy and Theology. 1. 1. pp. 34-45.*

Kanu, I. A. (2016a). *Igwebuike* as an Igbo-African hermeneutics of globalisation. *IGWEBUIKE: An African Journal of Arts and Humanities*, Vol. 2 No.1. pp. 61-66.

Kanu, I. A. (2016a). *Igwebuike* as the consummate foundation of African Bioethical principles. *An African journal of Arts and Humanities* Vol.2 No1 June, pp.23-40.

Kanu, I. A. (2016b) *Igwebuike* as an expressive modality of being in African ontology. *Journal of Environmental and Construction Management. 6. 3.* pp.12-21.

Kanu, I. A. (2017). *Igwebuike* as an Igbo-African philosophy for Christian-Muslim relations in Northern Nigeria. In Mahmoud Misaeli (Ed.). *Spirituality and Global Ethics* (pp. 300-310). United Kingdom: Cambridge Scholars.

Kanu, I. A. (2017). *Igwebuike* as an Igbo-African philosophy for the protection of the environment. *Nightingale International Journal of Humanities and Social Sciences.* Vol. 3. No. 4. pp. 28-38.

Kanu, I. A. (2017). *Igwebuike* as the hermeneutic of individuality and communality in African ontology. *NAJOP: Nasara Journal of Philosophy.* Vol. 2. No. 1. pp. 162-179.

Kanu, I. A. (2017a). *Igwebuike* and question of superiority in the scientific community of knowledge. *Igwebuike: An African Journal of Arts and Humanities.*Vol.3 No1. pp. 131-138.

Kanu, I. A. (2017a). *Igwebuike as a philosophical attribute of Africa in portraying the image of life.* A paper presented at the 2017 Oracle of Wisdom International Conference by the Department of Philosophy, Tansian University, Umunya, Anambra State, 27-29 April.

Kanu, I. A. (2017b). *Igwebuike* as a complementary approach to the issue of girl-child education. *Nightingale International Journal of Contemporary Education and Research.* Vol. 3. No. 6. pp. 11-17.

Kanu, I. A. (2017b). *Igwebuike* as a wholistic response to the problem of evil and human suffering. *Igwebuike: An African Journal of Arts and Humanities.* Vol. 3 No 2, March.

Kanu, I. A. (2017e). *Igwebuike* as an Igbo-African modality of peace and conflict resolution. *Journal of African Traditional Religion and Philosophy Scholars. Vol. 1. No. 1. pp. 31-40.*

Kanu, I. A. (2017g). *Igwebuike* and the logic (Nka) of African philosophy. *Igwebuike: An African Journal of Arts and Humanities. 3. 1.* pp. 1-13.

Kanu, I. A. (2017h). *Igwebuike* philosophy and human rights violation in Africa. *IGWEBUIKE: An African Journal of Arts and Humanities.* Vol. 3. No. 7. pp. 117-136.

Kanu, I. A. (2017i). *Igwebuike* as a hermeneutic of personal autonomy in African ontology. *Journal of African Traditional Religion and Philosophy Scholars. Vol. 2. No. 1. pp. 14-22.*

Kanu, I. A. (2018). *Igwe Bu Ike* as an Igbo-African hermeneutics of national development. *Igbo Studies Review. No. 6.* pp. 59-83.

Kanu, I. A. (2018). *Igwebuike* as an African integrative and progressive anthropology. *NAJOP: Nasara Journal of Philosophy.* Vol. 2. No. 1. pp. 151-161.

Kanu, I. A. (2018). New Africanism: *Igwebuike* as a philosophical Attribute of Africa in portraying the Image of Life. In Mahmoud Misaeli, Sanni Yaya and Rico Sneller (Eds.). *African Perspectives on Global on Global Development* (pp. 92-103). United Kingdom: Cambridge Scholars Publishing.

Ngas cultural festival - Pusdung. (2019). Circumcision in Ngas tradition. www.web.facebook. com/permalink.php?story_fbid=2285510651772436&id=1588390771484431&_xts_[0]=68. Accessed 5/22/2020.

Obindigbo.com (2020). Igbo Culture.http://obindigbo.com.ng/category/igbo-culture/. Accessed 5/11/2020.

Pankshin Local Government Area (2020). About Pankshin. *www.plateaustate.gov.ng/government/lgas/pankshin.Accessed 5/11/2020.*

Paulines Publications Africa (2020). Erection of the diocese of Pankshin and appointment of the first bishop. http://paulinesafrica.org/erection-of-the-diocese-of-pankshin-and-appointment-of-the-first-bishop/.Accessed 5/11/2020.

Puebla Document (1979). Third General Conference of the Latin American and Caribbean Bishops, 23 March.

Society of African Missions (2014).Pankshin: Nigeria's 56th diocese is born. https://sma.ie/pankshin-nigeria-s-56th-diocese-is-born/. Accessed 5/11/2020.

Tolu, (2020). Facts about the angas tribe of Nigeria. https://everyevery.ng/facts-about-the-angas-tribe-of-nigeria/. Accessed 5/11/2020.

Udeani, C.C (2007). Inculturation as dialogue: Igbo culture and the message of Christ. *Series: Intercultural Theology and Study of Religions.* Vol.2. [xv,228].DOI: https://doi.org/10.1163/9789401204606.

Umezinwa, C.C. (2014). Inculturation of the Church: Example of the Igboland, South-East, Nigeria. An International Journal of Arts and Humanities Bahir Dar, Ethiopia. AFRREV IJAH. Vol. 3 (1), S/No 9, [199-217].

2020 President and Fellows of Harvard College (2020). Catholicism in Nigeria. https://rlp.hds.harvard.edu/faq/catholicism-nigeria. Accessed 5/11/2020.

THE CODE OF CANON LAW AND THE SECOND VATICAN COUNCIL DOCUMENT: AN IGWEBUIKE PERSPECTIVE

IGBOECHESI, Emeka Stanley
Catholic Institute of West Africa
Port Harcourt, Rivers State
padrestantall@yahoo.com

ABSTRACT

The 1883 code effectuates and perfects the renewal of Christian life introduced by the Second Vatican Council. It puts into juridical formulae the principles of the council. This piece, through the underlying principle of Igwebuike philosophy, highlights the complementary relationship between these two essential documents of the Church. Igwebuike is employed here not only as a philosophy but as a methodology of research. It is employed as a transcendent complementary comprehensive systematic quest to penetrate the structure and dynamics of reality ultimately for the purpose of giving honest answers to fundamental questions or opinions to questions that arise within the arena of asking questions and questioning answers, and selfless enlightenment. In this search for truth, Igwebuike is, therefore, understood as an integrated systematic framework that strives beyond all forms of particularities, peculiarities, paradoxes and contradictions, and espouses the path of complementation, therefore, showing how realities can relate to one another in a mutually harmonized non-absolutistic mode. This piece discovers that there is a very strong connection between the Code of Canon Law and the Second Vatican Council Document, and that the two when studied together can be very enriching.

Keywords: Vatican II, Code of Canon Law, Complimentarity, Igwebuike, Methodology

INTRODUCTION

Stability is an essential quality of any good legal system, because a community's laws are an expression of its identity, and there is no identity without permanency. In a religious community where the source of its identity is in the common memory of a divine revelation, the demand for stability is even stronger. Fidelity to the Word of God and the teachings of the Church becomes the principal virtue. Yet, any good legal system must be open and receptive to developments. No community, secular or religious, can be frozen in time and live; absolute stillness means death. This work, therefore, in the spirit of *Igwebuike* is about the respective roles and desirable balance between Canon law and Vatican II.

VATICAN I AND THE CODE OF 1917

Any process of centralization requires the proliferation of universal laws in order to maintain harmony and promote unity. By the time of the First Vatican Council (1869-1870), the Church's legislative activity had resulted in a considerable confusion. While proclaiming the primacy and infallibility of the Pope, the Council Fathers realized that the Church's legal system needed to be completely revamped. Despite the significant historical attempts to coordinate the Church's laws, there had never been an authoritative or official codification. Even the *Corpus Juris Canonici* was unofficial, scholarly work. Several decades after the close of Vatican I, Pope Pius X attempted to accomplish this task. On March 19, 1904, he announced the establishment of a commission of Cardinals to gather into one authentic collection all the universal canonical legislation of the Latin-rite Church. This monumental task took thirteen years. Much of the work was done by the Secretary of the Commission, Pietro Cardinal Gasparri. This first Code of Canon Law was promulgated on Pentecost Sunday, May 19, 1918 (Komonchak, 1986).

Vatican I represents the final extrication of the Church from the medieval Christendom notion. With the loss of the Papal States, the Church emerged as entirely spiritual. The Church and State were seen as two separate but complete societies. It is only natural, therefore, that their legal systems should be similar, diverging only by reason of goal and means, but identical in the structures required by the nature of man (e.g., general norms, procedures and penalties).

VATICAN II AND THE 1983 CODE

Law is an evolving science and art. It reflects the changing practices and life of a community. It is inevitable that the Church's legal system would once again grow complicated, confusing and unwieldy. Within a relative short period of time, the interpretations clarifying various canons amounted to a printed volume larger than the code itself. The Church's first Codification achieved a great deal of clarity and precluded the massive confusion of former times, but eventually a total revision was necessary. This need for renewal was not simply one of legal technique. On the contrary, changing theological insights and pastoral values in the Church called for a thorough canonical reform of the Church's structures (Komonchak, 1986). Into this situation stepped Pope John XXIII, who ushered in another stage in the revision of canon law, linked to the movement of reform, crystallized in the Second Vatican Council.

Vatican II took an even more significant step towards a separate legal system. It recognized its law on its own model, according to its understanding of itself as a Church. The revised Code still bears some resemblance to civil law, but the similarities are diminished. Thus, the Code is organized differently based on the threefold office of Christ as king, prophet and priest. It considers people of God as a hierarchical communion in which all are commissioned to imitate Christ according to their own "juridic condition." The concrete effects are easily observable: "Governance" is described in General Norms and in Books II, V, VI, VII, "Teaching" is in Book III and "Sanctifying" is Book IV. In addition, penalties are reduced drastically. The second *Codex Juris Canonici* in the history of the Catholics of the Latin rite was promulgated by Pope John Paul II on January 25, 1983 and entered into effect on November 27, 1983. It contains 1,752 canons divided into seven books.

1983 CODE AND VATICAN II: AN IGWEBUIKE PERSPECTIVE

Igwebuike is an Igbo word. It literally means that there is strength in unity. However, philosophically, it points to the complementary nature of reality. It confronts discontinuity and the compartmentalization of reality. Although this philosophy is captured in an Igbo word, it has a universal taste and obvious in universal experience. It is a universal philosophy that is the incarnation and confirmation of the universal relevance of solidarity and complementarity (Kanu, 2017).

The philosophy of Igwebuike is clearly brought to the fore in the interwoven relationship between the 1983 Code and Vatican II. The Constitution, *Sacrae Disciplinae Leges,* in every distinct term notes the incorporation of the New Ecclesiology of Vatican Council II as one of the motivations of the 1983 code. The ecclesiology on which the New Code of Canon Law is based is predominantly that of the Second Vatican Council, for which the Code is rightly called the Code of the Second Vatican Council, to demonstrate the close relationship between the new code and Vatican Council II. A proper understanding of the canons will require close examination of the key features of ecclesiology of the Council as they relate to the canonical system, since the codification mirrors the new ecclesiology (Nwagwu, 2002).

The new code embraces the Council; it solemnly re-proposes fundamental institutions and major innovations and it establishes positive norms for implementing the Councils. There are several examples of conciliar innovations that can be found in the new Code of Canon Law:

The first is the doctrine regarding the episcopate and the relationship between the episcopate and the primate, that is, episcopal collegiality. This is not an entirely new doctrine in the deep consciousness of the Church, but rather a happy discovery. The code firstly, in canons 330-341, represents this clearly, and secondly, canons 342-348 accompany it with the positive view that constitutes the structure of the Synod of Bishops, allowing effective implementation of the structure of Episcopal collegiality (Olson, 2013).

A second example is the Council's teaching on the laity and, therefore, on the appropriate and active mission of the lay faithful in the life of the Church. Once again, this is not absolutely new, but more rediscovery. In canons 224-231, the revised Code of Canon Law reiterates this teaching through a series of regulations, regarding the diocesan pastoral council or the parochial pastoral council (Olson, 2013), structures that allow the laity to effectively participate in the pastoral decisions of the bishop or the pastor.

More than the mere necessity of updating the Church's legal system, the new code was meant to effectuate and perfect the renewal of Christian life introduced by the Council. The revision of the code was directly sought and requested by the Council itself. The Council Fathers were quite conscious of the canonical revision, which was to follow their deliberations. They left the specification of many disciplinary matters to the subsequent codification process. The code, therefore, became the instrument for carrying out the decisions of the Council. It was subsequently directed towards putting into juridical formulae the principles of the Council (Nwagwu, 2002).

The Commissions for Revision and the consultors who drafted the code referred continuously to the documents of the Council in the course of their work. The canons in their formulations reveal this close and dependant relationship on the Council. They frequently employed the concepts, language and expressions of the conciliar decrees. The code therefore depends on the previous work of the Council; it reflects its ecclesiology, its overall theological vision and manifests it spirit, not because of its content but because of its origin as both the code and the Council originated in a bid to renew Christian life.

In consonance with the creed of *Igwebuike*, much of the post-conciliar legislation implementing the Council's decrees, such as norms on dispensations, ecumenical marriages, annulment procedures and liturgical discipline, is incorporated into the revised code. This means that the code must be interpreted in the light of the conciliar documents. As Paul VI explained:

> Now, however, with changed conditions of things – for life seems to move along with greater speed – we must recognize with due prudence that canon law must be adapted; to the new mentality of the Second Vatican Ecumenical Council from which great contributions are being made to pastoral duties and new needs of the people of God.

To understand the canons properly, therefore, one must seek their meaning in their sources, that is, the documents of the Council. The conciliar teachings rule and guide the interpretation of the canons. It is, therefore, true to say that the Code of Canon Law is the fruit of the Second Vatican Council, the Council's final document. This means that the canons of the Code must be read in the light of the constitutions and decrees of the Council, which gave rise to them (Nwagwu, 2002).

At the 100th anniversary of the 1917 code that took place in 2017, Pope Francis stated that after the Second Vatican Council marked the passage from an ecclesiology modeled on canon law to a canon law conforming to ecclesiology. Canon law "should be the instrument for implementing the vision of the Second Vatican Council." Pope Francis continued by saying that, the new code should promote, "Collegiality, synodality in the governance of the church; valuing particular churches; the responsibility of all Christian faithful in the mission of the Church… and healthy collaboration between the Church and civil society in its various expressions" (Wooden, 2017).

CONCLUSION

Like any other piece of legislation or system of jurisprudence, the code is often difficult to decipher and there is a risk of missing some nuance in the text, or of being aware of some underlying legal principle if the principles of Igwebuike are not adhered to. Therefore, the documents of Second Vatican Council are necessary when exploring the Church's internal legal system. This is a fact every canonist or student of canon law should remember while delving into the code.

REFERENCES

Kanu, I. A. (2017). Sources of Igwebuike Philosophy: Towards a Social-Cultural Foundation. *IGWEBUIKE: An African Journal of Arts and Humanities.* 9.1. 1.

Kanu, I. A. (2015a). *African philosophy: An ontologico-existential hermeneutic approach to classical and contemporary issues.* Nigeria: Augustinian Publications.

Kanu, I. A. (2015b). *Igwebuike as an ontological precondition for African ethics.* International Conference of the Society for Research and Academic Excellence. University of Nigeria, Nsukka. 14th -16th September.

Kanu, I. A. (2015c). *Igwebuike as an Igbo-African philosophy of education.* A paper presented at the International Conference on Law, Education and Humanities. 25th -26th November 2015 University of Paris, France.

Kanu, I. A. (2016). *Igbo-African Christology: A cultural Christological construct in Post-Missionary Africa.* **Germany: Lambert Publications.**

Kanu, I. A. (2016a). African traditional folk songs as dialogue between education and entertainment. *Cambridge International Journal of Contemporary Education Research.* 6. 6. pp. 53-64.

Kanu, I. A. (2016a). *Igwebuike* as an Igbo-African hermeneutics of globalisation. *IGWEBUIKE: An African Journal of Arts and Humanities,* Vol. 2 No.1. pp. 61-66.

Kanu, I. A. (2016a). *Igwebuike* as the consummate foundation of African Bioethical principles. *An African journal of Arts and Humanities* Vol.2 No1 June, pp.23-40.

Kanu, I. A. (2016b) *Igwebuike* as an expressive modality of being in African ontology. *Journal of Environmental and Construction Management. 6. 3.* pp.12-21.

Kanu, I. A. (2016b). African traditional folktales as an integrated classroom. *Sub-Saharan African Journal of Contemporary Education Research.* Vol.3 No. 6. pp. 107-118.

Kanu, I. A. (2017). *Igwebuike* as an Igbo-African philosophy for Christian-Muslim relations in Northern Nigeria. In Mahmoud Misaeli (Ed.). *Spirituality and Global Ethics* (pp. 300-310). United Kingdom: Cambridge Scholars.

Kanu, I. A. (2017). *Igwebuike* as an Igbo-African philosophy for the protection of the environment. *Nightingale International Journal of Humanities and Social Sciences.* Vol. 3. No. 4. pp. 28-38.

Kanu, I. A. (2017). *Igwebuike* as the hermeneutic of individuality and communality in African ontology. *NAJOP: Nasara Journal of Philosophy.* Vol. 2. No. 1. pp. 162-179.

Kanu, I. A. (2017a). *Igwebuike* and question of superiority in the scientific community of knowledge. *Igwebuike: An African Journal of Arts and Humanities.* Vol.3 No1. pp. 131-138.

Kanu, I. A. (2017a). *Igwebuike as a philosophical attribute of Africa in portraying the image of life.* A paper presented at the 2017 Oracle of Wisdom International Conference by the Department of Philosophy, Tansian University, Umunya, Anambra State, 27-29 April.

Kanu, I. A. (2017b). *Igwebuike* as a complementary approach to the issue of girl-child education. *Nightingale International Journal of Contemporary Education and Research.* Vol. 3. No. 6. pp. 11-17.

Kanu, I. A. (2017b). *Igwebuike* as a wholistic response to the problem of evil and human suffering. *Igwebuike: An African Journal of Arts and Humanities.* Vol. 3 No 2, March.

Kanu, I. A. (2017e). *Igwebuike* as an Igbo-African modality of peace and conflict resolution. *Journal of African Traditional Religion and Philosophy Scholars. Vol. 1. No. 1. pp. 31-40.*

Kanu, I. A. (2017g). *Igwebuike* and the logic (Nka) of African philosophy. *Igwebuike: An African Journal of Arts and Humanities.* 3. 1. pp. 1-13.

Kanu, I. A. (2017h). *Igwebuike* philosophy and human rights violation in Africa. *IGWEBUIKE: An African Journal of Arts and Humanities.* Vol. 3. No. 7. pp. 117-136.

Kanu, I. A. (2017i). *Igwebuike* as a hermeneutic of personal autonomy in African ontology. *Journal of African Traditional Religion and Philosophy Scholars. Vol. 2. No. 1. pp. 14-22.*

Komonchak, A. J. (1986). Vatican II and New Code. *Archives de Sciences des Religion.* 62. 1.

Nwagwu, O. M. (2002). *Theology and Methodology of Canon Law.* Enugu: SNAAP Press LTD.

Olson, C. E. (2013). *Vatican II and the Code of Canon Law.* Retrieved 6/5/2020. https.//www. catholicworldreport.com/2013/01/22/Vatican-ii-and-the-code-of-canon-law.

Wooden, C. (2017). Canon Law Must Serve Vatican II Vision of the Church. Retrieved 6/6/2020. https.//www.ncroline.org.news/Vatican/canon-law-must-serve-vatican-ii-vision-of-the-church-pope-says.

THE CODE OF CANON LAW AND THE SCRIPTURE: AN IGWEBUIKE PERSPECTIVE

IGBOECHESI, Emeka Stanley
Catholic Institute of West Africa
Port Harcourt, Rivers State
padrestantall@yahoo.com

ABSTRACT

The purpose of the canon law is to help Catholics live well as Christians in line with the teachings of the Holy Bible. This piece studies the relationship between the canon law and the Scripture. It adopts Igwebuike as an Igbo-African philosophy for a complementary relationship between these two disciplines of the Church and their unique contributions to the development of Igwebuike philosophy. It is employed as a transcendent complementary comprehensive systematic quest to penetrate the structure and dynamics of reality ultimately for the purpose of giving honest answers to fundamental questions or opinions to questions that arise within the arena of asking questions and questioning answers, and selfless enlightenment. In this search for truth, Igwebuike is, therefore, understood as an integrated systematic framework that strives beyond all forms of particularities, peculiarities, paradoxes and contradictions, and espouses the path of complementation, therefore, showing how realities can relate to one another in a mutually harmonized non-absolutistic mode. This piece discovers that there is a very strong connection between the Code of Canon Law and the Scripture, and that the two, when studied together, can be very enriching.

Keywords: Igwebuike, Philosophy, Code of Canon Law, Scripture, Church, Catholic

INTRODUCTION

Rules are needed whenever people work or live together. The Church has its own system of law, known as 'Canon Law.' The purpose of canon law is to help Catholics live well as Christians in line with what the Scripture teaches. In consideration of the relationship between the canon law and the Scripture, some schools of thought in their approach propound for a virtual identity of the two. Such an approach makes the study of canonical science not only dependent on but subservient to theological discipline. This work, in accordance with the tenets of *Igwebuike*, seeks a more balanced relationship.

THE SCRIPTURE IN CANONICAL TEXTS

The Scripture is relevant to the development of the canon law. Gratian, the father of the study of canon law, suggested this in his first compilation. The opening *Distinctio* of Gratian's *Decretum* began by stating that the human race is ruled by two things, natural law and customary usages. Natural law consists of what is contained in the law and the gospel. The subsequent texts in the *Decretum* bear out this theoretical statement of the Sscripture's legal importance. Scriptural passages were cited frequently. Professor Gaudemet's calculations put the number of references to biblical texts in the *Decretum* at between thirteen and fourteen hundred. Early commentators on the *Decretum* followed this lead, themselves citing passages from the Scripture with regularity (Helmholz, 1994).

It is, however, safe to say that the influence of the Scripture on the canon law diminished after 1200 in favour of a more purely legal science; the Bible was clearly not excluded altogether by later developments. The law of the Church became a subject distinct from theology in a way that it had not earlier been, but the division did not necessarily spell the end of the Bible's utility in the law. Canons included in the Decretals continued to cite passages from the Scripture. Despite the reduction of influence, it is certain that the use of scriptural citation in the creation of law was neither excluded on principle nor ended in fact by the separation of law from theology (Helmholz, 1994). Nevertheless, the Bible played a quantitatively smaller role in the formation of the law than it had in the twelfth and early thirteenth centuries, and this was true in the works of canonists as in the *Corpus iuris canonici* itself.

CANONICAL UNDERSTANDING OF THE SCRIPTURE

When you think of law in the Scripture, it is apt to think of the detailed rules of conduct found in the Book of Leviticus or the Book of Deuteronomy. This, however, was not the approach of the Gratian, the father of canon law. He associated the Scriptures with natural law, a changeless source of law written on our hearts by God. This approach was also found in the writings of the canonists that followed Gratian (Helmholz, 1994). The attitude was amiable, even self-evident to them. They regarded the Bible and they used it, primarily as a way of showing what natural law required of the Church's legal system. The Bible provided juridical norms that were useful in evaluating legislation and in providing guidance for positive law of all sorts.

From the medieval point of view, at least, the approach characteristic of canonists made perfect sense. They held that the Bible showed, in particular ways, and in particular episodes, how men and women ought to arrange their lives. It was up to them to understand its lessons and now apply them. These lessons the canonists sought to draw from scriptural texts. The Bible is rarely used as enacted law. Canonists do not treat biblical texts as direct sources or as statutes; they do not take passages from the Bible and call them a *canon* or *lex*. Instead, they draw legal lessons and legal principles from them.

CANON LAW AND SCRIPTURE: AN IGWEBUIKE PERSPECTIVE

Igwebuike is an Igbo word that is characterized by three simple words. According to Kanu Anthony, the three words involved are identified and explained thus: *Igwe* is a noun which means 'number' or 'population', usually a huge number or population. *Bu* is a verb, which means 'is.' *Ike* is another verb, which means *strength* or *power*. Thus, put together, this means 'number is strength' or 'number is power;' that is, when human beings come together in solidarity and complementarity, they are powerful or can constitute an insurmountable force (kanu, 2017). From the etymological analysis, it is clear that the concept extends to solidarity, collectivism and interdependence.

In the light of the foregoing, many of the canons in the *Decretum* and some Decretals cited passages or events from the Bible as direct justifications for the rules enacted. A number of these were obvious. As a matter of fact, they were inevitable. The canons that dealt with the sacraments could not help but devote some attention to theological questions. Here, the universal appeal of *Igwebuike* comes into play as Scripture is given an important role. No lawyer could deal with a theological question or with the sacramental life of the Church without reference to the Bible. For instance, in accordance with the prescription of canon 849, the correct baptismal formula is determined by the commands of Jesus as found in the Bible, "…baptizing them in the name of the Father and of the Son and of the Holy Spirit…" (Mt28:19). Jesus directed his followers to baptize in the name of the Father, the Son and the Holy Spirit. The words must refer to the Trinity of persons, both individually and in their unity. If one refers to the Trinity by such terms as "creator, sustainer and sanctifier," as used in some circles to avoid so-called 'sexist' language, such a formula will be invalid, since it does not refer to the Three persons of the blessed trinity (Sheehy, 1999). No canonist or theologian could responsibly ignore the "proper form of words" as the Bible commands when discussing this subject in the canon law.

Under procedural law, the Book of Daniel chapter thirteen recounts the story of Susanna and the elders and how Daniel received testimonies in private and separate examination of each witness. According to the book, when Susanna resisted the advances of the elders, they resolved to revenge by accusing her of adultery with an imaginary young man. After Susanna had been condemned to death in an open trial, Daniel intervened. He questioned the two elders separately about the supposed crime. One of them placed her action under a yew tree, the other under a clove tree. Thus, their perjury was revealed and the life of the innocent woman was saved (Helmholz, 1994). Proceduralists see in this story a clear support for the system of canonical procedure. Canon 221 makes the point clear by insisting that procedural rights be respected in the penal process of the Church.

Genesis 3:9, "But the Lord God called to the man and said to him, "Where are you?" Thus, Adam was called to answer for his action. This passage is said to have established one of the basic elements of procedural law, the necessity of a sufficient summons (Helmholz, 1994). God knew where Adam was, yet He called out to Adam as if He was ignorant of Adam's whereabouts. He did that to demonstrate that defendants must be summoned before they are lawfully punished (c.2221). Procedural justice must be accorded to all, even the manifestly guilty. As stipulated in canon 220, everyone has the right to good reputation.

Ecclesiastical penalties have their sources in the Scripture. The Old Testament lays procedures where grievous sins like adultery, apostasy etc., (cf. Gen 20:9; Ex. 32, 21; 1Kgs 2:17; Jer. 19:11, Lev. 4:2, 13 and 27) were proportionately punished with penalties like death, temporary exclusion from the community for omission of circumcision (Gen. 17:14; Num. 9: 1-3) or of the feast of expiation (Lev. 23, 19:30) (Kii, 2019). Following the pattern set by the Bible, canon 1311 states that the Church has its own inherent right to constrain with penal sanctions Christ's faithful who commit offences.

Canonists sometimes see the admonition of Jesus in Mt. 22:21 and Mk.12:17, the things that belong to Caesar should be rendered to Caesar and things that belong to God should be rendered to God as an endorsement for ecclesiastical taxation (Helmholz, 1994). Canon 222 § 1 prescribes the obligation of Christ's faithful to provide for the needs of the Church. Canon 1263 goes further to state that the diocesan bishop, after consulting the finance committee and the council of priests, has the right to levy or tax juridical persons under his authority.

In the mind of a canonist, the biblical texts and examples rarely state straightforward legal rules. They are not laws in the sense of enactments that could be applied directly by a judge or lawyer. Instead, they demonstrate the existence of a norm or a basic legal principle. The passages of the Scripture where it appears that a literal rule of statute appears to have been laid down, are for the most part, not used and applied by canonists, but if ever used, they are used as apt illustrations for general legal standards rather than literal rules to be put into practice.

CONCLUSION

Canonists often consider their work to be more than human science. It is part of a divine plan for the world; hence, they must bear in mind at all times that the salvation of souls is the supreme goal (c.1752). Thus, the science of law in the Church is not simply a way of meeting societal needs. It is part of the unfolding of God's plan for mankind, a plan that is set forth preeminently in the Scripture. The philosophy of, therefore, provides a fundamental reason why canonists see no absurdity between biblical narratives and legal conclusions.

REFERENCES

Helmhoz, H. R. (1994). *The Bible in the Service of Canon Law.* 70 Chicago-Kent Law Review 1557.

Kanu, I. A. 2017. "Igwebuike as an Igbo-African Philosophy of Inclusive Leadership." *IGWEBUIKE: An African Journal of Arts and Humanities.* 3(7): 165-83.

Kanu, I. A. (2015a). *African philosophy: An ontologico-existential hermeneutic approach to classical and contemporary issues.* Nigeria: Augustinian Publications.

Kanu, I. A. (2015b). *Igwebuike as an ontological precondition for African ethics.* International Conference of the Society for Research and Academic Excellence. University of Nigeria, Nsukka. 14th -16th September.

Kanu, I. A. (2015c). *Igwebuike as an Igbo-African philosophy of education.* A paper presented at the International Conference on Law, Education and Humanities. 25th -26th November 2015 University of Paris, France.

Kanu, I. A. (2016). *Igbo-African Christology: A cultural Christological construct in Post-Missionary Africa.* **Germany: Lambert Publications.**

Kanu, I. A. (2016a). African traditional folk songs as dialogue between education and entertainment. *Cambridge International Journal of Contemporary Education Research.* 6. 6. pp. 53-64.

Kanu, I. A. (2016a). *Igwebuike* as an Igbo-African hermeneutics of globalisation. *IGWEBUIKE: An African Journal of Arts and Humanities,* Vol. 2 No.1. pp. 61-66.

Kanu, I. A. (2016a). *Igwebuike* as the consummate foundation of African Bioethical principles. *An African journal of Arts and Humanities* Vol.2 No1 June, pp.23-40.

Kanu, I. A. (2016b) *Igwebuike* as an expressive modality of being in African ontology. *Journal of Environmental and Construction Management.* 6. 3. pp.12-21.

Kanu, I. A. (2016b). African traditional folktales as an integrated classroom. *Sub-Saharan African Journal of Contemporary Education Research.* Vol.3 No. 6. pp. 107-118.

Kanu, I. A. (2017). *Igwebuike* as an Igbo-African philosophy for Christian-Muslim relations in Northern Nigeria. In Mahmoud Misaeli (Ed.). *Spirituality and Global Ethics* (pp. 300-310). United Kingdom: Cambridge Scholars.

Kanu, I. A. (2017). *Igwebuike* as an Igbo-African philosophy for the protection of the environment. *Nightingale International Journal of Humanities and Social Sciences.* Vol. 3. No. 4. pp. 28-38.

Kanu, I. A. (2017). *Igwebuike* as the hermeneutic of individuality and communality in African ontology. *NAJOP: Nasara Journal of Philosophy.* Vol. 2. No. 1. pp. 162-179.

Kanu, I. A. (2017a). *Igwebuike* and question of superiority in the scientific community of knowledge. *Igwebuike: An African Journal of Arts and Humanities.* Vol.3 No1. pp. 131-138.

Kanu, I. A. (2017a). *Igwebuike as a philosophical attribute of Africa in portraying the image of life.* A paper presented at the 2017 Oracle of Wisdom International Conference by the Department of Philosophy, Tansian University, Umunya, Anambra State, 27-29 April.

Kanu, I. A. (2017b). *Igwebuike* as a complementary approach to the issue of girl-child education. *Nightingale International Journal of Contemporary Education and Research.* Vol. 3. No. 6. pp. 11-17.

Kanu, I. A. (2017b). *Igwebuike* as a wholistic response to the problem of evil and human suffering. *Igwebuike: An African Journal of Arts and Humanities.* Vol. 3 No 2, March.

Kanu, I. A. (2017e). *Igwebuike* as an Igbo-African modality of peace and conflict resolution. *Journal of African Traditional Religion and Philosophy Scholars. Vol. 1. No. 1. pp. 31-40.*

Kanu, I. A. (2017g). *Igwebuike* and the logic (Nka) of African philosophy. *Igwebuike: An African Journal of Arts and Humanities.* 3. 1. pp. 1-13.

Kanu, I. A. (2017h). *Igwebuike* philosophy and human rights violation in Africa. *IGWEBUIKE: An African Journal of Arts and Humanities.* Vol. 3. No. 7. pp. 117-136.

Kanu, I. A. (2017i). *Igwebuike* as a hermeneutic of personal autonomy in African ontology. *Journal of African Traditional Religion and Philosophy Scholars. Vol. 2. No. 1. pp. 14-22.*

Kii, B. P. 2019. *Offences and Punishments in the Catholic Church.* Enugu: Fourth Dimension Publishing Co., Ltd.

Sheehy .G. et al. 1999. *The Canon Law Letter and Spirit.* London: Geoffrey Chapman.

THE CODE OF CANON LAW AND CATECHISM OF THE CATHOLIC CHURCH: AN IGWEBUIKE PERSPECTIVE

IGBOECHESI, Emeka Stanley
Catholic Institute of West Africa
Port Harcourt, Rivers State
padrestantall@yahoo.com

ABSTRACT

The Code of Canon Law and the Catechism of the Catholic Church are two very important documents in the Church. As important as each of these texts may be, they do not work in isolation. It is in this regard that this piece attends to the interdependent nature of CIC and CCC from an African lens via Igwebuike as an African complementary philosophy. It is employed as a transcendent complementary comprehensive systematic quest to penetrate the structure and dynamics of reality ultimately for the purpose of giving honest answers to fundamental questions or opinions to questions that arise within the arena of asking questions and questioning answers, and selfless enlightenment. In this search for truth, Igwebuike, is therefore, understood as an integrated systematic framework that strives beyond all forms of particularities, peculiarities, paradoxes and contradictions, and espouses the path of complementation, therefore, showing how realities can relate to one another in a mutually harmonized non-absolutistic mode. This piece discovers that there is a very strong connection between the Code of Canon Law and the Catechism of the Catholic Church, and that the two, when studied together, can be very enriching.

Keywords: Igwebuike, Catechism, Catholic Church, Code of Canon Law, Complementarity

INTRODUCTION

Every canonical norm is based on certain theological premise or doctrine. The search into the theological foundation of the canons in the 1983 code reveals theological presuppositions found in the official pronouncements of the Church on the matter. It takes into account the teaching documents of the Church, such as the Catechism of the Catholic Church, Papal Magisterium, etc. The code and Catechism do not contradict each other. Hence, there exists a level of solidarity which this work hopes to explore from the point of view of *Igwebuike* philosophy.

THE CATECHISM OF THE CATHOLIC CHURCH

The history of Catechisms in the Catholic Church goes back to the very earliest days of the Church. There is a document called the Didache, which sets out in a systematic way the beliefs, practices and moral imperatives of early Christians. The Didache dates from the end of the first century. It is an extraordinary ancient type of catechetical document. In 1566, the document commonly known as Roman Catechism was published in response to the request issued three years earlier before the Council of Trent (Bruskewitz, 1996). This was used until 1978; it inspired, as intended, the creation of many national catechisms.

In January 1985, Pope John Paul II convoked an extraordinary synod of the council of bishops to celebrate the 20th anniversary of the Second Vatican Council. The synod expressed a general desire for a new catechism for the universal Church, and so the following year the Pope organized a commission to draft one. Thus, this was done in the light of the Second Vatican Council and the whole of the Church's tradition. The text was approved by John Paul II on 25 June, 1992 and promulgated by him on 11 October, 1992. On August 15, 1997, accompanied by the apostolic letter *Laetamur Magnopere,* Pope John Paul II promulgated the Latin typical edition (the "*editio typical*"). All other publications are derived from this edition (Bruskewitz, 1996).

The present Catechism of the Catholic Church follows the four-fold presentation structure which has been a tradition, since the earliest days of the Church. The first part sets forth the mystery of faith, that is, what Catholics believe. This is based on the creed. The second part is based on the celebration of faith, and the way in which the grace and salvation of Jesus is mediated to the world. This has to do with the sacraments. The third part of the catechism concerns the faith working through love as it is expressed in Christian life, that is, what we must not only believe and celebrate, but what we must do in order to be saved. The basis of this is the Ten Commandments. The final part of the Catechism's structure is about how we are related in our belief, our celebration and our action to God Himself, and this is based on prayer. Thirty-nine percent of the text of the Catechism of the Catholic Church is devoted to the creed; twenty-three percent is devoted to the Sacraments; twenty-seven percent to the commandments, and eleven percent to prayer.

THE CODE OF CANON LAW

The Code of Canon Law is specifically meant for Catholics, and more particularly for Catholics of the Latin rite. It is sometimes abbreviated as the *CIC,* an abbreviation of the Latin title, *Codex Iuris Canonici.* There is an analogous document, the Codex *Canonum Ecclesiarum Orientalium* or Code of Canons of the Eastern Churches, applying to the other *sui juris* churches of the Catholic Church.

The *CIC* is a body of regulations, the oldest continuously functioning legal system in the Western world. It is the internal legal system of the Catholic Church. Internal means that canon law lies wholly within the Church's authority to compose and administer. This is in contrast to the wide variety of external (usually civil) laws to which the Church generally defers in the pursuit of her divine mission.

Canon law operates according to the principles of law chiefly as set out in Aristotelian-Thomistic legal philosophy. This is in contrast to suggestions that canon law is simply applied theology, morals, or the rules of religious cult. Canon law affects virtually every aspect of the faith life of Catholics all over the world. The code, in the words of Pope John Paul II, is in no way intended as a substitute for faith, grace, charisms, and especially charity in the life of the Church and of the faithful. On the contrary, its purpose is rather to create such an order in the ecclesial society that, while assigning the primacy to love, grace and charisms, it at the same time renders their organic development easier in the life of both the ecclesial society and the individual persons who belong to it (Peters, N.D).

The most recent edition of the Code of Canon Law was promulgated in 1983 also by Pope John Paul II, suspending the first and previous code, the compilation of which started under the pontificate of Benedict XV and ended under the pontificate of Pius XI in 1917, hence it is known as *Pio Benedictine Code*.

1983 CODE AND CCC: AN IGWEBUIKE PERSPECTIVE

Igwebuike is the heart of African thought, and in fact, the modality of being in African philosophy. The underlying principle of *Igwebuike* philosophy is the principle of complementarity (Kanu, 2017). In consonance with the universal appeal of *Igwebuike*, the connection between the code and the CCC should not be a case of Canon Law or Catechism. If you ask a question starting with "Do Catholics believe in…?", you will probably find the answer in the Catechism. If you ask a question starting with "Are Catholics allowed, obliged or forbidden to…?" or "What happens if Catholics disobey…?", then the answer is probably in the Code of Canon Law. The foregoing, however, does not raise walls that exclude complementarity. For example, canon 1184 gives a list of those to be deprived of a Christian burial; to the surprise of many it does not mention suicide victims, meaning that they can receive Christian burial. The reason for the exclusion is found in the CCC 2280-2283. In line with most customs, the Catechism describes suicide as "Gravely contrary to the just love of self…." In the minds of many, those who die of suicide are hell-bound due to mortal sin. For a sin to be mortal or the sinner culpable, the following three criteria must be met: grave matter, knowledge that it is wrong and consent of free will. No doubt, suicide as an act constitutes a grave matter, but are all those who carry out the act in the proper frame of mind for all criteria to be met? The answer is for sure, no, because, "Grave psychological disturbances, anguish, or grave fear of hardship, suffering, or torture can diminish the responsibility of the one committing suicide" CCC2282).

The name catechesis, according to CCC 4, has to do with the "…totality of the Church's efforts to make disciples… to educate and instruct them in this life, thus building up the body of Christ." The CCC is, therefore, a teaching tool for bishops and various catechists; no wonder then, Chapter II of Book III in the 1983 Code dedicates Canons 773 – 780 to the second form of the ministry of the word, that is, catechetical formation.

The rule in Canon 773 states that it is a serious duty of pastors to catechize. It lays down in a general way the duties already mentioned with regard to catechesis by Canon 386 § 1 for the diocesan bishop and by Canon 528 § 1 for the parish priest (Sheehy, 1999). Under the new code, all the faithful have some responsibility for teaching catechesis but pastors and sacred ministers have the primary duty to supervise catechesis. Pastors of souls are to encourage and protect the faithful's multiform catechetical activity, supplementing their efforts whenever their initiatives are insufficient and assigning certain catechesis to be taught and directed by the faithful.

Canon 774 stipulates that the duty of catechesis belongs to all members of the Church. This canon, no doubt, emphasizes the priority of the parental role, but it also adds that those who take the place of parents, like guardians, foster parents, or godparents, also share in this solemn duty (Beal, 2013). As far as godparents are concerned, this obligation is to be understood, according to this canon, not as secondary to the parents' duty, but is an addition. Family catechesis is to be encouraged and fostered by ministers.

Canon 775 distinguishes among the nominative competence of the Apostolic See, the diocesan bishops, and the bishops' conferences over catechetical formation, particularly the approval and use of catechisms.

Canon 776 lists the duties of a parish priest in relation to catechetical instruction. He is to lead the catechetical formation of the local church. The catechetical responsibility of a parish priest is of extreme importance (Cann 528 § 1, 761, 733). He is to ensure that catechesis is taught in the local church placed under his care.

Canon 777 throws up a list of different types of catechesis entrusted in a special manner to the parish priest and his duty to attend to them. The use of the words, "the parish priest is to ensure" indicates that the parish priest does not necessarily have to carry out these catechetical activities all by himself but to see that these things are done. The canon also encourages diocesan bishops to draw up a guideline for catechesis, according to their unique sociological data.

Canon 778 puts forth the duty of religious superiors and superiors of societies of apostolic life (both local and major) with regard to catechesis, with specific reference to the catechesis which they should teach in their churches and place of apostolic work. Religious orders and congregation of men and women, though subject to their charisms and their obligation, are called to help with the catechetical task. To the extent they can, they should teach catechesis. This they may do at times at their own initiative as an institute or at other times at the bishop's request (Fuentes, 2004).

The key catechetical tool is the catechism (Canon 775). However, Canon 779 encourages the use of other tools and means to teach catechesis. The tools are to be selected bearing in mind sociological data, age and the capabilities of the catechists. In choosing catechetical methods, care must be taken to consider pastoral needs, the range of instructional materials and the need for pastors to encourage the highly varied initiatives that will be proposed by the faithful. The code does not state categorically the tools "out of respect for the authority, which is above all to proclaim magisterially and generally coordinate and supervise the various initiatives" (Fuentes, 2004).

The need for catechists to be properly trained is addressed by Canon 780. According to Jose Fuentes, a catechist is one of the faithful who directly provides catechetical instruction. Preparation is key for anyone working in evangelism. Local ordinaries (vicars general, Episcopal vicars, diocesan bishops) are encouraged to ensure proper formation for catechists. Canon 780 speaks of doctrinal formation and general formation in the discipline of pedagogy. This formation is to be continuous so that they are kept abreast of the magisterial teachings and methods of instruction. To achieve the goal of ongoing formation for catechists, it is advisable to have catechetical schools and institutes. It is also advised that catechetical formation be given in seminaries.

CONCLUSION

They, CIC and CCC, are two separate documents, with separate purposes but one goal, which is the salvation of souls. Thus, in the pursuit of this one goal, the essential principle of *Igwebuike* – complementarity - comes to play. The CIC quotes the CCC for explanation and clarification, and vice versa. Thus, this helps to foster a good relationship between the legal and teaching documents of the Church. Experience and study show that some canonical norms are better interpreted, applied and fully comprehended only from the background of their theological relevance, in so far as they articulate the doctrines of the Church, which have been translated into norms of action for practical life.

REFERENCES

Beal, P. J. et al. (2013). *New Commentary on the Code of Canon Law*. New York: Paulists.

Bruskewitz, W. F. (1996). *The New Catechism of the Catholic Church*. Retrieved 15/6/2020. www.ewtn.com/catholicism/library/new-catechism-of-the-catholic-church-1284.

Fuentes, J. (2004). "Catechetical Formation" in *Exegetical Commentary on the Code of Canon Law* Vol.III/1. Montreal: Wilson & Lafleur.

Kanu, I. A. (2017). Sources of Igwebuike Philosophy: Towards a Social-Cultural Foundation. *IGWEBUIKE: An African Journal of Arts and Humanities.* 9.1. 1.

Kanu, I. A. (2015a). *African philosophy: An ontologico-existential hermeneutic approach to classical and contemporary issues.* Nigeria: Augustinian Publications.

Kanu, I. A. (2015b). *Igwebuike as an ontological precondition for African ethics.* International Conference of the Society for Research and Academic Excellence. University of Nigeria, Nsukka. 14th -16th September.

Kanu, I. A. (2015c). *Igwebuike as an Igbo-African philosophy of education.* A paper presented at the International Conference on Law, Education and Humanities. 25th -26th November 2015 University of Paris, France.

Kanu, I. A. (2016). *Igbo-African Christology: A cultural Christological construct in Post-Missionary Africa.* **Germany: Lambert Publications.**

Kanu, I. A. (2016a). African traditional folk songs as dialogue between education and entertainment. *Cambridge International Journal of Contemporary Education Research.* 6. 6. pp. 53-64.

Kanu, I. A. (2016a). *Igwebuike* as an Igbo-African hermeneutics of globalisation. *IGWEBUIKE: An African Journal of Arts and Humanities,* Vol. 2 No.1. pp. 61-66.

Kanu, I. A. (2016a). *Igwebuike* as the consummate foundation of African Bioethical principles. *An African journal of Arts and Humanities* Vol.2 No1 June, pp.23-40.

Kanu, I. A. (2016b) *Igwebuike* as an expressive modality of being in African ontology. *Journal of Environmental and Construction Management.* 6. 3. pp.12-21.

Kanu, I. A. (2016b). African traditional folktales as an integrated classroom. *Sub-Saharan African Journal of Contemporary Education Research.* Vol.3 No. 6. pp. 107-118.

Kanu, I. A. (2017). *Igwebuike* as an Igbo-African philosophy for Christian-Muslim relations in Northern Nigeria. In Mahmoud Misaeli (Ed.). *Spirituality and Global Ethics* (pp. 300-310). United Kingdom: Cambridge Scholars.

Kanu, I. A. (2017). *Igwebuike* as an Igbo-African philosophy for the protection of the environment. *Nightingale International Journal of Humanities and Social Sciences.* Vol. 3. No. 4. pp. 28-38.

Kanu, I. A. (2017). *Igwebuike* as the hermeneutic of individuality and communality in African ontology. *NAJOP: Nasara Journal of Philosophy.* Vol. 2. No. 1. pp. 162-179.

Kanu, I. A. (2017a). *Igwebuike* and question of superiority in the scientific community of knowledge. *Igwebuike: An African Journal of Arts and Humanities.* Vol.3 No1. pp. 131-138.

Kanu, I. A. (2017a). *Igwebuike as a philosophical attribute of Africa in portraying the image of life.* A paper presented at the 2017 Oracle of Wisdom International Conference by the Department of Philosophy, Tansian University, Umunya, Anambra State, 27-29 April.

Kanu, I. A. (2017b). *Igwebuike* as a complementary approach to the issue of girl-child education. *Nightingale International Journal of Contemporary Education and Research.* Vol. 3. No. 6. pp. 11-17.

Kanu, I. A. (2017b). *Igwebuike* as a wholistic response to the problem of evil and human suffering. *Igwebuike: An African Journal of Arts and Humanities.* Vol. 3 No 2, March.

Kanu, I. A. (2017e). *Igwebuike* as an Igbo-African modality of peace and conflict resolution. *Journal of African Traditional Religion and Philosophy Scholars. Vol. 1. No. 1. pp. 31-40.*

Kanu, I. A. (2017g). *Igwebuike* and the logic (Nka) of African philosophy. *Igwebuike: An African Journal of Arts and Humanities.* 3. 1. pp. 1-13.

Kanu, I. A. (2017h). *Igwebuike* philosophy and human rights violation in Africa. *IGWEBUIKE: An African Journal of Arts and Humanities.* Vol. 3. No. 7. pp. 117-136.

Kanu, I. A. (2017i). *Igwebuike* as a hermeneutic of personal autonomy in African ontology. *Journal of African Traditional Religion and Philosophy Scholars. Vol. 2. No. 1. pp. 14-22.*

Peter, N. E. (N.D). *CanonLaw.info.* Retrieved 17/6/2020. <u>www.canonlaw.info</u>.

Sheehy .G. et al. 1999. *The Canon Law Letter and Spirit.* London: Geoffrey Chapman.

THE VIRTUOUS NINEVITES: ECHOES OF IGWEBUIKE THEOLOGY IN THE NARRATIVE ANALYSIS OF JONAH 3:1-10

Malachi Udochukwu Theophilus, OSA, PhD
Santa Clara University
California, United States of America
theophilusmalachy@gmail.com

ABSTRACT

This article argues that the Ninevites' reaction to Jonah's preaching of doom echoes an Igwebuike perspective. The text (Jonah 3:1-10) shows how, even animals, acted in solidarity with their human patrons to avert an impending danger. While Jonah would have preferred an outright extermination of his pagan enemy nation, the penitential solidarity of the people of Nineveh, man and beast alike, elicited the mercy of God. Thus, in this narrative, just as in Jonah chapter one, we see a God who is not only interested in Israel, the elect people of God, but also One whose mercy and love supersedes national and religious boundaries. While the attitude of the people of Nineveh shows unity of purpose and a deeper understanding of how God works in human history, Jonah's attitude shows the opposite. He couldn't see beyond his prejudice against Nineveh and its inhabitants to a deeper understanding of our common humanity and how God acts from the same point of view. The Ninevites seemed to understand this better, and as such, did not allow their religious difference or political history with Israel prevent them from drinking from the common ocean of divine mercy.

INTRODUCTION

At the close of chapter one of the book of Jonah, certain issues found resolutions, but, certainly, not the command of YHWH to Jonah in 1:1; a command that instructs Jonah to proclaim the word of YHWH to the people of Nineveh. This brings us to the second part of the book. In this part, the words of YHWH came to the prophet a second time. These divine words elicited different reactions from the different characters. Reactions like obedience, anger, repentance and dispute. But one thing that is significant in this part of the book of Jonah is the reaction of the Ninevites, even though they are a pagan nation, to the preaching of Jonah. In their acts of penitence, we see echoes of *Igwebuike* theology, for even the animals acted in solidarity with their human patrons to avert an impending danger. While Jonah would have preferred an outright extermination of his pagan enemy nation, the penitential solidarity of the people of Nineveh, man and beast alike, elicited the mercy of God. Thus, in this narrative, just as in Jonah chapter one, we see a God who is not only interested in Israel, the elect people of God, but also One whose mercy and love supersedes national and religious boundaries.

Thus said, employing the art of biblical narrative, this article will do a close reading of Jonah 3:1-10, concentrating on the response of the Ninevites and their king to the preaching of Jonah. The aim is to show, not just the virtuousness of the Ninevites, but also how their actions echo *Igwebuike* theology. To do this, I will be contrasting the prophet Jonah with the pagan Ninevites. In Jonah 3:1-3a, the divine injunction, which seems to be interrupted by the scenes at the sea (cf. Jonah 1:4-2:11), is now taken up anew through what I may call "a second chance to the prophet" (cf. Jonah 3:1). The end of chapter two breaks the downward movement, which had characterised the plot, so that Jonah could emerge from within the belly of the fish to the dry ground. Again we have the change of the *compositio loci,* no more in the belly of the fish, but on the dry ground. However, the major protagonists remain the same: YHWH and Jonah. Thus, chapter three can be divided into two: first, Jonah 3:1- 3a relates to the reiteration of the divine order, the reaction of Jonah and his execution of the order. In the second part, Jonah 3: 3b-10, the narrative becomes centred on Nineveh and its inhabitants.[1]

A SECOND CHANCE TO THE PROPHET (3:1-3A)

> Now the word of the LORD came to Jonah a second time, saying, "Arise, go to Nineveh, that great city, and proclaim to it the message that I tell you." So Jonah arose and went to Nineveh, according to the word of the LORD

> I would like to divide this first part into two segments: the reiteration of the divine command (vv1-2) and the reaction of Jonah to this command (v. 3a).

THE REITERATION OF THE DIVINE COMMAND (3:1-2)

Jonah 3:1 is reminiscent of Jonah 1:1 as shown in the table below:

JONAH 1:1	JONAH 3:1
וַיְהִי֙ דְּבַר־יְהֹוָ֔ה אֶל־יוֹנָ֥ה בֶן־אֲמִתַּ֖י	וַיְהִ֧י דְבַר־יְהֹוָ֛ה אֶל־יוֹנָ֖ה שֵׁנִ֥ית
לֵאמֹֽר׃	לֵאמֹֽר׃
Now the word of YHWH came to Jonah, *son of Amittai*	**Now the word of YHWH came to Jonah** *a second time*
saying:	saying:

---

[1] Cf. D. Scaiola, *Abdia, Giona, Michea: Introduzione, Traduzione e Commento,* NVBTA (Milano: San Paolo, 2012), 45.

Almost word for word, in a *telling* mode, the prophetic formula of the call of YHWH to his prophets is repeated: "Then the word of YHWH came to Jonah…saying" (3:1). The slight difference lies in the omission of the paternal identification: "son of Amittai" (cf.1:1), and the addition of a temporal specification: "a second time" (3:1). Our protagonists remain YHWH and Jonah.

Among the differences between Jonah 1:1-3 and 3:1-3 is the adverb שֵׁנִית that replaces the prophet's patronym. Some scholars see this as an indication of the hand of the redactor who wants to knit together the two parts of the book (chapters 1-2 and 3-4).[2] However, Jack Sasson disagrees. For him, this purpose is too heavy a burden for an adverb. There is a construction in Haggai that is reminiscent of Jonah's. That book opens with "time setting" + "the word of the Lord came by Haggai […]" + "to Zerubbabel" (cf. Hag 2:1-2). Subsequent occurrences (between 2:1 and 2:10) drop the 'el clause and address the message directly. But in Hag 2:20, the book's introductory sentence is reformulated as follows: "then the word of the Lord came to Haggai *a second time* (שֵׁנִית) […]." Here, *šēnît* does not necessarily imply repetition of the previously received message, or a deliberate paralleling the two messages; rather, it emphasizes that this particular message is the second one to be delivered on that same day. Thus, Sasson concludes that in Jonah, the narrator knowingly used *šēnît* to belittle the passage of time as a dominant factor in this tale, possibly to have us concentrate on the renewed opportunity given to Jonah to make amend his disobedience.[3]

Therefore, without denying the possibility of a redactional process outright, I would rather say that this phenomenon of repetition marks, from the narrative point of view, a second chance for Jonah. Besides the reference to Jonah 1:1, the verb וַיְהִי also connects chapter three with chapter two, thus, continuing the plot. At the end of chapter two, the plot of the story is left pending: What will happen after the fish has vomited Jonah onto dry land? What about the message of God for the people of Nineveh? The reiteration of the divine command answers these questions and continues the plot of the story. YHWH's words carry no rebuke for Jonah and no warning of what would happen if he once again fails to obey. So, in this merciful manner, the plot rewinds and begins anew.

THE DIVINE COMMAND (3:2)

After the narrative introduction of the divine speech, the narrator re-presents YHWH's command to Jonah in direct speech:

> "Arise, go to Nineveh, that great city, and proclaim to it the message that I tell you" (v.2).

---

[2] Cf. Cyrus H. Gordon, "Build-up and Climax," in Y. Avishur – J. Blau, ed., *Creation, Genesis and Flood*, (Jerusalem: Rubinstein, 1978), 30; Phyllis Trible, *Studies in the Book of Jonah*, un published dissertation (Columbia University, New York, 1963), 185.

[3] Cf. Jack M. Sasson, *Jonah*. Anchor Bible 24B (New York: Doubleday, 1990), 225.

This verse again resumes the beginning of the book of Jonah (1:2), that is, the mission formula. The divine command to Jonah consists of three imperatives in direct speech. However, one notes a slight difference in the wording of this mission injunction in comparison with the first in Jonah 1:2. The table below highlights the difference:

JON 1:2	JON 3:2
Arise,	**Arise,**
Go to Nineveh, the great city, and *proclaim against* (עַל) *it* for their wickedness has come up before me.	**Go to Nineveh, the great city**, and *proclaim to* (אֶל) *it* <u>the message that I tell you</u>

If the first two imperatives קוּם לֵךְ ("Arise, go") in 1:2 and 3:2 are the same, the third imperatives: וּקְרָא עָלֶיהָ ("proclaim against it") in 1:2 and וּקְרָא אֵלֶיהָ ("proclaim to it") in 3:2 show a notable variation in the change of prepositions from עַל in 1:2 to אֶל in 3:2. These two prepositions often seem to be used interchangeably, but they are not synonymous and, consequently, not interchangeable. The LXX translates 1:2 and 3:2 identically and neutrally: κήρυξον ἐν αὐτῇ "preach in it."[4]

However, אֶל is most commonly translated as "to" while עַל could be translated as "against, above, over, upon" in the Hebrew Scriptures. Thus, Wolff observes that the change of prepositions from עַל to אֶל may be connected with the modification of the divine command given to Jonah in 3:2. In 1:2 the wickedness of Nineveh is the reason Jonah is to speak "against" the city (עַל). But in 3:2, it appears that the emphasis is on the message itself which has to be *carried to* (אֶל) the city.[5] Giving this understanding, Jonah 1:2 is rightly translated as "proclaim or call out against it" and 3:2 as "proclaim to it." But does this variation in repetition have any narrative significance? According to Lessing:

> The literary technique of repetition is a common feature of the Old Testament narrative. Often there is some minor but significant change in the repeated version, reflecting a different standpoint or interpretation of events between the first and the second texts.[6]

Thus, in the case of Jonah 1:2 and 3:2, one notes that the content of what Jonah was to preach was not made clear in 1:2; but from the context, one could deduce that it was meant to be a message of judgement. However, the change from עַל in 1:2 to אֶל in 3:2 suggests a more neutral directive. Thus, it is plausible that the shift from עַל to אֶל involves a change in YHWH's

---

[4] Reed R. Lessing, *Jonah*, Concordia Commentary (St. Louis: Concordia Publishing House, 2007), 270.

[5] Cf. Walter H. Wolff, *Obadiah and Jonah.* (Minneapolis: Augsburg, 1986), 139.

[6] Lessing, 271. For example, compare Gen 24:1-22 with Gen 24:34-49 (especially 24:3-4 with 24:41). Also compare the three versions of the interaction between Potiphar's wife and Joseph in Gen. 39 (especially 39:12-13 and 39:17-18).

instruction to his prophet. Whereas in 1:2 YHWH instructed Jonah to preach "against the city," now in 3:2 YHWH commands him to "proclaim to it the message *which I am going to tell you*." This means that the message is yet to be specified;[7] it will not be revealed to Jonah until he enters the city. Furthermore, this shift from עַל to אֶל tells us something about the prophetic status of Jonah. In 1:2 he had every freedom to word the content of the message the way he wanted; but 3:2 specifies that Jonah is to be completely dependent on YHWH for the wording of his prophetic statement, which will not be given to him until it is time to proclaim it.[8] Therefore, it appears, with this prepositional variation, the narrator without explicitly saying it, lets us into the mind of YHWH, who, owing to Jonah's rebellious tendencies, decides to personally word the content of his prophetic message this time around. As if, knowing His prophet well, God decides to directly put on his lips an *ad hoc* announcement. So, Jonah must proclaim to Nineveh what has been proclaimed by God.

The expression: "proclaim to it the message that I tell you" uses an unusual *qal* participle of the root verb דבר, usually in *piel* form. This form, insisting on the present form of the verb "to say,"[9] is found 31 times in the Old Testament,[10] but of note is in Ex 6:29, where YHWH instructed Moses to tell Pharaoh what He (YHWH) says. In this context, the prophet is obliged to say what he has been told by God. If Moses obeyed the divine order, will it also be so with Jonah?

In addition to the participle *qal*, the proclamation formula is also expressed through the repetition of the root word קרא, but this time with a definite article: אֶת־הַקְּרִיאָה. This cognate accusative construction is a *hapax*,[11] which may be translated as "message." The word is also a neutral term, in that it does not indicate whether the message is a message of salvation or a message of judgement. So, with this unspecified message, the narrator, therefore, creates a *gap* here through the techniques of reticence, leaving the reader with a blank space for his imagination. In this first part, the phenomena of repetition enter into a common dynamic, thus indicating that it is a new principle. Then it creates a suspenseful effect that raises the question: Will Jonah seize the opportunity offered by God as a second chance? Or will he again flee (cf. Jonah 1:3)?

THE OBEDIENCE OF THE PROPHET (V.3A)

Once again, the word of YHWH sets everything in motion, but this time in the mode of obedience rather than flight:

---

[7] Ibid., 270-71.
[8] Ibid, 271.
[9] Uriel Simon, *Jonah: The Traditional Hebrew Text with the New JPS Translations* (Philadelphia: Jewish Publication Society, 1999), 26.
[10] Cf. Scaiola, 68.
[11] *Hapax* is a word or an expression that appears only in one place in the Bible, in this case, in the Old Testament.

"So Jonah arose and went to Nineveh, according to the word of the LORD" (3: 3a)

After rising, Jonah does not flee "to Tarshish away from the face of Yahweh" (cf. 1: 3), but he goes "to Nineveh according to the word of Yahweh" (3:3). This connotes obedience. The difference is made word for word using verbs of motion. While "He arose to escape," at the first instance, (1:3); now, "He arose," "and went" (3:3). While the *waw* in 1:3 is disjunctive, in 3:3 it is consecutive, emphasising Jonah's obedience to the word of YHWH. At the level of the city, we have Nineveh (3:3), as opposed to Tarshish (1:3); and from the point of view of relationship to YHWH, we have: "according to the word of YHWH" (3:3) as opposed to "away from the face of YHWH" in 1:3. These whole variations in the expressions, as noted above, show a total change on the part of Jonah. His movement becomes in conformity with the word of the Lord who instructed him to go to Nineveh. The last word: "according to the word of the Lord," summarizes this conformity to the divine command, and characterizes the prophetic obedience.

Thus, at this point, the first two imperatives ("Arise, go") of the divine command immediately find their fulfilment, but the third ("proclaim") delays. Uriel Simon notes that, even though Jonah had been subdued to "arise and go in accordance to the word of YHWH," he has not been persuaded. His silence still conceals the content of his heart.[12] This makes the lector suspect: *will he obey and proclaim the message which is about to be given to him?* However, we know nothing of how soon he left, how the trip went, when he arrived in Nineveh, or any such detail. At present, we can only assume that he recognizes the futility of further disobedience to his God and would attempt no further rebellion, at least in terms of his actions.[13]

THE NINEVITE'S RESPONSE TO JONAH'S PREACHING (3:3B-10)

"Now Nineveh was a great city to God, a three days' walk across" (3:3b).

In 3:3b, the narrator interrupts the narrative catena with a *waw-x-qatal*,[14] and using a delay tactic, he seizes the opportunity to present something concerning the city of Nineveh. The opening of a narrative unit with the circumstantial *wav* is not unusual (e.g., "Now Moses,

---

[12] Cf. Simon, 26.

[13] Cf. Douglas Stuart, *Hosea-Jonah*, WBC 31, (Dallas: Thomas Nelson Inc. 1987), 482.

[14] Although the Hebrew verbal system can be categorized into tenses (the perfect and the imperfect, technically referred to as *Qatal* and *Yiqtol* respectively), the precise implication of these tenses is complex, but suffice it to know that the Hebrew Perfect does not necessarily indicate tense (does not have tense or time of action) apart from context and issues of syntax. It rather signifies type of action (Aspect). It designates a verbal action with its conclusion envisioned in the mind of the speaker or writer. Likewise the Hebrew Imperfect, it does not necessarily denote tense. It has predominantly an indicative meaning. It is used to denote incomplete action, whether in the past, present or future. Which means it does not have tense or time of action apart from context and syntactical considerations. The *waw*-prefixed forms: *wayyiqtol* and *weqatal* are sequential forms, used in clauses depicting sequential events, while the free-standing forms *qatal* and *yiqtol* are non-sequential

tending the flock of his father-in-law Jethro" (cf. Ex 3:1); "now King David was old, advanced in years" (cf. 1 Kg 1:1). Even though here it comes in the middle of a verse, there is no doubt that the circumstantial clause is anticipatory, since it serves as an exposition that gives us an insight into the city.[15]

The expression: "Nineveh was a great city to God" has generated different interpretations among scholars. Some see it as expressing a superlative. For example, according to Simon, the expression "a great city to God" is placed on a godly scale: "Everything that [an author] wishes to present as being very large is associated with God as a way of magnifying it."[16] Thus, Simon sees the expression as a superlative. However, Hebrew has several customary ways of expressing a superlative.[17] This is not a common way, nor do all grammarians agree that the phrase here should be regarded as a superlative. Sasson objects to this superlative interpretation of the expression. He argues that if it is indeed a superlative, then it will be very unique to Scripture because such superlatives normally have a noun in construct with *elōhîm/ʾēl*. So, the text in question should read something like *ʾîr ʾelōhîm* or even *ʾîr-ʾelōhîm gedôlâ*. But here, what we have is *lēʾlōhîm*.[18]

Winton D. Thomas discusses eight passages in which either לֵא or מֵיהְלֵא is allegedly used to form a superlative. He concludes that "the divine names have a superlative force so long as we understand that the superlative force is imparted, not by the addition of the divine names as intensifying epithets, but by the fact that a person or thing is brought into a relationship with God."[19] In the case of Jonah 3:3, Thomas argues that Nineveh was "great to God," that is, *even to God*, who has a different standard of greatness from men.

In seven of the eight passages considered by Thomas, a noun is in construct with a term for "God." Jonah 3:3 is the only one of the eight passages in which a superlative is allegedly formed by "God" in a prepositional phrase.[20] So for him, the greatness of Nineveh is not just a mere superlative; rather, the narrator meant to let us know that "Nineveh is great to God," as rightly captured by the LXX: μεγάλη τῷ θεω (3:3). A city which is a symbol of enmity to Israel is great to God. This is a theological affirmation.

However, I think the addition of the preposition לְ in the expression, לֵאלֹהִים, is not just superfluous; it must be taken seriously. It is a circumlocution for a genitive, as such, "the greatness of Nineveh" could be said "to belong to God." So, Nineveh belongs to God, just as Israel belongs to God. This suggests a divine perspective that readily explains God's merciful

---

[15] Cf. Simon, 27.

[16] Ibid, 28.

[17] Cf. B. K. Waltke - M. O'Connor, *An Introduction to Biblical Hebrew Syntax.* (Indiana: Eisenbrauns, 1990), § § 14.3.3b; 14.5; P. Joüon - T. Muraoka, *A Grammar of Biblical Hebrew.* SB 27 (Rome: GB Press, 2011), § 141 j.

[18] Sasson, 228.

[19] W. D. Thomas, "A Consideration of Some Universal Ways of Expressing the Superlative in Hebrew," *Vetus Testamentum 3* (1953), 216.

[20] Cf. Ibid, 209-24.

disposition towards Nineveh. Even though this merciful attribute is part of the nature of God, but its disposition towards mankind is not always automatic; it must be activated by human actions or response to the divine (cf. 2 Chron 7:14; Jer 15:9; Zech 1:3; Mal 3:7). Therefore, the greatness of Nineveh exceeds a mere superlative; it suggests divine ownership: Nineveh is a city that belongs to God.

This theological interpretation of Nineveh has a significant narrative implication in the plot of Jonah. The affirmation here that Nineveh is a great city *belonging to God* fits with Jonah's confession in 1:9 that YHWH is the God "who made the sea and the dry land," since all creation belongs to Him. It is also consistent with what YHWH Himself would say about the city in Jonah 4:10-11, where YHWH compares Nineveh to the *qiqayon* plant. Using the verbs "to labour" and "make grow" for the plant in 4:10, YHWH implies in 4:11 that He Himself cultivated the city, just as He did the plant. As earlier noted, the author of Jonah repeats key words and phrases, which take on added significance with each new repetition, until the climactic one reveals the full import. In this way, the narrative progresses towards its goal. Lessing captures the progressive descriptions of Nineveh as follows:

1. "Arise, go to Nineveh, the great city" (1:2).
2. "Arise, go to Nineveh, the great city" (3:2).
3. "Now Nineveh is a great city (*belonging*) to God" (3:3) [21]

Thus, the fourth climactic description of Nineveh confirms the interpretation that 3:3 declares that Nineveh is great and that it belongs to God, even though the full extent of YHWH's compassion for the city is not revealed until 4:11.[22] Therefore, from the literary point of view, 3:3b is an unusual circumstantial sentence (cf. Ex 3:1), the value of which is *proleptic*.[23] The narrator makes this information on the city an essential element in order to understand the rest of the narrative plot centred on Jonah's entrance into the city. This information shows how the narrator uses the technique of repetition to build up and give a deeper meaning to a particular word or concept. In this case, the information about the theological greatness of Nineveh is carefully given to grow the plot. Therefore, in addition to the repetition of the expression: "the great city," we now know that the city has a relationship "to YHWH." Finally, we are given a spatial expression with respect to the city: "a journey of three days." Without going into mathematical reflections of the width and circumference of the city, I think this spatial information is intended to draw the attention of the reader to something very important, because the biblical narrator does not say something just for the sake of it.

---

[21] Ibid, 280.
[22] Cf. Ibid, 281.
[23] Cf Scaiola, 69.

JONAH'S OBEDIENCE (V.4)

> Jonah began to go into the city, going **a day's walk**. And he cried out, "Forty days more, and Nineveh shall be overthrown!"

In fact, Jonah did not go through the city in three days, but he begins to enter the city only "for a day's journey" (3:4). So, Jonah finds himself outside the gates of Nineveh. The longest period of *narrated* time, the journey, is reported in the briefest of *narrative* time.[24] This imperfect parallelism shows a difference of temporal order: "only a day's journey" (3:4) connoting a readiness that contrasts with the reluctance and slowness of Jonah in fulfilling his mission. Even though he obeyed to go to Nineveh after a near-death experience in the belly of the fish (see Jonah 2), his body language, as evident in his one day preaching instead of three days, shows his inner disposition. Jonah does not want the salvation of Nineveh; he would rather prefer they are destroyed. This is even more obvious in the way he worded his preaching. It makes one wonder: what will happen after the proclamation of a single day's walk in a city that takes a three-day walk? The slowness of the narration created by the description of the city, and the slow entrance of Jonah in Nineveh, accentuates the suspense, but leads to the fulfilment of the divine order by Jonah.

In verse 4b, which tells the story of the proclamation of Jonah to Nineveh for a journey of one day, the reader enters the realm of direct discourse: "And he called and said [...]" The introduction to it relieves the suspense about Jonah's response to YHWH's third imperative: "call."[25] And the content of the proclamation that the reader has been expecting from the first two chapters of the book is now about to be made known. The pace of the narrative after the slowdown is now accelerated. Before now, I noted that only two of the three divine commands given to Jonah in 3:2 were fulfilled. But now we have a perfect correspondence, word for word, of the three divine commands (in three *wayyiqtols*), as shown in the table below: This completes the obedience of the prophet to the divine command.

YHWH'S INSTRUCTION	JONAH'S OBEDIENCE
קוּם "Arise" (3:2)	וַיָּקָם "And he Arose" (3:3)
לֵךְ "Go" (3:2)	וַיֵּלֶךְ "And he went" (3:3)
וּקְרָא "And Call" (3:2)	וַיִּקְרָא "And he called" (3:4b)

In the earlier command (1:2), God does not specify the message for Jonah to transmit, as we have already seen; God shows faith that Jonah will know what to say. In chapter three, however, God dictates a message to Jonah, thereby making it more difficult for him to deviate from

---

[24] Cf. Golka W. Friedemann, *The Revelations of God: A Commentary on the Books of Song of Songs and Jonah.* (Grand Rapids: Eerdmanns, 1988), 102.

[25] Cf. Trible, 179.

his renewed assignment. Moreover, let's recall that the wording of this divine command to Jonah in chapter three ("proclaim/call to it") is different from what we have in chapter one ("call out against it"). The former connotes a message of repentance and not condemnation. But does Jonah understand the theological implication of the divine instruction: "to proclaim to it (Nineveh)?"

JONAH'S CALL TO THE NINEVITES

He cried and said, "Another forty days, and Nineveh shall be overturned!" (3:4)

Instead of urging the people to repent, Jonah announces their imminent doom, reverting to the original command: "call out against it." Jonah does not want the people of Nineveh to repent; on the contrary, he prefers to witness their demise. Jonah begins to preach his message: "Forty days and Nineveh would be הפך (destroyed or overturned?)." In the Bible, the number forty indicates a time of trial or testing that leads to renewal and salvation. Thus, the duration of "forty" here is reminiscent of Noah's flood (Gen 7:4.12.17; 8:6), the forty days of Moses on Sinai (Ex 24:18; 34:28), of Ezekiel bearing the iniquity of Judah for forty days (Ezek 4:6). Most pragmatic is Israel's forty years in the wilderness.<?>Yet, these events relate to an elapsed time during which the actions take place. But in our case, it is rather a *tuned delay*: A postponement of execution that provides opportunity to escape destruction, and to give room for efforts to earn God's forgiveness. In the words of Uriel Simon:

Forty days is a typological number that indicates a relatively long period of time (cf. Dt 9:18; also 1 Kgs 19:8). Here it is the period of grace until it comes due. This stay of execution presents an opportunity to escape the impending destruction.<?>

I think the narrator's choice of the *Niphal* participle of the verb הפך to describe the fate of Nineveh, as proclaimed by Jonah, is very deliberate. The verb is the same used in the overthrow of Sodom and Gomorrah (Gen 19:21,25,29). As such, it becomes part of biblical cliché used to describe wrath and destruction that is as bad as *when the Lord overturned Sodom and Gomorrah.* Evidently, Jonah finds comfort in this word. If Nineveh's fate is like that of Sodom and Gomorrah, he will of all, be very happy.<?> The temporal force of the *Niphal* participial verb: נֶהְפָּכֶת can be determined from the context. Participles, generally, are mostly used for imminent actions that will take place soon.<?> Hence, Jonah may well have hoped that no change would take place in Nineveh until it is destroyed in forty days' time. This may as well explain the lethargic attitude with which he approached the message: "Yet in forty days, and Nineveh would be destroyed" (3:4). In a day, Jonah was done with his message to a city that takes three days walk (3:3b-4a). But, will the Ninevites be really destroyed in "forty days' time?"

It suffices to say, though, that the verb הפך for certain recalls what happened to Sodom and Gomorrah, but it also has certain subtlety in its nuance. The verb, which is usually translated as "destroy," also means "upset, overturn, or change." The verb can refer to a radical reversal from one extreme to another, including a change of heart. For example, In Dt 23:6, Moses reminded the sons of Israel that "YHWH your God turned [וַיַּהֲפֹךְ, Qal imperfect] for you the curse [of Balaam] into a blessing, because YHWH your God loves you."<?> Hence, this double sense of the verb calls the reader to expect the unexpected. J-P Sonnet opines that the verb appropriate to this logic of "overturning" is הפך, because it represents the *overturning* of *all in all*, which only God is capable of doing.<?> As such, the question that confronts the lector at this point is: will the city be reversed or overturned in the sense of being ruined, or will it be reversed in the sense of repentance? But we must also wonder whether Jonah is really aware of the double sense of that word. Therefore, it appears as if the narrator, using the forty days of respite for the upheaval of the city, creates a verbal irony of the double sense of the verb, הפך. This further creates the effect of suspense that opens up the future of the narration and makes conversion possible. "Yet, forty days Nineveh will be overturned" could refer to its destruction like Sodom and Gomorrah or to its change from impenitent wickedness to repentance and faith. Either way, Nineveh will be changed!<?>Jonah likely would have understood his message to be one of impending doom of the sort that befell Sodom, and the Ninevites clearly took it as a warning that they would perish, if they did not repent.<?>

And as such, they overturned their way of life to avert the overturning of their city and its inhabitants. The two possible meanings of the verb allow for a fact that YHWH seeks a change in the people's hearts (see 3:9-10), while Jonah longs for their destruction (see 4:1,5). Jonah's distress in chapter four is partly because he does not realize that his sermon came true in the sense YHWH intended. How ironic!<?> However, at the macro level of the story, this verse marks the resolution, not only of the divine command of 3:2, but also the plot that had begun in 1:3 with the first complication, that is; of Jonah fleeing to Tarshish. Finally, he obeys and proclaims, not minding his reluctance and desire for the doom of Nineveh.

THE REACTION OF THE NINEVITES

> And the people of Nineveh believed God; they proclaimed a fast, and everyone, great and small, put on sackcloth (3:5).

In 3:4, we see God's words as reported by Jonah, "yet forty days and Nineveh will be overturned/ destroyed." Jonah never claimed divine authority for this statement, however, the people of Nineveh gave a theological response to it: "they believed God" (3:5). Coming from the Hebrew root אמן, this verb has never been used in the course of our story; it forms a play on words with the name of the father of Jonah, Amittai, which is derived from the same root and therefore connotes trust or faith. Hence, the announcement to the Ninevites by Jonah, the son of one whose name means "God's faithfulness or trust in God," inspires the Ninevites to trust in

God.<?> Scaiola observes that the swiftness of their belief in God contrasts ironically with the slowness of Jonah, who only accepted his divine commission towards Nineveh after a three-day and three-night ordeal in the belly of the fish.<?> Even when he finally accepts to preach to the Ninevites, he presents it lethargically in five Hebrew words, translated: "Yet, forty days, Nineveh will be destroyed." But, despite Jonah's seemingly nonchalant attitude towards the preaching, the people of Nineveh all believed in God. Phillip Cary said that it will be difficult to resist adding: "And it was counted to them as righteousness,"<?> just as it was said of Abraham (cf. Gen 15:6). The loftiness of the repentance of the people of Nineveh to the preaching of the Israelite prophet shines out when compared with the attitude of the Israelites given the same circumstances. A close look at certain biblical passages shows that the very response of faith that Israel could not give without signs and wonders (cf. Ex 4:9) or even refused to give despite miracles (Isaiah 7), the pagan Ninevites gave after a sermon of a reluctant preacher.<?>

"Calling a fast and putting on sackcloth" is the same language used for calling a solemn assembly in order to sanctify a fast in Israel (cf. Joel 1:14; 2:15). The first word comes from the root verb קרא (they *call* or *proclaim* a fast) which is the same verb that Jonah used to announce to the people of Nineveh the words of God in 3:4. The second comes from the root verb לבשׁ (they *put-on* sackcloth). This is a new word thus far in the story. However, both phrases are used to express penitential acts. But it is not used for a non-Israelite, except in Jonah. The expression: "from the largest to the smallest of them" gives an emphatic character to the absolute repentance of the people of Nineveh. Uriel Simon observes here that "in the Sodom periscope, it is the all-inclusive scope of the guilt that is emphasized, 'from young to old' (Gen. 19:4). Here, however, the comprehensive guilt is overcome by the all-inclusive scope of the repentance."<?>

One thing that surprises the reader is the ease and immediacy with which they believed in the message of a foreign prophet, or better still, "an enemy prophet." Also, they were not in any concrete danger at the moment, like the sailors in chapter one,<?> whose conversion was occasioned in the midst of an actual peril. Thus, the repentance of these pagan characters appears surprising. This raises the curiosity of the reader: is there an element of the past that escapes us? This narrative *blank*, which is never filled-up in the story, keeps the lector in tension and pushes him to formulate for himself a *reading key*, a key which J.-P. Sonnet supplies. He says that this *blank* exists "so that the project of God, which constitutes the substratum of the narrated story, acts through the spring of curiosity."<?> In the reaction of the people of Nineveh, we see how a minimum means (Jonah's five-words-preaching) produced a maximum effect. As if one should say, like *Yesua ben David*, "Nowhere in Israel have I seen a *repentance* like this" (cf. Matthew 8:10).

THE REACTION OF THE KING OF NINEVEH

> When the news reached the king of Nineveh, he rose from his throne, removed
> his robe, covered himself with sackcloth, and sat in ashes (3:6).

The news reaches the king of Nineveh, and now it's the subjects who dictate the order of the day, pushing the king by their example to make penitential acts. The King's appearance on the scene, who is also not named in the story, matches the appearance of the captain of the ship in 1:6; but this instance is even more insightful. He is exemplary, both in his response to the word of God and in his actions. With no storm blowing, no boat about to sink, just one brief and ambiguous message, he realizes the city is in great danger and that something has to be done to save it. Learning that his people have called a fast and put on sackcloth, he follows suit. He formalises their effort of penitence with a decree. In the words of Phillip Cary: "It seems he is not above following his own people (how many kings are this wise?), jumping on the bandwagon when he sees it carrying them toward life, not death."<?> He doesn't merely follow the example of his subjects, but he acts even further: he strips himself of his regalia, making a journey back from the royal dignity to penitential humility.<?> Or better still, according to Lessing, "in response to Jonah's message that Nineveh would "be changed" (3:4), the king himself changed, both in dwelling, in dress, and in dignity."<?> This portrays, not just contrition, but true repentance. His action begins with his rising from his throne, and ends with his sitting in ashes:<?>

A He rose from his throne

    B removed his royal robe

    B' covered himself with sackcloth

A' and sat upon the ash heap.

The narrator probably represented the action of the king in this chiastic summary, to underline the change the king underwent in an effort to show his repentance. Unlike Jonah's descent which was in disobedience, the king descends in humility before the word of God, from his throne to an ash heap. Thus, while Jonah in 1:3 arises *to go down in disobedience*, the king of Nineveh arises and *sat down in humble obedience* to the word of YHWH preached by Jonah. God did not speak directly to the king of Nineveh, as he did to Jonah. But even at that, the king responds in a humble and ready way, as if the word of God had been given to him without mediation. The king's response to the דבר (word) YHWH is quite exemplary and this is exactly what Jonah could not get around to, until he finds himself helpless in the deep waters. So, the king and Jonah are antitypes. Jonah's first response to the דבר YHWH was to flee, but the king's immediate reaction was to abase himself in obedient response to the word of God.

It is interesting to see how the king spontaneously steps away from his regal status as he arises from his throne to sit down in ashes and exchanges his royal regalia for sackcloth.<?> The action of the king does not surprise the reader, who has already been prepared by the narrator in the previous verse, when he learned that the people of Nineveh believed God and they immediately performed penitential acts; but what surprises the reader here is that the actors follow inverse paths which one would not ordinarily expect of them: a king, rather than controlling, follows the example of his subjects; and instead of the normal course: "from grass to grace," he follows an opposite route: "from grace to grass." All this points to the genuineness of the repentance of the king and his people.

Furthermore, the reaction of the king of Nineveh is all the more very remarkable in that, elsewhere in the Old Testament, Assyrian kings are portrayed as arrogant, boasting monarchs who not only defy YHWH and threaten Jerusalem, but also argue that their power is greater than YHWH's because they have been able to *defeat* the God of Israel/Judah just as they defeated the gods of other nations (cf. Is 10:5-34; 2Kgs 18-19; Nahum 2-3).<?> On the contrary, the king in Jonah (3:6) acted, not in the manner one would expect from an Assyrian ruler, but in a way one would expect from a king after God's own heart, like David (cf. 2 Sam 12:16). In fact, the king is not only distinctive among Assyrian rulers, his actions also dwarf that of many kings in Israel. For example, Jer 36:9-31 makes clear that Jehoiakim of Jerusalem was notably unmoved by Jeremiah's words and, therefore, was denounced for his obstinacy. But this pagan king of Nineveh, acted quite differently.

THE DECREE OF THE KING (VV. 7-9)

> Then he had a proclamation made in Nineveh: "By the decree of the king and his nobles: No human being or animal, no herd or flock, shall taste anything. They shall not feed, nor shall they drink water ..." (3:7-9).

In 3:7, the focus shifts from the king's personal response back to the city's communal response. Only after humbling himself does the king issue an edict to institutionalise the "overturning." There is something very striking here. The edict issued by the king has almost a prophetic function. Normally, when the word of God comes to the prophet, as regards an impending doom, the prophet either intercedes on behalf of the people, or calls the people to repentance (cf. Abraham in Gen 18:23-32; and Moses in Ex 32). Jonah obviously acted like the opposite of Abraham and Moses. However, since Jonah did not behave like a prophet, the king of Nineveh filled the gap, playing the role of a prophet and calling his people to repentance.<?>

More so, even the process by which the Ninevites arrive at their particular form of repentance is a kind of overturning for Nineveh's social status: the highs (the king and his nobles) following the lows (the common people of Nineveh).<?>Scaiola observes that there is a play on words based on the term טַעַם, which means decree only in ancient Hebrew, while, customarily, it assumes the sense of "taste," "judgment" or "discernment." As such, it recalls the content of the decree through the root verb טעם; which indicates the prohibition to taste food. The interesting thing here, though, is that the verb that is normally used with respect to human beings now affects also animals.<?> Scaiola further observes that this vocabulary has a broader resonance in wisdom literature. It has a sensual nuance. So here it could indicate that men and animals have to give up any form of pleasure.<?> The king's decree involves both men and animals, emphasising that the penitence comprises the totality of Nineveh. The entire city has to make a penitential movement, or rather should refrain from all the normal actions that serve life and, moreover, produce a gratification of the senses.

It may seem an ironic trait that even animals are involved in fasting, but we find a similar nuance elsewhere in Scripture (cf. Joel 1:18-20; Judt 4:9-10). Thus, this simply shows that, even the animals are more responsive to YHWH than the Israelite prophet, Jonah. The animals are in solidarity with their human patrons in the effort to avert the impending doom. Animals participate in fast when they are not pastured or watered (cf. Judith 4,9-11). In this way, they call on God in their hunger and thirst, for even the bellowing of animals is a sort of prayer, as attested to by the prophet Joel: "The very beasts of the field cry out to You; for the watercourses are dried up" (Joel 1:20).

The King's decree continues. After the three negative commands in the previous verse follows the three positive commands here. And at the beginning of each of this part, the phrase 'men and animals' is repeated. Therefore, with this strong call to repentance, addressed to each and every one (man and beast alike), without exception, we see the true contrition of the inhabitants of Nineveh, man and beast alike. The force of this radical change is seen in the last decree of the king: "Let everyone turn from his evil way and from the violence that is in their hands;" the people of Nineveh have to turn, that is, convert. The verb used is from the root שוב. Interestingly, the expression: "They must turn, each from his evil ways" is prevalent in the Old Testament, particularly in the book of Jeremiah (cf. Jer 18:11; 23:14,22; 25:5; 26:3; 35:15; 36:3,7). However, here in the book of Jonah, this expression is made, not by an Israelite prophet, but by a pagan king. As such, Lessing succinctly observes:

> That this king speaks the same words YHWH utters through his prophet Jeremiah recalls the similar situation in Jonah 1, where the pagan captain used commands spoken earlier by YHWH: "Arise, ... call" (1:2). When the captain and the king quote God, the satire is evident: the Israelite Jonah is unfaithful to YHWH's Word, but the pagan Gentiles are converted to faith in accord with YHWH's Word. <?>

Here, the Israelite prophet is *out propheted* by Gentile converts. In fact, this pagan king showed a knowledge of God that outclassed Jonah's understanding of the way God works. The King said in his decree: "Who knows? God may repent and change his mind ..." (v.9). The fact that the king of Nineveh expressed a certain kind of uncertainty regarding the reaction of God to their repentance, with a question full of hope, but without any real certainty, indicates his awareness of how God works. God's compassion and mercy are not to be taken for granted; they come solely from the love of God. God alone will decide the fate of Nineveh. The citizens of Nineveh can believe and repent, but sincerity alone cannot control what God is free to do for them or against them. They can hope for deliverance, but cannot surely expect it (3:9). The hearer/reader does not know what will happen either. This understanding of God's activity that the king of Nineveh has is quite different from the one that Jonah shows in his behaviour (cf. 4:2). The expression highlights the fact that in the Bible, the culprit has no right to redress. In other words, "who knows if God may repent?" (3:9) does not denote lack of faith; rather, it is an expression of the discrete hope<?> of one who knows that He (God) will be gracious to whom He intends to be gracious to, and will show compassion on whom He wills to show compassion (cf. Ex. 34:19).

The *Nifal* verb נחם ("to repent") semantically defines the retraction of a judgment already issued or to a previously planned action; but more deeply, it expresses the divine freedom that can move without restriction from one attribute to another, from justice to mercy, mercy to justice, without being accused of caprice or inconstancy. It's a reversibility appropriate to the God who, in Exodus 3:14, reveals Himself to Moses as "I am who I am." In other words, "I can be whoever and whatever I want to be," claiming the possibility of alternation of His attributes.<?>

Jonah, uttering the oracle in 3:4 "Yet forty days and Nineveh will be overturned," had perhaps intended it as a terrible announcement of punishment which will definitely come to pass, but the people of Nineveh interpreted differently; for them, it was an urgent call to repentance, and as such, they entered in the dynamic of divine reversibility that they now wonder if God would turn back from His anger and repent: It's not a certainty, but a trust in the love of God. Even *Yesua ben David* recognised the remarkable significance of the attitude of the people of Nineveh towards the preaching of Jonah that he accorded them the right to condemn his generation (cf. Luke 11:32). Thus, he makes the people of Nineveh models of true repentance and calls his followers to emulate it.

GOD'S RESPONSE TO THE "WHO KNOWS?"

> "When God saw what they did, how they turned from their evil ways, God changed his mind/repented ... " (3:10)

In vv. 8-9, one notes the connection between the action and the decree of the king in vv. 8-9, on one hand, and God's reaction, on the other. The king's exhortation: "and let everyone return from his evil way" (v. 8) is confirmed in the conduct of the people of Nineveh: "and God saw that they had all returned from their evil way" (v. 10). The king had hoped: "who knows, God will return and repent, and return from the fierce of his wrath" (v. 9); and now it is assured: "and God repented of the evil" (v. 10). This underlines the substantial difference between the divine and the human responses: God's answer comes in the way of God, in an unpredictable way. Thus, just as Trible rightly observed, "human action does not dictate divine response."<?> The "Who knows," of the king of Nineveh confirms this dictum. God, in His own way, overturns the dreaded harm into salvation.

ECHOES OF IGWEBUIKE<?> THEOLOGY IN JONAH 3:1-10

From this close reading of Jonah chapter three, two things stand out: Jonah's attitude towards an enemy nation and the Ninevites uprightness, despite being an "other" in this narrative. The Other against whom Israel's identity is forged is abhorred, abject, impure, and in the *Old Testament*, a vast number of them obliterated, while in the *New Testament*, vast numbers are colonized. *Igwebuike* theology erases the line between "Us" and "Them," a line which Jonah, by his attitude, tries to maintain. His reluctance to go and preach the message of repentance to an enemy nation and the lethargic attitude with which he eventually does it show his ill disposition towards Nineveh. Jonah would rather God destroys Nineveh; this explains why he was greatly distressed when God showed His gracious mercy towards the people of Nineveh (cf. Jonah 4:1).

However, the *adonai* of Israel (לֵאלֹהֵי יִשְׂרָאֵל יְהֹוָה) is also God the most High (וְיֹדֵעַ לֹא אֵל), who created the heavens and the earth (cf. Gen 14:22). This is an aspect of God that Jonah didn't want to accept. He acted as if to say the enemy of Israel should also be the enemy of YHWH; the nation which Israel hates, God should also hate. The narrator did not tell us of the antecedent relationship between Nineveh and Israel, nor did he let us into the reason why Jonah was particularly angry at the mercy of God towards the people of Nineveh. But from biblical evidence, we could suppose that Jonah was reluctant to go to Nineveh, owing to the antecedent hostile relationship between the two nations (Israel and Assyria). Secondly, Jonah knew that God is rich in mercy (cf. Jonah 4:2) and will eventually forgive Nineveh, the arch enemy of Israel, should it repent. But, Jonah would not want such mercy over a city like Nineveh. The city, apart from being mentioned in an etiology concerning the origin of several Mesopotamian cities in Gen 10:8-12; is also mentioned in 2 Kgs 19:36; Is 37:37; and in Nahum and Zephaniah. Both of those prophetic books emphasize Nineveh's role as the symbol of the Assyrian Empire, the mortal enemy of Israel, renowned for brutal conquest and butchery.<?>However, God's mercy towards Nineveh "challenges every separatist theology that tries to exclude people based on religion, tribe, ethnicity, nationality or moral ideology. It tells us from biblical perspective that "to belong" does not necessarily mean conformity to a particular standard or people. It simply means "to be" — to be available for the divine as part of the global human family."<?>

More so, this sovereign God, who alone is *Good* (cf. Mk 10,18) by His very nature, reacts to evil, no matter who commits it, whether Israel or any other nation of the earth. The predicament of man is the predicament of God who has a stake in human situation. Sin, guilt and suffering cannot be separated from the divine situation. The life of sin is more than a failure of man; it is a frustration to God who is involved in human history.<?> Therefore, the YHWH of Israel is the sovereign Lord over all nations. He is the God of Jonah, the God of the sailors and the God of the Ninevites. This understanding calls us to rise above our differences which, in themselves, should not constitute a threat or be a factor that divides us; rather, they can be basic notes for a beautiful musical symphony.

Furthermore, God seemed to be drawn by the beautiful solidarity in the penitential acts of the inhabitants of Nineveh. For even the animals, through their bellowing, were in solidarity with their human patrons in seeking for divine mercy. Nineveh's repentance manifests itself in a form that rivals even the most pious Israelite times of repentance. Not only the king, but all the people and even the livestock put on sackcloth and fasted (Jonah 3:5-8). Jonah 3:8 is worded to suggest that just like the people, the livestock too, cover themselves with sackcloth! In that way, the Ninevites' penitence exceeds any recorded for Israel. This powerful unity in their penitential gestures appeared to move God, in His sovereign freedom, to act in favour of Nineveh and its inhabitants.

CONCLUSION

From the foregoing, we see how Jonah, urged repeatedly by God's command, went to Nineveh, proclaimed the word of YHWH, and then left the scene for the people of Nineveh, the king of Nineveh and of course YHWH. The Ninevites and their king performed penitential acts and made a real change of direction. While the attitude of the people of Nineveh shows unity of purpose and a deeper understanding of how God works in human history, Jonah's attitude shows the opposite. He couldn't see beyond his prejudice against Nineveh and its inhabitants to a deeper understanding of our common humanity, and how God acts from the same point of view. The Ninevites seemed to understand this better and, as such, did not allow their religious difference or political history with Israel prevent them from drinking from the common ocean of divine mercy.

Of course, the reader would be wondering what happened to Jonah; what will his reaction be to this unexpected and positive action of the Ninevites, on one hand, and God's mercy, on the other: Will he really *grow up* and avail himself to the ways of God, who "shows favour to whom he wants, and grants mercy to whom he wants" (cf. Ex 34:19)? Will he really realise that just as Israel is "a people of God," so too Nineveh is "a great city unto God" (Jonah 3:3b)? I do not have the answers to these questions. But it suffices to say that the book of Jonah is the only biblical book that ends with a question mark. Through such ending, the narrator calls us, not just to participate in the conflict between Jonah and God's ways, but more importantly, to participate in the theology of the book and confront our own inclination that assumes salvation is only for us.

BIBLIOGRAPHY

Bovati, P. *Cosi Parla Il Signore: Studio sul Profetismo Biblico*. Bib. Bologna: EDB, 2008.

Cary, P. *Jonah: Brazos Theological Commentary on the Bible*. Michigan: Brazos Press, 2008.

Friedemann, G. W. *The Revelations of God: A Commentary on the Books of Song of Songs and Jonah*. Grand Rapids: Eerdmanns, 1988.

Gordon, C. H. "Build-up and Climax," in *Creation, Genesis and Flood*. Edited by Y. Avishur – J. Blau. Jerusalem: Rubinstein, 1978.

Heschel, A. J. *The Prophets*. New York: HarperCollins Publishers, 2001.

Joüon, P. - Muraoka, T. *A Grammar of Biblical Hebrew*. SB 27. Rome: GB Press, 2011.

Kanu I. A. *A hermeneutic approach to African traditional religion, theology and philosophy*. Nigeria: Augustinian Publications. 2015

Kanu I. A. *Igwebuikeconomics*: Towards an inclusive economy for economic development. *Igwebuike: An African Journal of Arts and Humanities. Vol. 3. No. 6*. 113-140. 2017

Kanu I. A. Sources of *Igwebuike* philosophy. *International Journal of Religion and Human Relations*. 9. 1. pp. 1-23. 2017

Kanu, A. I. *Igwebuike* as a trend in African philosophy. *IGWEBUIKE: An African Journal of Arts and Humanities. 2. 1.* 97-101. 2016

Kanu, A. I. *Igwebuike* as an Igbo-African philosophy of inclusive leadership. *Igwebuike: An African Journal of Arts and Humanities*. Vol. 3 No 7. pp. 165-183. 2017

Kanu, A. I. *Igwebuike* philosophy and the issue of national development. *Igwebuike: An African Journal of Arts and Humanities*. Vol. 3 No 6. pp. 16-50. 2017

Kanu, A. I. *Igwebuike* as an Igbo-African ethic of reciprocity. *IGWEBUIKE: An African Journal of Arts and Humanities. 3. 2. pp.* 153-160. 2017

Kanu, I. A. Towards an African cultural renaissance. *Professor Bassey Andah Journal of Cultural Studies. Volume 3*, pp. 146-155. *2010*

Kanu, I. A. A metaphysical epistemological study of African Medical practitioners. In O. E. Ezenweke and I. A. Kanu (2012). *Issues in African traditional religion and philosophy* (pp. *227-240)*. Nigeria: Augustinian Publications. 2012

Kanu, I. A. Being qua belongingness: The Provenance and Implications of Pantaleon's redefinition of being. *Uche: Journal of the Department of Philosophy, University of Nigeria, Nsukka.* Vol. 17. pp. 57-58. 2012

Kanu, I. A. From 'Onye' to 'Ife' hypothesis: The contribution of Edeh to the development of the concept of being. *Lwati: A Journal of Contemporary Research.* 9, 4. 218-223. 2012

Kanu, I. A. Inculturation and Christianity in Africa. *International Journal of Humanities and Social Science.* Vol. 2. No. 17. pp. 236-244. 2012

Kanu, I. A. The functionality of being in Pantaleon's operative metaphysics vis-a-vis the Niger Delta conflict. *African Research Review: An International Multi-Disciplinary Journal.* Vol.6. No.1. pp. 212-222. 2012

Kanu. I. A. Towards an Igbo Christology, In Ezenweke, E.O and Kanu, A.I. (Eds) *Issues in African traditional religion and philosophy,* Jos: Augustinian Publications. 2012

Kanu, I. A. The problem of being in metaphysics. *African Research Review: An International Multi-Disciplinary Journal.* Vol.6. No.2. April. pp. 113-122. 2012

Kanu, I. A. The problem of personal identity in metaphysics. *International Journal of Arts and Humanities.* Vol.1. No.2. pp.1-13. 2012

Kanu, I. A. The concept of life and person in African anthropology. In E. Ezenweke and I. A. Kanu (Eds.). *Issues in African traditional religion and philosophy* (pp. 61-71). Nigeria: Augustinian. 2012

Kanu, I. A. Towards an Igbo Christology. In E. Ezenweke and I. A. Kanu (Eds.). *Issues in African traditional religion and philosophy* (pp. 75-98). Nigeria: Augustinian. 2012

Kanu, I. A. African identity and the emergence of globalization. *American International Journal of Contemporary Research.* Vol. 3. No. 6. pp. 34-42. 2013

Kanu, I. A. Globalisation, globalism and African philosophy. C. Umezinwa (Ed.). *African philosophy: A pragmatic approach to African probems* (pp. 151-165). Germany: Lambert. 2013

Lessing, R. Reed. *Jonah.* Concordia Commentary, St. Louis: Concordia Publishing House 2007.

Sasson, J. M. *Jonah.* Anchor Bible 24B. New York: Doubleday, 1990.

Scaiola, D. *Abdia, Giona, Michea: Introduzione, Traduzione e Commento.* NVBTA. Milano: San Paolo, 2012.

Simon, U. *Jonah: The Traditional Hebrew Text with the New JPS Translations*. Philadelphia: JPS, 1999.

Sonnet, J.-P. "God's Repentance and "False Starts" in Biblical History." *Congress Volume Ljubljana* (2007): 469-494.

Sonnet, J.-P. "Jonas est-il parmi les prophètes? Une réécriture narrative sur les attributs divins,» in *Écritures réécriture*. Edited by C. Clivaz - *et al. BEThL* 247 Leuven (2012): 137-157.

Sonnet, J.-P. "L'analisi Narrativa dei Racconti Biblici," in *Manuale di Esegesi dell'Antico Testamento*: *Testi e Commenti*. Edited by M. Bauks – C. Nihan. Bologna: Edizioni Dehoniane, 2015.

Stuart, D., *Hosea-Jonah*, WBC 31, Dallas: Word, Incorporated, 1987.

Theophilus, M. "The Role of Rehab in the Conquest Story of Joshua as a Manifestation of Igwebuike Theology: A Narrative Analysis of Joshua 2," in *Igwebuike: An African Journal of Arts and Humanities*. Vol. 5, no. 8 (2019): 72-92.

Thomas, W. D. "A Consideration of Some Universal Ways of Expressing the Superlative in Hebrew." *Vetus Testamentum 3* (1953): 209-224.

Timmer, D. "Jonah's Theology Of The Nations: The Interface Of Religious And Ethnic Identity." *RivBib* 120 (2013): 13-23.

Trible, P. "Studies in the Book of Jonah." An unpublished dissertation. Columbia University, New York, 1963.

Waltke, B. K. - O'Connor, M. *An Introduction to Biblical Hebrew Syntax*. Indiana: Eisenbrauns, 1990.

Wiseman, D. J. "Jonah's Nineveh," *Tyndale Bulletin 30* (1979): 29-51.

Wolff, W. H. *Obadiah and Jonah*. Minneapolis: Augsburg, 1986.

Zakovitch, Y. "Through the Looking Glass," *BI* 12 (1993): 139-152.

A NARRATIVE ANALYSIS OF JONAH/SAILORS IRONIES IN JONAH 1:1-16: AN IGWEBUIKE PERSPECTIVE

Malachi Udochukwu Theophilus, OSA, PhD
Santa Clara University
California, United States of America
theophilusmalachy@gmail.com

ABSTRACT

This article reviews the journey of Jonah, paying attention to his failings. This helps to highlight, not just the virtuousness of the pagan characters in the first chapter of the book of Jonah, but also shows an Igwebuike theological perspective, a theology that shows the power in unity. The outcome of such theology is life, its opposite being death. The narrative is radical because it joggles so many preconceived ideas of the biblical Israel who believe that God is only interested in Israel, the elect people of God. But this assumption has not only proved to be misguided, but also completely wrong. The God of the Israelite prophet Jonah is also the God of the pagan sailors. The sailors' unity of purpose in the face of a near-death situation stands them out in the narrative in contrast to Jonah, the prophet. Their theological understanding gained them life, while Jonah opted for death. This tells us, from a theological view point, that the special relationship between YHWH and Israel does not preclude other nations and people from the mercy of God and from being used by God towards the salvation of others, for God's sovereignty is a world-wide sovereignty.

Keywords: Igwebuike Perspective, Narrative Analysis, Jonah, Sailors, Ironies

INTRODUCTION

The book of Jonah, even though short, is theologically a very rich story about a prophet, the prophet's relation to his God, and God's relation to all His creation. The narrative is radical because it joggles so many preconceived ideas of the biblical Israel about how God operates in our world: Is it not the case that He is only interested in Israel, the elect people of God? This assumption has not only shown to be misguided, but also flat out wrong. One thing that stands out in the book is its interest in non-Israelites, which is my focus in this paper. Prophets in Israel are known, not just as the mouthpiece of YHWH, but also as those who stand in the gap on behalf of the nation. They rally the nation together for a particular salvific purpose. However, that was not the case with Jonah, son of Amittai. Jonah went counter-current to the basic principles of *prophetism,* and as such, betrays the principle of *Igwebuike*<?> theology, meaning, "there is strength in solidarity." He preferred to stand alone and aloof from every other person, including God. His sentiments and body language preach nationalism instead of globalization or the unity of the human family. However, the sailors, even though minor characters and "pagans," confirm the strength in solidarity.

Therefore, my aim in this paper is to look at the sailors in the story of Jonah and demonstrate how their virtuousness overshadows the action of the prophet Jonah. In other words, I will be looking at the book of Jonah from the perspective of the supporting casts, with the aim of establishing that the key to unlocking the theology of Jonah chapter one lies in the actions of the sailors, even though they are supporting casts or minor characters.

To demonstrate this, I intend to use the *arts of biblical narrative* to show that the book of Jonah is one of the biblical narrations in which the supporting casts assume an important role that aids the development of the plot of the story. The narrator masterfully, through the power of words, enrobes these characters with a *virtuous garment* that that makes them stand out in sharp contrast to the primary character. The literary *vehicle* through which the narrator conveys the virtuousness of these characters and highlights their importance in the plot is called *irony.* By this, the narrator, on the one hand, attributes to the them certain qualities that one would have expected of a believer in YHWH; while on the other hand, he presents the prophet Jonah in a manner that appears to contradict the expected conformations of a prophet.

In the light of the above, I will sometimes refer to these supporting casts (the sailors) as pagans. This is not intended to be derogatory, but is used with the aim to bring out the ironies between them and Jonah, the prophet of YHWH. After all, Israel in the Bible sees the worship of any divinity outside YHWH, the God of Israel, as paganism or idolatry (cf. Exod 20:2; Deut 5:6; 18:9-14).

Thus said, I intend to follow Jonah in his journey in this narrative unit (Jonah 1:1-16), paying attention to his failings so as to see how they help to highlight the heroism and the uprightness of the sailors. The story goes from surprise to surprise, following complications, resolutions and revelations. I intend to go into this great journey of conversion as a reader and the narrator will be my guide as I pay close attention to the finesse of his narrative art. Jonah 1:1-3 immediately throws us into the heart of the story: the call of Jonah and his flight. So let's begin our journey with Jonah as I retell the story from the point of view of the art of biblical narrative.

EXPOSITIO - THE CALL AND THE FLIGHT OF JONAH (1:1-3)

From the point of view of the Hebrew verbal form, וַיְהִי begins the story, rather abruptly. No historical superscription or any other introduction preceded this first episode. The Hebrew word, וַיְהִי, normally translates as "and it happened" or "it came to pass." Among the twelve Minor Prophets, Jonah is the only book to open with the word וַיְהִי, a term that often begins narratives. Such a beginning suggests continuation; it implies that the background of the story is already known to the reader. Even though the book of Ezekiel (1:1) begins the same way, it's a first person narrative. It differs from Jonah (1:1) which is a third person narrative. Thus, Jonah is a narrative whose own beginning is elusive and whose ending remains unwritten. "And it came to pass" signals a tale told *in medias res (in the middle of things).*

Therefore, it is possible to conclude that Jonah is in the first place a narrative that begins prior to Jonah 1:1, making the brief description of Jonah in 2Kings 14:25 the starting point. This could mean that our narrator assumes his audience has a previous knowledge of the prophet from 2 Kings 14.<?>

THE ANNOUNCEMENT OF THE INTERVENTION OF YHWH (JONAH 1:1)

The story begins with a minimal description of the two interlocutors: YHWH and Jonah, "the son of Amittai." YHWH, the first protagonist to appear, addressed Jonah with the formulation of the prophetic oracle well known in the Bible. The clause <?>קוּם לֵךְ אֶל־ lit., "Get up and go to [...]") appears for example, in 1 Kings 17:9: "Arise and go to Zarephath [...]" (as an imperative to Elijah); also in Jeremiah 13:6, "Get up and go to the Euphrates [...]." With this formula, let's suppose, without being explicitly told, that the recipient of the word is a prophet.

Jonah, as the second protagonist, is introduced by his full name, "Jonah, son of Amittai." "Jonah" in Hebrew means "dove," a bird used to describe the folly and inconstancy of Israel (cf. Hos 7:11-12).<?> Our dove also goes counter-current to those of Is 60:8-9, where doves are used as a metaphor for the ship that came to Jerusalem from Tarshish. אֲמִתַּי - his father's name is based on the verb אָמַן, which in the *Hiphil* means "to believe" and in *Niphal* could either mean "faithful or be certain." However, אֲמִתַּי is closer in form to the noun אֱמֶת (truth or faithfulness), which is derived from the verb, אָמַן.<?> Based on this lexicographical dimension of the name Jonah, some authors observed that the *yod* at the end of אֲמִתַּי may be regarded as a hypocoristicon (shortened form of יָה or יהוה), allowing *Amittai* to mean something like "YHWH is true/faithful.<?> So, our Jonah is *the son of one whose name means the faithfulness of YHWH.* But do his actions and inactions demonstrate this? In Jonah, we will see that the one who was surnamed "the faithfulness of YHWH" is being unfaithful to the call and mission entrusted to him by YHWH.

THE MISSION OF JONAH (V.2)

The word of YHWH involves three main verbs in imperative: "Arise; go and call or proclaim." The imperative קוּם ("arise") represents the emergence of YHWH who puts the story in motion, inviting Jonah to act. Such an order will reoccur two times in the story, always addressed to Jonah, but not always from the mouth of YHWH (cf. 1:6 and 3:2). The imperative "go" (לֵךְ) translates a dynamic mission that Jonah must follow. Finally, the expression קְרָא עָלֶיהָ "call or proclaim against it" could imply a dimension of disapproval and reproach common in the prophetic ministry (cf. 1 kings 1:2; Jer 25:29).<?> It could also imply a call to repentance. However, the reader, like Jonah, already knows the recipient of the message: "Nineveh, that great city." But how would Jonah respond to these divine imperatives?

INCITING MOMENT: THE FLIGHT OF JONAH (V.3)

The first description of Jonah's reaction corresponds perfectly to the order of the Lord: קוּם "Arise" (cf. v. 2).<?> However, the second verb of his response leaves the reader puzzled: לִבְרֹחַ ("to flee"). The Qal infinitive construct of ברח, "to flee" with the preposition לְ, <?> informs us about the purpose of his *rising*, which indicates an act of rebellion and flight. Up until this verse, the reader is expected to follow the plot of the conversion of Nineveh, which was the starting point of the book. However, with the disjunctive *waw*, the narrator introduces the *inciting moment* to the plot.<?> At this point, the reader would expect a sentence like: "And Jonah arose and went to Nineveh," as this is the normal response to divine instructions, but that is not the case here. A question surges immediately in the mind of the reader: "But why did Jonah not go to Nineveh in accordance to the divine injunction?"<?> The narrator, not telling us anything in this regard, creates a narrative *gap* which puts the reader in *suspense* and arouses his *curiosity*.<?> Other prophets, like Moses, Gideon, or Jeremiah, who attempted to resist a divine command, expressed their opposition in words (Ex 3:11; Jdg 6:11-19; Jer 1:6) so that it is possible for the Lord to persuade them to bow to His yoke.<?> Here, on the other hand, the escape from and opposition to the divine command are silent, and look very determined. Jonah goes indeed to a very specific place, described with two designations: 1) the name of the city: "Tarshish;" and 2) its position with regard to God: "away from the presence of the Lord." After this brief introduction, which moves the excitement from "where?" to "how?," we now have the description, action after action, of Jonah's flight. We read:

> He went down to Joppa and found a ship going to Tarshish and paid the price, and went down into it, to go with them to Tarshish from the presence of YHWH (v. 3cd).

Four verbs punctuate the flight: דרי (twice) - "to go down," מצא - "to find" נתן - "to give" and אוב - "to enter." Jonah, who had "risen" (v. 3a), now starts a double descent, which will continue all through this narrative unit, describing the principal aspect of his attitude — first, to Joppa, the port city of Israel, and second, for which the "down" use of the verb is most unusual, in a ship. A Concatenation of verbs, in *wayyiqtol*, mostly demonstrates a certain speed in the actions of Jonah. The Hebrew text is very interesting here because it constructs a play of words between the situation that provokes the decision of God to send his prophet, namely, "the evil that *rises up* to him;" and the reaction of Jonah who *rises*, but "to go down." This verb "to go down" is a key word, particularly in the first part of this story. It does not only connote "physical or geographical movement, but most of all, the refusal of the prophet with regards to the mission entrusted to him by God."<?> Thus, it connotes rebelliousness on the part of Jonah. Another thing to note in this flight of Jonah is its irony couched in a chiastic structure:

A: Jonah arose to flee to Tarshish away from the presence of YHWH.

B: He went on to Joppa and found a ship and paid its price and boarded it.

A: To go with them to Tarshish away from the presence of YHWH.<?>

The irony of Jonah's flight is made evident in the structure above: the presence of YHWH surrounded Jonah, even in his flight to Tarshish. Who can escape the presence of God? No wonder the Psalmist says in Ps. 139:7-10 (NJB):

> Where shall I go to escape your spirit? Where shall I flee from your presence?
> If I scale the heavens you are there, if I lie flat in Sheol, there you are. If I speed
> away on the wings of the dawn, if I dwell beyond the ocean, even there your
> hand will be guiding me, your right hand holding me fast.

But it appears Jonah did not know this aspect of God; he is still determined to flee. The story did not end with this ironic but *inciting moment*; rather, it is only the beginning of its further complications.

COMPLICATIO - THE STORM AT THE SEA (1:4-16)

In this scene, the complication of verse 4 is resolved in verses 15 and 16. The scene is structured in a concentric manner. The first half of the scene (1:4-10a) is progressively enriched by the second half (1:10b-16). The fear, tension, vain efforts and prayers all find resolution in the second half of the scene, thanks to the self-revelation of Jonah in v. 9. This self-revelation marks the epicentre of the scene and propels the story to its final resolution. This movement from complication to resolution is obviously not automatic. It goes through certain exigencies (like surprises, vain efforts, fears, prayers and revelations) that highlight the activity of the sailors and the passivity of Jonah before reaching its final resolution.

COMPLICATION I: GOD THROWS A STORM THAT INSPIRES FEAR (V. 4-5A)

In this second scene, the narrator introduces us to another group of personages, outside the main protagonists of the story (YHWH and Jonah), namely:הַמַּלָּחִים "the sailors." However, it is remarkable that the sailors in Jonah, unlike the מַלָּח in Ezekiel 27:9, are completely devoid of any ethnic or national identity (except for the fact that they are non-Israelite), while their religious identity receives comparatively ample description.<?> Nonetheless, they are non-Israelites and supposedly *pagans*, from Israel's perspective. The narrator tells us succinctly that YHWH caused the wind, which caused the storm, which caused the ship to be in danger of sinking. These complicate the story and arouse the curiosity of the reader. The reader, at this point, does not know what would become of Jonah and the divine message to Nineveh, owing to the tension caused by the storm. This complication of the story (cf. *waw* disjunctive indicating a break in the momentum of Jonah)<?> opens the second stage of the chapter. Here, we have a situation of *Reader-elevating position*; that is, a situation where the reader knows more than the characters in the story.<?> The characters do not know the cause of the storm, but thanks to the omniscient narrator, we know that it was God who threw "a great wind on the sea." Meanwhile, the sailors' response was: וַיִּירְאוּ הַמַּלָּחִים - "and the sailors were afraid." Out of fear, "they cried out, each to his god."

THE EFFORTS OF THE SAILORS (V. 5BC)

Their first action is religious in nature. The sailors have realized that a god can be hidden behind this mysterious storm, because among the ancients, every cosmic calamity is attributed to a divine intervention.<?>As such, they became afraid and cried (זעק) each to his own god. The insight of Bruna Costacurta on the relationship between "fear" and "cry" is very pertinent here. The cry of the sailors is not just a mere instinctive cry as a result of fear. Rather, it is "a cry for help which man, threatened and gripped by fear, addresses both to men and to God. In this case, fear does not paralyse the faculty, but rather expresses itself in a search to find an escape."<?> Thus, in their cry, the sailors made recourse, "each to his own god," in the bid to save themselves and to salvage the ship. Here, we see the unity of purpose among these sailors. They all prayed, each to his own god, for the common purpose of salvaging the situation. Their action resonates with the words of Anthony I. Kanu, that "when human beings come together in solidarity and complementarity, they are powerful and can constitute an insurmountable force."<?> The second action is mechanical: throwing (with the return of the טול verb) the vessels in the sea to lighten the ship. Since the prayer does not seem to work, the sailors throw their goods overboard, without knowing yet that Jonah is the only load that puts the ship in distress. And indeed Jonah, at this time, continues his descent. He cuts off himself from the group and continues with his descent into the world of *aloneness*. He forgets the popular maxim attributed to the ancient Greek storyteller, Aesop, that says: "united we stand, but divided we fall."

The religious identity of the sailors may not be *Yahwistic*; however, they had faith in their god(s); and they called upon them in their time of danger. Jonah, on the other hand, a prophet of YHWH, is deep asleep. In the words of Hayyim Angel, "How ironic it is that Jonah contrasts himself with the sailors: he is righteous and aware of God's plan; they are idolatrous and ignorant of God's ways. Comparatively, the reader sees that the sailors acted admirably, praying and acting to save themselves,"<?> and to save Jonah as well. So while the sailors move from inner emotion to outward cry to vigorous action, Jonah, below the deck, moves from action to inaction and finally to total withdrawal. As the sailors increase, Jonah decreases.

The verbs "to become afraid" (יָרֵא) and "to call out" (זעק or צָעַק) are used together only in Jonah 1:5 and Exodus 14:10, which have an almost identical expression: "They became very afraid, and they call out" (וַיִּירְאוּ מְאֹד וַיִּצְעָקוּ).<?> Thus, looking at it from the point of view of Exodus 14:10, it shows that even the non-Israelite sailors did what an average Israelite should do in times of trouble, namely: "call upon the divine." However, the storm still rages. Since their prayer does not amount to a solution, they rightly conclude that the answer must lie in someone else: Jonah, of course! But he who is guilty lies indifferently fast asleep.

SURPRISE I: JONAH ECLIPSED (V.5D)

> "Jonah, meanwhile, had gone down into the hold of the ship and had lain down, and was fast asleep."

The order of the words in Hebrew expresses a contrast to that which has just been told.<?> While the sailors are doing everything to survive, Jonah runs away even further from his responsibility and is eclipsed in his sleep, as if it were nothing. Nonchalance is emphasized here by the contrast between the three verbs that describe the action of the sailors: "fear, scream and throw," and the three used to describe the action of Jonah: "go down, lie down, and fall deep asleep." Hence, Jonah is inactive, contrary to the active sailors. According to Simon, "his ability to sleep at such a time is the first manifestation of his preferred inclination of death to life."<?> Scaiola observes that "the verb רדם used here is derived from the substantive תַּרְדֵּמָה which could imply either a profound sleep (cf. 1 Sam 26,12; Is 29,10) or a state of trance (cf. Gen 2,21; 15,12, Dan 8,18)."<?> Jonah sleeps profoundly, but his sleep is not a trance, but an escape from YHWH and from his prophetic responsibility. To describe the place where Jonah had gone down, the narrator makes use of an unusual term: יְרְכָה, usually used to describe the most extreme and profound part of a place.<?> This Jonah's new descent, therefore, emphasizes his estrangement from God and from the stage, to the depths of the ship, in a total detachment from life and the story around him. At this stage, the reader wonders what the fate of the sailors would be, owing to the fact of their ignorance of the person responsible for the danger that had befallen them.

TURNING POINT: JONAH IS FOUND AND SUMMONED TO HELP (V. 6)

> "The captain (of the sailors) came and said to him, "What are you doing sound asleep? Arise, call on your god! Perhaps the god will spare us a thought so that we do not perish"

This new complication of the story finds a turning point with the intervention of the captain of the ship. After a rhetorical question that implies a rebuke,<?> the captain repeats without knowing the divine imperative: קוּם קְרָא אֶל ("Arise, call on your god!"). Upon awakening, Jonah meets with the word from which he is fleeing. He who refuses to rebuke Nineveh is reproached with irony, and most of all, by a non-Israelite who re-proposes the word of YHWH, the God of Israel: "Arise and call." This officer is the first human character to make a direct speech. He orders Jonah to "arise" and "call" to God, whose own command, "arise … call" Jonah had already spurned. He is thus called by a new authority to his intercessory mission to save the lives of men. He is called to align himself with the attitude of the sailors, who cried out "each to his own god" (v. 5). Perhaps his God will do something to the ship.

If YHWH, the God of Israel, found in a *pagan*, the captain, a worthy instrument for His Word, it obviously bespeaks of the place of these supporting characters in this narrative unit. It tells us something about the God of the Bible. It tells us that despite one's "otherness," in relation to Israel, he/she can still be an instrument in the hands of the creator.<?> The captain assumed the role of a prophet, a responsibility which the Israelite Jonah abnegated. In other words, God used a *pagan* as His mouthpiece to speak to his prophet Jonah, to remind him of his prophetic responsibility. Anyone familiar with the prophetic books of the Bible knows that the fundamental vocation of the prophet is the "word," or more specifically, דְּבַר־יְהוָה (the word of YHWH). Thus, the prophet is one who speaks.<?> However, ironically here, we have a prophet who refuses to speak. God, using a pagan as his "mouthpiece," is not peculiar to the book of Jonah, it is found elsewhere in the Old Testament. For example, in Jeremiah 40,1-5, God used a pagan Captain, Nebuzaradan to talk to his Prophet Jeremiah. But here in Jonah, it tells us that we are before a narrative in which the supporting characters assume an important role in accordance with the theology of the book. All this makes Jonah look like a "prodigal prophet." The captain is more aware of the power of prayer than the fleeing prophet! The heathen captain seeks divine deliverance, while Jonah seeks oblivion. Prophets are often expected to intercede in a time of crisis (cf. Moses at Israel's golden calf apostasy in Exodus 32, 11-14 and Amos in the locust and fire disasters in Amos 7, 1-6). But Jonah remained adamant. His silence is deafening! He is a prophet who does not speak!<?> These repetitions of key words are common features throughout the book, and they convey some important ideas. קוּם and קְרָא in both 1:2 and 1:6 reiterate the huge gulf between the active praying sailors and the sleeping disobedient *Prophet* of YHWH, who refuses to arise and call to Nineveh. Also, the repetition indicates that Jonah has not escaped the presence of God.<?>

THE REVELATION OF THE GUILTY BY CASTING OF LOTS (V.7)

> "The sailors said to one another, "Come, let us cast lots, so that we may know on whose account this calamity has come upon us". So they cast lots, and the lot fell on Jonah."

If in v. 6 we are at the bottom of the ship, where the captain spoke to Jonah, who, uninterested in what happens and wanting to stay away from all worries, retires most probably to sleep. In v. 7, the narrator, in a dramatic way, makes evident an action that most likely took place where all the sailors were present, that is, far away from the bottom and on the deck of the ship. So, it is remarkable how the narrator moves the reader from one place to another, without the reader realizing it at a first glance.

Another highlight is the curiosity that the narrator evokes from the reader by omitting the reaction of Jonah to the imperatives קוּם קְרָא (v. 6) of the captain: What did Jonah do in response to the imperatives? Did he pray? Or did he again ignore the command to "arise and call..."? Verse 7 does not tell us what happens, but it makes us imagine what happens: Jonah's probable silence brings the sailors into focus as they propose the casting of lots to determine who among them is responsible for the evil. It is as if we are in front of theatrical action: the sailors cast lots and they talk among themselves. Not knowing the cause of the tempest, the sailors must have believed that once the culprit was found, the final destruction could be prevented. The phrase that the reader hears, "Come, let us cast lots, so that we may know on whose account this calamity has come upon us," also has the effect of creating a little suspense and curiosity: *will the lot fall on Jonah?*

THE SAILORS' LOT CASTING: TYPICAL OF ISRAELITE'S DIVINATION

The casting of lots is widely attested to in the ancient world<?> as well as in the Hebrew Bible. The precise *lots* in question vary, both within ancient Israel and outside it.<?> However, giving the prevalent nature of "lot casting tradition" in the ancient Near East, it wouldn't be surprising that the sailors adopted this option in such dire circumstances.<?> But a closer look at this, in the context of Jonah, "suggests that the sailors' activity is rather unusual and, literarily- speaking, delightful."<?>

B. A. Strawn rightly observed that in the majority of instances where lots or lot casting are mentioned in the Hebrew Bible, the language used is not of foreigners, but of Israelites. Apart from Jonah 1:7, "only five other passages speak of foreigners employing the practice: Esth 3:7; 9:24; Joel 4:3; Obad 11; and Nah 3:10. All other instances concern intra- Israelite use of lots for a rather wide variety of purposes, the majority of which are connected to YHWH (see, e.g., Josh 18:8,10; 1 Sam 10:20-24; 14:41; Prov 16:33), the cult (e.g., Lev 16:8-10; Neh 10:35), or the land of Israel itself" (Num 36:2; Josh 14:1-2; 15:1).<?> Even among those five additional passages (besides Jonah) that mention foreigners casting lots, at least four reflect an intra-Israelite perspective - mentioning Israel or YHWH in some fashion (cf. Esth 3,7; 9,24; Joel 4,3; Obad 11).<?>

The same might be said of the lot casting in the book of Jonah. Even though it involves foreigners, the situation that prompted the casting of lots was caused by YHWH, and rightly, the lot fell on YHWH's prophet. On this note, Limburg states that "Jonah's sailors 'make some theological assumptions in connection with the lot casting. One such assumption is that the storm is divine punishment; another is that God communicates through the casting of lots."<?> Similarly, Trible holds that "theologically, the use of lots to disclose the truth elevates chance to the level of divine will."<?> So one may say that Jonah's sailors, though not unusual in employing divination, but "the fact that they are specifically said to cast lots (נפל +גּוֹרָלוֹת); an oft-attested Israelite practice, using Israelite terminology (cf. Esth 3:7; 9:24) suggests an *Israelite* perspective on the scene."<?> Thus, our sailors are not just painted in Israelite garb, but more importantly, are depicted as familiar with Israelite ritual. In this, we see the sailors as supporting casts, aiding the development of the plot. Their action of casting lots leads to the discovery of the culprit and subsequently moves the story forward.

In all this, of course, as is customary in Scripture, the story is led by God, who brings into play the human freedom so as to bring man to victory over fear and the recognition of the Holy One as the God of life. So, if Jonah sought the sea that God Himself created, to escape from the face of YHWH, it is God again who guides the story by making the lot to fall on Jonah. Here, we see a significant relation between human liberty and sovereign dominion of the God of history.

QUESTIONS TO DETERMINE THE NATURE OF THE CRIME (V. 8)

> "Then they said to him, "Tell us why this calamity has come upon us. What is your occupation? Where do you come from? What is your country? And of what people are you?"

The sailors do not automatically lash out against the guilty prophet, since they have identified the culprit. Instead, they simply ask him: "Tell us why this calamity has come upon us." This is followed by further questions. Sweeney notes that this kind of question is conventional and generally made to know the identity of a person.<?> Here, we have a true and proper interrogation. In ancient Israel, there are different steps and processes of establishing justice. Even though the lot fell on Jonah, the sailors didn't stop at that. They went a step further. They implored the interrogative step. This step functions to ascertain facts and responsibility (cf. Gen 3:13; 4:10; Judg 18:18).<?> Thus, this shows that the sailors are very attentive to establishing the truth. They don't want to give anything to chance. They want to be sure beyond all reasonable doubt about what they are doing.

The first question is the most crucial. Its answer is not obvious. The crew quite naturally wonders if somehow they might have done some wrong deserving of this calamity. Have they offended Jonah? Are they helping him do something wrong? Is it guilt by association? Or is Jonah alone to blame? Are they transporting someone who has committed a great crime? They are still genuinely wondering why the lot fell on Jonah and what it means for them. The crew is also desperate to know exactly who Jonah is, because they only know that he is somehow the focus of the problem. Until they know his identity, they can't expect to know, for example, which god he has offended, and how. Thus, the sailors asked him further questions. His occupation, once they know it, will tell them much, if he is a priest, or a prophet, or an executioner, or an idol-maker, or has any one of many other religiously sensitive occupations. The final three questions all concern Jonah's origin. The answer to these would also have religious significance, since one's national god was usually the most important divinity in one's life at this point in history. During Jonah's time, people's personal destinies were inextricably linked with their national destinies, and national gods functioned increasingly as personal gods, at least in Palestine.<?>

REVELATION: JONAH'S SELF-IDENTIFICATION AND THE REACTION OF THE SAILORS (V. 9)

> "I am a Hebrew, he replied. "I fear YHWH, the God of heaven, who made the sea and the dry land". Then the men were even more afraid"

These questions make us get into the heart of the story of the first chapter of the book of Jonah. At last, Jonah finally speaks: "I am a Hebrew ... I fear YHWH ..." James Ackerman says that this answer, taken out of context, is presented as a confession of faith.<?> The problem is that until now Jonah has not shown any faith in the God of Israel. So, in what sense does he fear God? Antonio Nepi observes here that Jonah's *profession of faith* in YHWH, the God of heaven, of earth and of the seas "is an example of dramatic irony, because it clashes with the claim of escaping a God who transcends the ethnic boundaries of Israel and controls the wind and waves."<?> In other words, if he really "fears" this omnipresent God, why does he try to escape from him?

The term עִבְרִי "Hebrew," on the other hand, is often used when contrasting Israelites with non-Israelites. In this vein, Jonah's usage of *Ivri* in 1:9 is expected, since he was contrasting himself with *pagans*. Jonah's perceived dissimilarity to the sailors is the main emphasis of Jonah 1. We are before a revelation, an important stage in the development of the plot that directs the story towards a resolution. In fact, the sailors' realization of who their interlocutor is and what he would say to them about his escape from YHWH will lead them to take a dramatic decision. This awareness takes away from the sailors the initial curiosity they had about Jonah, particularly, about his identity. However, this contrast with the sailors was most important to

Jonah; therefore, the narrator placed only these words in his direct quotation. This response caused a reaction from the sailors.

In all this, however, one notes that Jonah avoided the question about his occupation. He didn't say he was a prophet. This omission seems very significant. Scaiola opines that this is so "because maybe, given the situation, he finds it difficult to say he is a prophet."<?> But, I would rather think that this omission highlights his continuous desire to flee from his prophetic responsibility.

Our narrator tells us, "and the men feared a great fear" (1:10a). This יָרֵא here links the preceding section to subsequent efforts by the sailors to avert disaster. According to Lessing, "the narrator uses יָרֵא in different ways to indicate that the events in chapter 1 transform the sailors from sheer terror (1:5) to an awe at the awareness of being in YHWH's presence and finally to trust, belief, and worship of this great God."<?> In other words, Jonah's confession brings the sailors from fear (in verse 5) to awe (in verse 10) of the God of the heavens, who created the sea and the dry land. The sailors react in a way more indicative of faith than does the Israelite Jonah. He is reacting in a manner one would expect from an unbeliever. The sailors are unable to imagine anyone treating his deity in such a fashion. They, unlike Jonah, have fear and respect for the divine. They display greater reverence and understanding than the Israelite Jonah.

FLASHBACKS: THE QUESTION ABOUT THE CRIME (V. 10)

> "They said to him, "What is this that you have done?" For the men knew that
> he was fleeing from the presence of the YHWH, because he had told them so."

This interrogation of Jonah by the sailors to Jonah refers us back to the past of the prophet. This tells us that we are faced with an *analepsis*, or a flashback, which, in turn, echoes God's question to Eve: "What have you done?" (Gen 3:13). The narrator withheld the information on how the sailors realised that Jonah was running away from YHWH, only to let us into that knowledge now, by telling us that "the men knew because Jonah had told them." The question of the sailors is not merely intended to know what they ask, because they already knew through the express confession of Jonah, but it seems that they want to rebuke him for what he had done. It may sound like: "How could you do this to your God?" Thus, this question is not just a mere desire to seek for information. Rather, having established the truth, "because Jonah had told them so," the men, through this question, express their perplexity in the fact that a man, who "fears YHWH, the God of heaven, who made the sea and the dry land," could attempt to flee from this same YHWH. So, it appears that with this question that expressed their perplexity, they wanted to bring Jonah into the perspective of the gravity of what he had done.

JONAH IS CALLED TO HELP (V.11)

> "Then they said to him, 'What shall we do to you, that the sea may quiet down for us?' For the sea was growing more and more tempestuous."

There is something very interesting here. The sailors had established the truth: "Jonah is the culprit, and YHWH, the God of Jonah knows about the storm." And more still, the situation at the sea wasn't encouraging either, "For the sea was growing all the more tempestuous." But despite all this, and as upright men, the sailors do not take the law into their hands. Instead, they cordially ask Jonah: "What shall we do to you[...]?" I think Douglas Stuart captures the situation even better. In his words:

> The sailors are not *Yahwists*, and certainly not prophets. Jonah is both the guilty party and the expert here. So Jonah is the only one who can tell them what YHWH would require to turn aside His wrath. They ask him what to do. There must be some punishment of Jonah which they can instigate that will stop the storm. The sea was churning ever higher, so the lightening of the ship by throwing cargo overboard had only bought time; it had not really gotten them out of danger.<?>

The sailors want to save their lives. There are no elements suggestive of hostility towards the prophet; indeed, it will soon become evident in their attempt to save his life.

REVELATION: JONAH REVEALS WHAT TO DO TO END THE STORM (1, 12)

> "He said to them, 'Pick me up and throw me into the sea; then the sea will quiet down for you; for I know it is because of me that this great storm has come upon you.'"

Here, the prophet is well aware of why the storm is raging: it is his disobedience to the will of YHWH that has caused all this. Thus, to avert the danger, he asks to be thrown into the sea. The sailors have done everything to avoid ending up in the sea with their ship and Jonah, but Jonah, on the contrary, asks to be thrown into the sea. Here, Ska observes that "water, from biblical point of view, is synonymous with the place of death."<?> This contrast is alarming. Jonah, the עִבְרִי, who in v. 9 made what almost looked like a confession of faith: "I fear the Lord, the God who of heaven, who made the sea and the dry land," now wants to end up in the sea, the world of death.<?>Jonah obviously does not want to obey anyone except his own whims. He, who bears the name of the *dove*, refuses to go to Nineveh, does not pray to his God as the captain had asked of him, and now wants to end up in the world of the dead. While the sailors continue to make efforts to bring the prophet to focus about his mistake so he can choose life together with them instead of death, Jonah, on the other hand, prefers aloneness and death, instead of unity and life. But the sailors want none of that. They choose life instead; hence, they try to save him at all costs.

It is interesting to imagine the passivity of Jonah when he asked to be thrown into the sea. He could jump into the water by his own freewill, and assume alone all the responsibility. Instead, choosing once again passivity and running away from responsibility, he questions the freedom of the sailors themselves, and involves them in a risky and compromising operation.

THE EFFORTS OF THE SAILORS (V. 13)

> "Nevertheless the men rowed hard to bring the ship back to land, but they could not, for the sea grew more and more stormy against them."

The Qal of the verb חתר (here third common plural imperfect with *waw* consecutive) could be translated as "to dig, burrow, hollow out." Lessing believes חתר was used metaphorically, as for example, in Amos 9:2, where YHWH speaks of people who *burrow* into *Sheol*, seeking to escape his wrath. So here it could mean the sailors *dug* into the water with their oars, which means they rowed harder.<?> Also, it is important to note that the verb, "to row," exists in Hebrew, and it is not חתר. In most cases, Hebrew uses the root verb שוט to represent the act of rowing, or moving to-and-fro (cf. Num 11:8; 2 Sam 24,2; Ezek 27:6,29). חתר, on the hand, is used in Hebrew to represent the act of digging, tunneling or burrowing through (cf. Job 24:16; Ezek 12:5,7). Therefore, leaning on the insightful view of Christopher Meredith, I would rather concur that, by using חתר and not שוט, "the author seems most concerned not with the motion of rowing — the action of *digging* into the water, but with the severity of the storm and the ship's progress through it. The sailors have to tunnel through waves as the tempest swells around them."<?> In other words, this presents us with a picture where a terrestrial word is used to describe a marine action. This crucial strain between land and sea is what the narrator tries to underline here. "The sailors insist on being back on land, the land lubing Jonah insists on being given over to the water."<?>

Evidently, these sailors did their utmost best to save, not only their own lives, but also the life of the Hebrew. If Jonah seemed inclined to die, they do not want any death. In a climate of even more growing tension, due to the force of an unleashed sea, these *pagans* were going against the will of the prophet and against the stormy sea. This desire to save the unfortunate man who had disobeyed YHWH depicts obviously the *virtuousness* of these sailors. Now, given that all their efforts had proven abortive, will they succumb to the request of the *runaway prophet* of YHWH and *hurl* him into the sea? The narrator is a teacher who raises this question in the reader: *curiosity* and *suspense* pervade these lines. Worthy of note is the fact that all this underlines the place of the sailors in this story. Even though Jonah requested that he should be picked up and hurled into the sea (1:12), they still did everything to save their lives and that of the prophet from Israel. They feared killing a man, even when he requested it, and even when doing so would eventually save their lives. The ethical standard of these Gentiles is far higher than that of Jonah. They have been thrown into a life-threatening storm through no fault of theirs. They have lost their cargo, yet they still seek to save the life of the man who is responsible for all the chaos.

THE AUTHENTIC PRAYERS OF THE SAILORS (V. 14)

> "Then they cried out to the YHWH, 'Please, YHWH, we pray, do not let us perish on account of this man's life. Do not make us guilty of innocent blood; for you, O YHWH, have done as it pleased you.'"

The journey of faith, therefore, seems to be well under way. In fact, we are not in front of people shouting at their own god (1:5), but in front of people calling YHWH, וַיִּקְרְאוּ אֶל־יְהוָה ("They cried out to YHWH"). This is contextually similar to the expression that the Bible usually puts on the lips of the children of Israel -וַיִּזְעֲקוּ בְנֵי־יִשְׂרָאֵל אֶל־יְהוָה — "And the sons of Israel cried to YHWH [...]" (cf. Ex 14:10; Jdg 3:15; 4:3). I would like to pay particular attention to this part of the exemplary action of the sailors because, to me, it forms the climax of their progressive journey of faith and demonstrates their uprightness.

Now the sailors were in a no-win situation. If they throw him overboard, they may bring YHWH's wrath upon themselves; and if Jonah stays on board, they may perish. So, what should they do? They narrator tells us: וַיִּקְרְאוּ אֶל־יְהוָה- "They called to YHWH." The only recourse is to plead for acquittal from YHWH. So, unlike Jonah, the sailors did not flee from YHWH (1:3) nor remain silent like Jonah who never said a single word to YHWH throughout chapter one. Rather, they prayed to God. Their prayer was a true supplication to God. In 1:5 "they called out each to his god." But here in verse 14 they invoked the name of YHWH. They have come to believe that Israel's God is the God over the universe, whose power is felt even in the stormy sea.

According to Lessing, their prayer is in the pattern of the most common Hebrew prose prayers:

1. Invocation ("O YHWH")
2. Petition ("Do not let us perish on the account of the life of this man, do not place against us innocent blood")
3. Motivation for the petition ("For you are YHWH; just as you please, you do")[26]

In this prayer, as represented above, one sees that it is not only the narrator that says "they invoked YHWH," but the sailors themselves called God "YHWH." This shows a *Yhwhistic* faith. Now, let's take a closer look at this prayer pattern used by the sailors. First of all, one notices that apart from their acknowledgement of the sovereignty of YHWH, they also

---

[26] Lessing, 135.

acknowledge that murder is a capital crime for which they could perish if YHWH holds them responsible. In fact, Theodore Laetsch writes: "These Gentiles had the fifth commandment (Ex 20:13; Dt 5:17) written in their hearts... and revolted from slaying a man."[27]

The sailors' second request: "Do not place against us innocent blood" echoes YHWH's instruction through Moses to the people of Israel for the expiation of untraced murder in Dt 21:8-9. In other words, if Jonah has misled them, they are not to be held responsible. Hence, they want to be sure that they are doing the will of YHWH, which Jonah the prophet never bothered about.[28]

Finally, they articulated the last part of their prayer in a way one would expect of Jonah or any ardent believer of YHWH: "For you are YHWH; just as you please, you do" (יְהֹוָה כַּאֲשֶׁר חָפַצְתָּ עָשִׂיתָ כִּי־אַתָּה). This expression, writes Jack M. Sasson, "looks very much as if it could be used at any time that a Hebrew wanted to compare God's limitless freedom of action to the pagan god's more restricted movement."[29] All this confirms what Laetsch says, with regard to the word of the Lord being written in the hearts of these pagans. They, in conformity with words of the Scripture, confess that "YHWH does as he pleases" (Is 46:10; Ps115: 3; 135: 6), while Jonah, in chapter four, expresses his frustration because YHWH does exactly as He pleases. What an irony!

RESOLUTION: JONAH IS HURLED INTO THE SEA, THE TEMPEST CEASED, AND THE SAILORS OFFERED SACRIFICES AND MADE VOWS (VV. 15-16)

> "So they picked Jonah up and hurled him into the sea; and the sea ceased from its raging. Then the men feared YHWH even more, and they offered a sacrifice to the YHWH and made vows."

After their prayers, they threw Jonah overboard; and the tempest ceased. This confirms that it is indeed YHWH, the God of Jonah (1:9), and now, the God of the sailors (1:14), who controls the seas and the waves. So, surely they are safe, the sailors and all in the ship.

Now, the narrator, playing on the verb יָרֵא, tells us again: "Then the men feared a great fear (literally) of the Lord, and they offered a sacrifice to the Lord and made vows" (1:16). This brings the spiritual ascent of the sailors to its climax. They moved from sheer fear of danger (1:5) to fear of the presence of YHWH in the storm (1:10) and finally to fear as a reverence to YHWH (1:14,16). The response of these sailors is striking in its simplicity and overpowering in its implications. If Jonah, in his "confession of faith," professed a reverence (couched in fear and disobedience) to the God of heaven, these sailor's on the other hand, worshiped YHWH

---

[27] Theodore Laetsch, *The Minor Prophets*. (St. Louis: Concordia, 1956), 227.

[28] Cf. Lessing, 136.

[29] Sasson, 136.

in an unalloyed manner. They demonstrated commitment to YHWH by offering sacrifice and making vows to him. This is almost certainly a description of whole-hearted conversion to YHWH. "Sacrifice" and "vows" mentioned in the same verse confirm this interpretation, since the Hebrew Bible elsewhere associates these actions with a permanent commitment to YHWH (cf. Ps 50:14; Is 19:21). It will not be an overstatement to conclude that, in the first and second scenes of the book of Jonah, God's true heroes are the sailors, and not the prophet.

CONCLUSION

From the foregoing, it is evident that the sailors, even though supporting casts, took the centre stage in Jonah 1. Jonah, the primary character of the story, in the light of this first chapter, can rightly be described as a *round character*. "Round characters" have more depth and their personality often contains conflicting, even contradicting tendencies."[30] The complexity of Jonah's character is made evident when compared with those of the sailors. But the sailors, on the other hand, even though secondary characters, acted as main protagonists of the second scene. The sailors progressively move from "each crying to his own god" (1:5a), to lot casting: a typical Israelite divination practice, with the aim of establishing the truth.[31] From there, they progressed to an eloquent prayer to YHWH (1:14), which culminates in vow-making and sacrifice to YHWH (1:16). These actions of the sailors evolve the plot. After the general fear caused by the storm, they implored their gods (1:5b); and then, in a progressive manner, turned to YHWH in faith who then averted the danger. But one thing that stands out in this story is the unity of purpose with which the sailors approached their near-death situation. Their action, in most part of the story, shows an implicit understanding of *Igwebuike* theology, a theology that shows the power in unity. The outcome of such theology is life, while its opposite outcome is death. This is evident in this story. The sailors were saved because of the unity of purpose in their orientation towards the divine. But Jonah, in his quest to stand alone and faraway from God, ended up in the waters, which, symbolically, represents death.[32]

The narrative concludes with the offering of sacrifices and vows made by the sailors to YHWH, not in sheer fear, but in outright devotion to YHWH as a culmination of their journey of faith. Thus, it is evident that "the sailors are personages linked strictly to the scene of the tempest. They entered the scene after YHWH had unleashed the tempest on the sea, and went out of the scene when the tempest ceased."[33] This makes them agent characters, not in the sense of flat characters who are not important in themselves, but in the sense of their functional role at the service of the plot. This tells us, from theological view point, that the special relationship between YHWH and Israel does not preclude other nations and people from the mercy of God and from being used by God towards the salvation of others, for God's sovereignty is

---

[30] Ska, *Our Father Have Told us*, 84.
[31] Cf. Strawn, 66-76.
[32] Cf. Gen 7:4; Ex 14:21-22; Josh 3:15-16.
[33] A. Niccacci – M. Pazzini – R. Tadiello, *Il Libro di Giona* (Milano: Analecta, 2013), 117.

a world-wide sovereignty. It is undisputable that Israel, in the Bible, is a "Vineyard which God himself has planted" (cf. Ps 80:7-15). But this does not exclude other nations as part of the universal family of God's children. This further shows that it is not the possession of the truth that counts, but how ready we are to live in the light of the truth we possess. Jonah, the "son of God's faithfulness," possessed the Word (cf. Jonah 1:1-2), but he wasn't faithful to the Word he possessed. The sailors, on the other hand, were supposedly ignorant of the Word, but their actions throughout the story were indicative of the fact that the Word of God was actually written in their hearts. They, rather than the prophet, are the heroes of uprightness in this story.

BIBLIOGRAPHY

Ackerman, J. S. "Jonah." in R. Alter, - F. Kermode, ed., *The Literary Guide to the Bible*, Cambridge: Harvard University Press, 1987

Bovati, P. *Cosi Parla Il Signore*: *Studio sul Profetismo Biblico*. Bib. Bologna: EDB, 2008.

Bovati, P. *Ristabilire la Giustizia. Procedure, vocabolario, orientamenti*. AnBib 110. Roma: Pontificio Istituto Biblico, 1986.

Brody, J. A. *Each Man Cried Out to His God: The Specialized Religion of Canaanite and Phoenician*. Atlanta: Brill, 1998.

Costacurta, B. *La Vita Minacciata*: *Il Tema della Paura nella Bibbia Ebraica*. AnBib 119. Roma: Pontificio Istituto Biblico, 1988.

Dam, C. V. *The Urim and Thummim. A Means of Revelation in Ancient Israel*. Indiana: Eisenbrauns, 1997.

Hayyim, A. "The Book of Jonah: A Call to Personal Responsibility." *TRADITION 30* (1995): 56-67.

Kanu, I. A. "Igwebuike as an Igbo-African Hermeneutic of Globalization," in *Igwebuike: An African Journal of Arts and Humanities*, Vol. 2 no. 1 (March, 2016):1-6.

Kanu, I. A. (2018). *Igwe Bu Ike* as an Igbo-African hermeneutics of national development. *Igbo Studies Review. No. 6*. pp. 59-83.

Kanu, I. A. (2018). *Igwebuike* as an African integrative and progressive anthropology. *NAJOP: Nasara Journal of Philosophy*. Vol. 2. No. 1. pp. 151-161.

Kanu, I. A. (2018). New Africanism: *Igwebuike* as a philosophical Attribute of Africa in portraying the Image of Life. In Mahmoud Misaeli, Sanni Yaya and Rico Sneller (Eds.). *African Perspectives on Global on Global Development* (pp. 92-103). United Kingdom: Cambridge Scholars Publishing.

Kanu, I. A. (2019). Collaboration within the ecology of mission: An African cultural perspective. *The Catholic Voyage: African Journal of Consecrated Life*. Vol. 15. pp. 125-149.

Kanu, I. A. (2019). *Igwebuike* research methodology: A new trend for scientific and wholistic investigation. *IGWEBUIKE: An African Journal of Arts and Humanities (IAAJAH)*. *5. 4. pp. 95-105.*

Kanu, I. A. (2019). *Igwebuikeconomics*: The Igbo apprenticeship for wealth creation. *IGWEBUIKE: An African Journal of Arts and Humanities (IAAJAH)*. *5. 4. pp. 56-70.*

Kanu, I. A. (2019). *Igwebuikecracy*: The Igbo-African participatory cocio-political system of governance. *TOLLE LEGE: An Augustinian Journal of the Philosophy and Theology. 1. 1.* pp. 34-45.

Kanu, I. A. (2019). On the origin and principles of *Igwebuike* philosophy. *International Journal of Religion and Human Relations*. Vol. 11. No. 1. pp. 159-176.

Kanu, I. A. (2019b). An *Igwebuike* approach to the study of African traditional naming ceremony and baptism. *International Journal of Religion and Human Relations*. Vol. 11. No. 1. pp. 25-50.

Kanu, I. A. (2017). *Igwebuike* as an Igbo-African philosophy for Christian-Muslim relations in Northern Nigeria. In Mahmoud Misaeli (Ed.). *Spirituality and Global Ethics* (pp. 300-310). United Kingdom: Cambridge Scholars.

Kanu, I. A. (2017). *Igwebuike* as an Igbo-African philosophy for the protection of the environment. *Nightingale International Journal of Humanities and Social Sciences*. Vol. 3. No. 4. pp. 28-38.

Kanu, I. A. (2017). *Igwebuike* as the hermeneutic of individuality and communality in African ontology. *NAJOP: Nasara Journal of Philosophy*. Vol. 2. No. 1. pp. 162-179.

Kanu, I. A. (2017a). *Igwebuike* and question of superiority in the scientific community of knowledge. *Igwebuike: An African Journal of Arts and Humanities*. Vol.3 No1. pp. 131-138.

Kanu, I. A. (2017a). *Igwebuike as a philosophical attribute of Africa in portraying the image of life*. A paper presented at the 2017 Oracle of Wisdom International Conference by the Department of Philosophy, Tansian University, Umunya, Anambra State, 27-29 April.

Kanu, I. A. (2017b). *Igwebuike* as a complementary approach to the issue of girl-child education. *Nightingale International Journal of Contemporary Education and Research*. Vol. 3. No. 6. pp. 11-17.

Kanu, I. A. (2017b). *Igwebuike* as a wholistic response to the problem of evil and human suffering. *Igwebuike: An African Journal of Arts and Humanities*. Vol. 3 No 2, March.

Kanu, I. A. (2017e). *Igwebuike* as an Igbo-African modality of peace and conflict resolution. *Journal of African Traditional Religion and Philosophy Scholars*. Vol. 1. No. 1. pp. 31-40.

Kanu, I. A. (2017g). *Igwebuike* and the logic (Nka) of African philosophy. *Igwebuike: An African Journal of Arts and Humanities*. 3. 1. pp. 1-13.

Kanu, I. A. (2017h). *Igwebuike* philosophy and human rights violation in Africa. *IGWEBUIKE: An African Journal of Arts and Humanities*. Vol. 3. No. 7. pp. 117-136.

Kanu, I. A. (2017i). *Igwebuike* as a hermeneutic of personal autonomy in African ontology. *Journal of African Traditional Religion and Philosophy Scholars*. Vol. 2. No. 1. pp. 14-22.

Laetsch, T. *The Minor Prophets*. St. Louis: Concordia, 1956.

Lessing, R. Reed. *Jonah*. Concordia Commentary, St. Louis: Concordia Publishing House 2007.

Limburg, J. *Jonah: A Commentary*. Louisville: John Knox Press, 1993.

Meredith, C. "The Conodrum of *htr* in Jonah 1:13." *Vetus Testamentum* 64 (2014): 147-15

Nepi, A. *Dal Fondale alla Ribalta: I Personaggi Secondari nella Bibbia Ebraica*. Bologna: Epinia della Parola, 2015.

Niccacci, A. – Pazzini, M. – Tadiello, R. *Il Libro di Giona*, Milano: Analecta: 2013.

Sasson, J. M. *Jonah*. Anchor Bible 24B. New York: Doubleday, 1990.

Scaiola, D. *Abdia, Giona, Michea: Introduzione, Traduzione e Commento*. NVBTA. Milano: San Paolo, 2012.

Simon, U. *Jonah: The Traditional Hebrew Text with the New JPS Translations*. Philadelphia: JPS, 1999.

Ska, J.-L. "Giona sei tu! La Creazione del Lettore nel Libro di Giona." An unpublished Paper presented at a Conference in the Theological Institute of Triveneto, Italy (2013): 5-22.

Ska, J.-L. *Our Father Have Told us*, Roma: Biblical Press, 2000.

Sternberg, M. *The Poetics of Biblical Narrative: Ideological Literature and the Drama of Reading*. Indiana: Indiana University Press, 1985.

Strawn, B. A., "Jonah's Sailors and Their Lot Casting: A Rhetorical Critical Observation." *Biblica* 91 (2010): 66-76.

Stuart, D., *Hosea-Jonah*, WBC 31, Dallas: Word, Incorporated, 1987.

Sweeney, M. A. "Jonah" in Cotter, D.W., ed., *The Twelve Prophets*. BERIT OLAM, Collegeville: Liturgical Press, 2016.

Theophilus, M. "The Role of Rehab in the Conquest Story of Joshua as a Manifestation of Igwebuike Theology: A Narrative Analysis of Joshua 2," in *Igwebuike: An African Journal of Arts and Humanities*. Vol. 5, no. 8 (2019): 72-92.

Trible, P. "Studies in the Book of Jonah." An unpublished dissertation. Columbia University, New York, 1963.

Trible, P. *Rhetorical Criticism: Context, Method, and the Book of Jonah*. Minneapolis: Fortress Press, 1994.

THIRDSPACING THE EXILE IN EZEKIEL'S THEOLOGY OF DIVINE PRESENCE AND ITS IMPLICATIONS FOR THE ABRAHAMIC RELIGIONS: AN IGWEBUIKE PERSPECTIVE

Malachi Udochukwu Theophilus, OSA, PhD
Santa Clara University
California, United States of America
theophilusmalachy@gmail.com

ABSTRACT

While the community in Judah considered those in exile as "other" because they had no temple and were not within the geographical location called "Judah" (cf. Ezek 11:15), this study leans on the critical spatial theories of Edward W. Soja and Wesley A. Kort to show that location does not guarantee the experience of the divine. What counts is not location, but praxis, that is, our orientation towards the Holy One. YHWH's expression (cf. Ezek 11:16), in reaction to the tension that existed between the exilic community and the remnant community in Judah, challenges the religious tension and religious exclusivism that characterize our world today. It shows that despite the existential peculiarities of each community of faith, there exists a theological minimum that can form the basis of our experience of the divine. Sometimes, we may think we possess the fullness of truth, as symbolized in the temple with its sacred adornments or as contained in the Torah, the Holy Bible or the Koran, but the reality of the experience of the divine does not necessarily lie in the one who possesses the truth. It is not the possession of the truth that matters, but how prepared we are to walk in the light of the truth that we possess, irrespective of our religious affiliations.

Keywords: Igwebuike, Ezekiel, Theology, Divine Presence, Abrahamic Religions

INTRODUCTION

The idea of divine presence was imperative to the people of the ancient Near East. This was evident in their cultic practices. Temples, sacrifices and rituals ensured the deities were present to those who revered them. The kingdoms of Israel and Judah were not exceptions to this concern for the presence of the divine. They may have depended upon the theologies of the ancient Near East in the construction of their theology of divine presence. However, "around the time of the neo-Babylonian empire, the Israelite prophetic writings began to show unambiguous evidence of a changing attitude towards some widely shared assumptions about divine presence."[34] Notable among these literatures is the book of Ezekiel.

The book of Ezekiel is punctuated by three great visions linked together by the experience of divine glory. In the first vision (Ezek 1-3), the glory of YHWH comes to Ezekiel and his fellow captives in exile beside the river *Chebar* of Babylon (cf. Ezek 1:1). In Ezek 8-11 (the second vision), the glory of YHWH leaves the temple and takes a stand on the mountain to the east of the city (cf. Ezek 11:23). In the last part of Ezekiel's prophecy (Ezek 40-48), Ezekiel sees another vision of the divine glory returning and inhabiting the glorious temple.

In the above-stated visions (Ezek 1-3; 8-11; 40-48), one observes that the presence of YHWH is experienced in three different spaces: in the temple, in exile and on the mountain east of the city. These manifestations of the divine presence in different spaces challenge, not only the traditional priestly understanding of YHWH as exclusively "tabernacled" in the Jerusalem temple, but also the claims of monopoly on God from different religious groups in our world today. The religious struggles in our world today echo the religious tension that existed between the exilic group and those that remained in Judah, as both claimed to be the true *qahal* (assembly) of YHWH (cf. Ezek 11:15-16; 33:25-29). We live in a world polarized by religious conflicts and faith leaders' claim to exclusivity of truth and monopoly on God. This study will illuminate the reality that God cannot be monopolized or restricted to any particular group, a truth that echoes an *Igwebuike* perspective.

To demonstrate this, I will, first and foremost, put the *Igwebuike* theology in dialogue with Ezekiel's visions of divine presence, particularly with respect to the stands of the Jerusalemite community against the exilic community (cf. Ezek 11:15-16). Then I will lean on the critical spatial theories of Edward W. Soja and Wesley A. Kort, to show how praxis and mobility in the visions of Ezekiel bridge the gap between the sacred and "non-sacred" spaces. To achieve my objective in this study, I will also interpret the *exile* space as *thirdspace*. Since the exile motif is theologically rich and entrenched in the formation of Israel's self-consciousness, I will focus on the importance of space and memory, looking at the place of the temple/Jerusalem in the consciousness of Israel through the ages. This will enable us see the significance of the exile space - in its *firstspace, secondpace* and *thidspace* elements. In discussing the exile as *thirdspace*, I will show how praxis determines the presence or absence of the divine.

The fruits of this study will subsequently shed some light on religion in our contemporary world, especially as it is practiced among the three *Abrahamic* faiths. The aim is to show how this study, on one hand, challenges the religious tension and religious *exclusivism* that

---

[34] Nathan MacDonald, *Divine Presence and Absence in Exilic and Post Exilic Judaism*, FZAT 61, eds. Nathan MacDonald and Izaak D. de Hulster. (Tubingen: Mohr Siebeck 2013), XI.

characterize our world today and, on the other hand, lends its voice to the efforts and progress made so far in the area of inter-religious dialogue.

EZEKIEL'S THEOLOGY OF DIVINE PRESENCE IN DIALOGUE WITH *IGWEBUIKE*[35] THEOLOGY

In Ezekiel, the presence of God is experienced, not only through the כּבוֹד (glory), but also through the divine רוּחַ (spirit) and יָד (hand) [cf. Ezek 3:12, 14; 8:3; 11:1, 24; 40:1; 43:5]. The spirit and the hand of YHWH share a connotation of power; they are, therefore, closely related concepts and are used in the visions of Ezekiel as instruments of divine presence and activity.

---

[35] Kanu, Ikechukwu Anthony. *Igwebuike and the Logic (Nka) of African Philosophy,* 14. Kanu, I. A. (2018). *Igwe Bu Ike* as an Igbo-African hermeneutics of national development. *Igbo Studies Review. No. 6.* pp. 59-83. Kanu, I. A. (2018). *Igwebuike* as an African integrative and progressive anthropology. *NAJOP: Nasara Journal of Philosophy.* Vol. 2. No. 1. pp. 151-161. Kanu, I. A. (2018). New Africanism: *Igwebuike* as a philosophical Attribute of Africa in portraying the Image of Life. In Mahmoud Misaeli, Sanni Yaya and Rico Sneller (Eds.). *African Perspectives on Global on Global Development* (pp. 92-103). United Kingdom: Cambridge Scholars Publishing. Kanu, I. A. (2019). Collaboration within the ecology of mission: An African cultural perspective. *The Catholic Voyage: African Journal of Consecrated Life.* Vol. 15. pp. 125-149. Kanu, I. A. (2019). *Igwebuike* research methodology: A new trend for scientific and wholistic investigation. *IGWEBUIKE: An African Journal of Arts and Humanities* (IAAJAH). 5. 4. pp. 95-105. Kanu, I. A. (2019). *Igwebuikeconomics*: The Igbo apprenticeship for wealth creation. *IGWEBUIKE: An African Journal of Arts and Humanities* (IAAJAH). 5. 4. pp. 56-70. Kanu, I. A. (2019). *Igwebuikecracy*: The Igbo-African participatory cocio-political system of governance. *TOLLE LEGE: An Augustinian Journal of the Philosophy and Theology. 1. 1.* pp. 34-45. Kanu, I. A. (2019). On the origin and principles of *Igwebuike* philosophy. *International Journal of Religion and Human Relations.* Vol. 11. No. 1. pp. 159-176. Kanu, I. A. (2019b). An *Igwebuike* approach to the study of African traditional naming ceremony and baptism. *International Journal of Religion and Human Relations.* Vol. 11. No. 1. pp. 25-50. Kanu, I. A. (2017). *Igwebuike* as an Igbo-African philosophy for Christian-Muslim relations in Northern Nigeria. In Mahmoud Misaeli (Ed.). *Spirituality and Global Ethics* (pp. 300-310). United Kingdom: Cambridge Scholars. Kanu, I. A. (2017). *Igwebuike* as an Igbo-African philosophy for the protection of the environment. *Nightingale International Journal of Humanities and Social Sciences.* Vol. 3. No. 4. pp. 28-38. Kanu, I. A. (2017). *Igwebuike* as the hermeneutic of individuality and communality in African ontology. *NAJOP: Nasara Journal of Philosophy.* Vol. 2. No. 1. pp. 162-179. Kanu, I. A. (2017a). *Igwebuike* and question of superiority in the scientific community of knowledge. *Igwebuike: An African Journal of Arts and Humanities.* Vol.3 No1. pp. 131-138. Kanu, I. A. (2017a). *Igwebuike* as a philosophical attribute of Africa in portraying the image of life.* A paper presented at the 2017 Oracle of Wisdom International Conference by the Department of Philosophy, Tansian University, Umunya, Anambra State, 27-29 April. Kanu, I. A. (2017b). *Igwebuike* as a complementary approach to the issue of girl-child education. *Nightingale International Journal of Contemporary Education and Research.* Vol. 3. No. 6. pp. 11-17. Kanu, I. A. (2017b). *Igwebuike* as a wholistic response to the problem of evil and human suffering. *Igwebuike: An African Journal of Arts and Humanities.* Vol. 3 No 2, March. Kanu, I. A. (2017e). *Igwebuike* as an Igbo-African modality of peace and conflict resolution. *Journal of African Traditional Religion and Philosophy Scholars. Vol. 1. No. 1. pp. 31-40.* Kanu, I. A. (2017g). *Igwebuike* and the logic (Nka) of African philosophy. *Igwebuike: An African Journal of Arts and Humanities.* 3. 1. pp. 1-13. Kanu, I. A. (2017h). *Igwebuike* philosophy and human rights violation in Africa. *IGWEBUIKE: An African Journal of Arts and Humanities.* Vol. 3. No. 7. pp. 117-136. Kanu, I. A. (2017i). *Igwebuike* as a hermeneutic of personal autonomy in African ontology. *Journal of African Traditional Religion and Philosophy Scholars. Vol. 2. No. 1. pp. 14-22.*

However, for the sake of brevity, I will be looking at divine presence from the perspective of the כבוד YHWH. The כבוד (glory) represents an outward manifestation of the divine presence. It is what John T. Strong calls the "hypostasis of YHWH."[36] S. Dean McBride defines hypostasis as "a quality, epithet, attribute, manifestation or the like of a deity which through a process of personification and differentiation has become a distinct (if not fully independent) divine being in its own right."[37]

It is interesting to note that Ezekiel experienced this visible manifestation of presence of the divine while he was with his fellow exiles in Babylon, specifically, by the river *Chebar* (Ezek 1:1). According to Pieter de Vries, "the *Chebar* was a canal near the city of Nippur and was part of an extensive system of irrigation channels that distributed water from the Euphrates and Tigris to Nippur and the surrounding district."[38] It is probably not without significance that YHWH first calls Ezekiel beside a river. In fact, de Vries further notes that "the countries beyond Israel were regarded as unclean (cf. Ezek 4:13; Amos 7:17). So, Israelite exiles preferred to seek communion with God in the vicinity of flowing water, to which cleansing power was attributed (Lev. 14:5, 50; 15:13; Num. 19:17)."[39] This definitely resonates with the psalmist who also presented a picture of the exiles "by the rivers of Babylon" (cf. Ps 137:1-4).

It is significant, therefore, to realize that it is in this same unclean land, in which the song of Zion cannot be sung (cf. Ps 137:4), that Ezekiel experiences the מַרְאוֹת אֱלֹהִים ("visions of God"). In both the Priestly and the Zion theologies, the כבוד functions as a technical expression of God's presence.[40] The place in P (*priestly*) where God's glory descends[41] is the Tabernacle. In Exod 40:33b-35, we see how the Tabernacle is constructed and completed. But more importantly, the text provides us with information about the relationship of the כבוד to the Tabernacle:[42]

Thus, Moses finished the work. Then the cloud covered the Tent of Meeting, and the כבוד YHWH filled the Tabernacle. But Moses was not able to enter the Tent of Meeting, because the cloud settled upon it and the כבוד YHWH filled the Tabernacle (Exod 40:33b-35).

After the experience in Sinai, the Tabernacle itself "becomes a mobile sanctuary, a place of rendezvous for Moses and the כבוד YHWH."[43] However, even though the Tabernacle is a

---

[36] Cf. John T. Strong, God's *Kābôd*: "The Presence of YHWH in the Book of Ezekiel," in *The Book of Ezekiel: Theological and Anthropological Perspectives*, eds. Margaret S. Odell and John T. Strong SBLSS 9(Atlanta: SBL 2000), 69-95.

[37] S. Dean McBride, "The Deuteronomic Name Theology" (Ph.D diss. Harvard University, 1969), 5.

[38] Pieter de Vries, *Kābôd Yhwh in the Old Testament: with Particular Reference to the Book of Ezekiel*, (Leiden: Brill, 2016), 236.

[39] Ibid., 236.

[40] John F. Kutsko, Between Heaven and Earth: Divine Presence and Absence in Ezekiel (Winona Lake: Eisenbrauns, 2000), 83.

[41] except for the pre-Tabernacle texts in Exodus 16 and 24.

[42] Kutsko., 82.

[43] Kutsko, 82.

mobile sanctuary, it has no self-locomotive ability. The כָּבוֹדYHWH is housed in it, fixed and carried by its bearers until it has its final resting place in the temple, as the primary *locus* of divine presence for Israel.

Kutsko observes:

> The ideology that characterized Zion theology of divine presence, especially during the monarchic tradition, is represented by the divine epithet יְהוָה צְבָאוֹת יֹשֵׁב הַכְּרֻבִים, that is, the "YHWH, the God of hosts who sits enthroned above the cherubim" (cf. 1 Sam 4:4; 2Sam 6:2).[44]

The transfer of this ideology to the Temple of Solomon, according to Kutsko, "championed a theology of God's election of and permanent presence in the Jerusalem Temple (2 Kgs 19:15)."[45] Thus, Ezekiel's מַרְאוֹת אֱלֹהִים ("visions of God") in a foreign and *unclean* land demonstrates a shift in the *status quo*. It fashions an image of God who is not restricted to the temple and provides an effective image of God's presence in exile.

However, the inhabitants of Jerusalem do not see the exiles as faithful. In Ezek 11:15, they share their opinion about the exiles. They say that "[the exiles] have gone far from YHWH; to us this land is given for a possession." In other words, the inhabitants of Jerusalem believe that the exiles are cut off from the Lord. For them, exile is synonymous with punishment and with being distanced from God. They think of exile as abandonment by God, whereas Jerusalem is proof of nearness to God. But they are flat out wrong.

In Ezek 11:16, YHWH responds to the theological position of the inhabitants of Jerusalem with respect to the exiles. They believe that YHWH has disinherited the exiles. But YHWH responds that He has not disinherited the exiles; rather, He will be for them a מִקְדָּשׁ מְעַט — *a sanctuary in some measure*. Some translate this as "a sanctuary in small measure." But no matter the translation, the basic point is that YHWH is accessible also to the exilic community in Babylon.

God's presence is available for the exiles, even without the institution of the temple. Although the exiles are far from the temple, they are not far from YHWH. This echoes what I see as the basic tenet of *Igwebuike* theology, a theology that "challenges every separatist theory that tries to exclude people based on religion, tribe, ethnicity, nationality"[46] or even geographical location. In this theology, there is no "us" against "them." It is a theology that sees the entire human race as a family, a family of God's children. For, "when human beings come together in solidarity and complementarity, they are powerful and can constitute an insurmountable

---

[44] Ibid., 83.

[45] Ibid, 83.

[46] Malachy Theophilus, "The Role of Rehab in the Conquest Story of Joshua as a Manifestation of Igwebuike Theology: A Narrative Analysis of Joshua 2," in *Igwebuike: An African Journal of Arts and Humanities*. Vol. 5, no. 8 (2019), 91.

force."[47] Thus, as a theological reality, *Igwebuike* emphasizes that any human being, irrespective of religious affiliation or geographical location, is a child of God; has the capacity to experience God; and "can be an instrument in the hand of the divine for the global picture of salvation. It de-emphasizes those things that separate us."[48] Edward W. Soja and Wesley A. Kort shed more light on this, albeit, from a different perspective, using their spatial theories.

CRITICAL SPATIAL THEORY

This study is influenced by works published in the field of critical spatial theory. These works have not only inspired biblical scholars, but in recent decades, the theoretical perspectives of this theory have been applied by scholars of biblical and religious studies in their respective works.[49] Liv Ingeborg Lied observes that in recent times, there has been a rise of theoretical interests in the human conception of space and place.[50] He further notes:

> This field of theoretical debate has primarily developed in the social sciences, but contributions have also come from other academic disciplines such as philosophy, architecture, and geography.[51]

Among the scholars who have greatly ignited the interest in space and spatiality are E.W. Soja and Wesley A. Kort. According to Lied, "the works of the French philosopher Lefebvre[52] and the American geographer Soja[53] have held a special position in the field of biblical and religious studies. This is likely due to the investment in their works by the scholars affiliated with the productive SBL-forum: *Construction of Ancient Space Seminar.*"[54]

---

[47] Anthony I. Kanu, "Igwebuike as an Igbo-African Hermeneutic of Globalization," in *Igwebuike: An African Journal of Arts and Humanities*, Vol. 2 no. 1 (March 2016), 3.

[48] Theophilus, "The Role of Rehab in the Conquest Story of Joshua," 73.

[49] See Liv Ingeborg Lied, *The Other Lands of Israel: Imagination of the Land in 2 Baruch*, (Leiden. Boston: Brill, 2008), 13.

[50] Ibid., 13.

[51] Ibid., 13.

[52] Henri Lefebvre's *La Production de L'espace* (Paris: Anthropos, 1974) was published as early as 1974. It was however mostly unknown to the wider circles of scholars until it was translated into English in 1991 (H. Lefebvre, *The Production of Space* (trans. D. Nicholson-Smith, Oxford: Blackwell, 1991).

[53] Cf. Edward W. Soja, *Postmodern Geographies: The Research of Space in Critical Social Theory* (London/New York: Verso, 1989); Edward W. Soja, *Third Space: Journeys to Los Angeles and Other Real-and-Imagined Places* (Oxford: Blackwell 1996).

[54] Lied, 13. The Constructions of Ancient Space Seminar ran as a joint project of the AAR (American Academy of Religion) and SBL (Society of Biblical Literature) from 2000-2005, the only cross-society venture of its time. For the first time in the development of biblical studies, participants in the seminar attempted to foreground and critically analyze space with the same theoretical nuance that biblical scholars have traditionally devoted to history. Cf. www.case.edu/affil/GAIR/Constructions/Constructions.html. Cf. among others J.L. Berquist, "Critical Spatiality and the Use of Theory," n.p. Online: http: // www. cwru.edu / affl / GAIR / papers / 2002 papers/berquist.html; J.L. Berquist, "Critical Spatiality and the Construction of Ancient Worlds," in

Soja and his master, Lefebvre, propose "a change of spatial epistemology."[55] They do this in reaction to modern notions that interpret space as "passively-existing materiality."[56] For Soja, we create and form space by our practices. As such, space is not like an empty box; it is a cultural and social construct.[57]

Another important contribution of Soja is his focus on lived experience and social praxis as the decisive aspect of human spatiality.[58]Soja sees space as both material and as a product of imagination,[59] and describes the reconfiguration of both the material and the mental as *thirdspace*.[60]According to him, this space "is a product of a *thirding* of the spatial imagination, the creation of another mode of thinking about space that draws upon the material and the mental spaces of the traditional dualism but extends well beyond them in scope, substance and meaning."[61] Lied's felicitous representation of Soja captures the idea even better. In his words, Soja sees space as the "comprehensive recombination of material perceptions ('Firstspace') and mental conceptions of space ('Secondspace') in lived experience ('Thirdspace')."[62]

Furthermore, Wesley Kort adds another nuance to critical spatial theory. He observes that place-relations[63] are often valued at the expense of mobility and the temporal associations carried by mobility. Indeed, this evaluation of place-relations over mobility often implies a contrast between attitudes that are in some way or to some degree judged as traditional and "sacred" in contrast to mobility and temporality, which are judged as modern and "profane" or "non-sacred."[64] Kort further notes that "many studies and literatures have ignored the value of mobility, and have thus overvalued the less mobile by assuming that rootedness is morally and spiritually superior."[65]

The high value currently placed on rootedness affects the status of the category of "sacred space." It becomes easy to pit "sacred space" against the "profane." Kort alludes to the work of Mircea Eliade as an example, holding that Eliade "continues to exert influence not because

---

Imagining Biblical Worlds: Studies in Spatial, Social and Historical Constructs in Honor of James H. Flanagan (eds D.M. Gunn and P.M. McNutt, Sheffield: Sheffield Academic Press, 2002), 64-80.

[55] Lied, 14. Also see Soja, "Thirdspace: Expanding the Scope of the Geographical Imagination," in *Architecturally Speaking: Practice of Art, Architecture and the Everyday* (ed. Alan Read, London: Routledge, 2000), 19-20.

[56] Lied, 14.

[57] See Soja, *Third Space: Journeys to Los Angeles*, 13. See also Lied, 14.

[58] Lied, 14.

[59] Soja, *Third Space: Journeys to Los Angeles*, 11.

[60] Ibid., 11.

[61] Ibid., 11.

[62] Lied, 14. Also cf. "Thirdspace: Expanding the Scope," 21-22.

[63] By "place-relations" Kort means human attitude towards a particular geographical location. This is what Soja technically calls "praxis." See Wesley A. Kort, "Sacred/Profane and an Adequate Theory of Human Place-Relations," in *Constructions of Space: Theory, Geography, and Narrative* vol. 1 edited by Jon L. Berquist - Claudia V. Camp (New York. London: T & T Clark 2007)33-34.

[64] Kort, 33.

[65] Ibid, 34.

of the Idealism of his phenomenology of sacred space but because he posits sacred space as a contrary to modern history, which is profane."[66] Eliade says in the beginning of his work, *The Sacred and the Profane*, that "the first possible definition of the *sacred* is that it is the opposite of the profane."[67] Kort concludes that the theories of sacred space, if they are to regain substance, should be based on a more adequate theory of positive place-relations, rather than on history constructed as sacred space's negative contrary.[68]

If we begin our investigation of the locus of divine presence from the concept of Soja's *praxis* or Kort's positive *place-relations,* rather than the sacred/profane dichotomy, then we will realize, as Larry E. Shiner says, that "space is a homogenous continuum ... Homogeneity means that every point is of equal value to every other point, that no direction has any privilege over any other, that space is continuous and infinite."[69]This does not mean that there are no places of awe. Places exist where we feel compelled to "take off our shoes" because of a perceived connection with the transcendent. However, it does not also diminish the possibility of a supernatural encounter in places that are not that awe-inspiring.

APPLICATION OF THE SPATIAL THEORIES TO EZEKIEL'S THEOLOGY OF DIVINE PRESENCE WITH PARTICULAR REFERENCE TO THE SACRED AND NON-SACRED SPACES

Applying the theories of Soja and Kort to Ezekiel's theology of divine presence will help to understand the theological implication of the divine movements from the temple in Jerusalem (sacred space) to the exiles in Babylon (non-sacred space) in the visions of Ezekiel. But to do this, it will be pertinent to understand first, how the world of the ancient Near East saw and understood "exile," and second, the place Jerusalem and its temple held in the consciousness of the average Jew.

Dalit Rom-Shiloni notes that exile was a military punishment forced upon peoples, and usually designated as the last stage in a war. According to him, "subjugating peoples and territories led the neo-Assyrian, and later on the neo-Babylonian empires to rearrange daily life at both the center and the periphery of their domains in diverse ways."[70]Exile in the ancient Near Eastern world was mostly partial. Not all the defeated and captured peoples were taken into exile. In most cases, some were taken into captivity, while others remained in the homeland. This is

---

[66] Ibid., 34-35.

[67] Mircea Eliade, *The Sacred and the Profane* (New York: Harper & Row Publishers, 1959), 10.

[68] Wesley A. Kort, "Sacred/Profane and an Adequate Theory of Human Place-Relations," 34-35.

[69] Larry E. Shiner, "Sacred Space, Profane Space, Human Space," Journal of the American Academy of Religion, Vol. 40, No. 4 (1972), 427.

[70] Dalit Rom-Shiloni, "Ezekiel as the voice of the Exiles and Constructor of the Exilic Community," **Hebrew Union College Annual** 76 (2005),1-2. Rom - Shiloni also observed that "exile" had become an international imperial policy in the neo-Assyrian period, mainly under Tiglath-Pilesser III (745-27 B.C.E.) and his successors.

exactly the case with the deportations of Israel and Judah reported in the biblical literature (cf. 2 Kgs 15-17 and 24-25).

Historically, the kingdoms of Israel and Judah experienced a number of exiles. Worthy of note was the exile of 720 B.C.E., the exile of the northern kingdom of Israel at the hand of the Assyrians. Those exiled were supposedly deported and scattered throughout the empire, although biblical archaeology has shown that many migrated to the southern kingdom of Judah.[71]Another important exile in the history of Israel as a people was the exile of the southern kingdom of Judah, otherwise known as the Babylonian deportations. In 597 B.C.E., the noble members of the society in the southern kingdom of Judah, including the prophet Ezekiel, were exiled during the reign of Nebuchadnezzar II of Babylon. In 586 B.C.E., when the temple was destroyed, a new batch of the Judean exiles arrived in Babylon, but there was a significant number of Judeans who remained behind in Judah.

Alluding to biblical sources, Rom-Shiloni observes that the event of the exile" divided the Judean people into two communities, the exiles with King Jehoiachin in Babylon on one hand, and the People who remained in the Land under King Zedekiah (Jeremiah 40:6), on the other."[72]

For the exiled community, living in exile outside their homeland posed a theological crisis, a crisis that is poignantly captured by the psalmist:

> By the Rivers of Babylon we sat mourning and weeping when we remembered Zion. On the poplars of that land we hung up our harps. There our captors asked us for the words of a song; our tormentors, for a joyful song: "Sing for us a song of Zion!" But how could we sing the LORD's song in a foreign land? If I forget you Jerusalem, let my right hand wither. May my tongue cling to the roof of my mouth if I do not remember you, if I do not consider Jerusalem my highest joy" (Ps 137:1-6, *NAB*).

Thus, living outside the Promised Land without the temple was indeed a crisis of faith for the exiles. The ongoing existence of the temple and the daily life in Jerusalem advantaged the remnant community, who saw the exiles as the outcasts or better put, as "distant from YHWH" (Ezek 11:15). Following the Priestly and the Deuteronomic concepts of exile, the community in Jerusalem believed the exile community was punished for their sins (Deuteronomy 4:25-28; 8:19-20; Leviticus 18:24-30; 20:22-24). In other words, the temple and Jerusalem became for them the sign of *election*, as exile represents for them a sign of divine punishment.

---

[71] See Israel Finkelstein and Thomas Römer, "Comments of the Historical Background of the Jacob Narrative in Genesis," ZAW 126.3 (2014): 317-338.

[72] Dalit Rom-Shiloni, *Exclusive Inclusivity: Identity Conflicts Between the Exiles and the People who Remained (6th -5th Centuries BCE).* (New York - London: Bloomsbury, 2013), xvi.

Unlike the exile space, Jerusalem, in the history of Jewish religion, is a holy city, a *locus sanctus*, or an *axis mundi*[73] associated with historical events and eschatological expectations. It was the place for God to deal with God's people and to be a focal center of God's restored people.

Emile Benveniste, in his study of the ancient European languages, particularly Latin and Greek, observes that Biblical Hebrew does not differentiate the idea of the sacred from that of holiness, unlike Latin and Greek.[74] In Hebrew, both notions are rendered solely by *qodeš* and words composed from that same root. In the semantic field of Hebrew, according to Francis Schmidt, sacredness is situated between the positive and the negative poles. In his words:

> Positively, *qodeš* refers to that which is in a relationship of belonging to the divine, that which is consecrated to it. Negatively, *qodeš* is defined by opposition to the profane, *tāmēʿ*.[75]

Thus, in the above sense, the sacred in which holy objects or sanctified persons circulate, like the temple, is only understood in its relation to the profane. Thus, sacred and profane are characterized by their *proximity to the Divine*. Jerusalem and its temple are sacred because in the eyes of the biblical Jews, God dwells there.

The temple is believed to be the epicenter of holiness because it is the abode of the divine and the primary locus of divine presence. This understanding of the temple is evident in Jewish religious history. The first book of Maccabeus recorded an event that happened around 165 BCE. The story was about Judas Maccabeus, son of Mattathias, a priest, who set up camp at *Mizpah* to the north of Jerusalem. He and his brothers fasted and wore sack clothes. Their faces were turned towards heaven: what were they to do since the abode of the divine had been profaned? The foreigners had profaned the temple.[76] These penitential acts show how important the temple was to them.

Also in the book of Baruch, we read about the man Baruch, who "wasted from fasting, his clothing torn, climbs the steps of the temple mount and goes to sit before the doors that the sun lights up in the morning."[77] He laments:

> Why from now on sow in the countryside? Why should the vine give wine?
> What good are the reservoirs for rain, of what use the heat of the sun? Why

---

[73] A perceived center of the world, where Heaven and Earth are connected.

[74] Cf. E. Benveniste, *Le vocabulaire des institutions indo-européennes. II. Pouvoir, droit, religion* (Paris: Minuit, 1969), 187–207; H. Fugier, *Recherches sur l'expression du sacré dans la langue latine*, II (Paris: Belles Lettres, 1963), 25–86.

[75] Francis Schmidt, How the Temple Thinks: Identity and Social Cohesion in Ancient Judaism (Sheffield: Academic Press, 2001), 90. One of the most characteristic formulations of this opposition is found in Lev 10:10 and Ezra 22:26; 44:23.

[76] Ibid., 86. Cf. also 1 Macc. 3:46–59.

[77] Ibid., 86. Also see 2 Bar. 10.5–19.

should the moon continue to set the sequence of months? Of what use are marriages and births? Since the Meeting Place with the Divine is destroyed, "how can they still speak of beauty, how can there still be question of grace!" (2 Bar. 10:17).[78]

This lament of Baruch echoes the plight of the people of Israel because the epicenter of their relationship with YHWH has been destroyed. In fact, in the two examples above, the main theological question is: since the primary locus of divine presence is destroyed, where and how can we encounter the Divine?

This understanding of the sacredness of Jerusalem and its temple informed the attitude of the remnant community in Jerusalem against the exile community in the book of Ezekiel. Ezek 11:15 reads: "son of man, your brothers, (even your brothers), your own kin, the whole house of Israel, all of them, are those of whom the inhabitants of Jerusalem have said, *'They have gone far from YHWH; to us this land is given for a possession.'"* Thus, the exile community is the *impure* that cannot be mixed with the pure, namely, the remnant community in Judah. The two spaces cannot meet in the eyes of the Jews.

THE EXILE AS A THIRDSPACE

The exile space is not a neutral space but a contested one, or as Soja coins it, a *thirdspace*. For Soja, *thirdspace* encompasses *firstspace* and *secondspace* and is always vibrant, flexible and open to (re)interpretation.[79]

Soja holds that *firstspace* privileges objectivity and materiality. It aims at a formal science of space.[80]Thus, *firstspatially*, the reader is told where Ezekiel received his מַרְאוֹת אֱלֹהִים (*visions of God*). He was "among the exiles by the river *Chebar*"(1:1). Here, the *firstspace* is his *existential* location. Ezekiel and his fellow exiles were in a susceptible and helpless situation, a situation that creates a crisis faith. It appears as if their patron, God YHWH, allowed them to be taken into exile, a reality that marked victory for Babylonian gods. Brandon Fredenburg captures this idea even better:

> The Babylonian gods removed a contingent of leading Judeans for Judah's failure to meet its vassal duties. YHWH, the patron God of Israel, had permitted their deportation. The "official" view of those in Jerusalem was that YHWH had finally cleansed the capital of its troublemakers and allowed the favored to remain (cf. 11:3).[81]

---

[78] Cf. Ibid., 86-87

[79] Cf. Soja, "Thirdspace: Expanding the Scope," 23.

[80] Soja, *Third Space: Journeys to Los Angeles.*75.

[81] Brandon Fredenburg, *Ezekiel.* The College Press NIV Commentary (Joplin : College Press Pub. Co., 2002), 37-38

Even though we do not know the exact location of the *real space* (*Firstspace*) of the exiles, the text tells us that it is beside the river *Chebar*. Daniel I. Block notes that the "Hebrew *nĕhar kĕbār* is the equivalent of Akkadian *nār kabari/u*, "Kabaru canal," which occurs several times in the 5th-century B.C. archives of the *Murashu* family in Babylon."[82] It is believed that *nĕhar kĕbār* is located in the vicinity of Nippur. Its conduit was "one of many branches of an elaborate canal system that distributed water from the Tigris and the Euphrates throughout the city and its environs."[83] It does appear that after the city was destroyed, the Babylonian king at that time, "repopulated the region with deportees from many parts of the empire; among them were Ezekiel and his fellow Judeans."[84] As earlier noted, we do not know for sure if the reference to *the Chebar Canal* means that Ezekiel was physically beside the canal at the time of the vision, or if the expression functions as a general description for the region where the Judean exiles lived. In any case, it tells us something, even if only partially, about the existential reality of Ezekiel and his fellow exiles.

The exile's *secondspace* would be the conceived or the mental space, which is culturally conditioned. According to Soja, "*Secondspace* is entirely ideational, made up of projections into the empirical world."[85] This viewpoint highlights the fact that the exiles are away from their native land, "removed from Jerusalem and the temple, the place from which YHWH's glory had emanated in the past."[86] Thus, in this sense, the exiles' fate becomes an incontrovertible proof of divine rejection. Exile's *secondspace* is thus a place of divine punishment (cf. Deuteronomy 4:25-28; 8:19-20; Leviticus 18:24-30; 20:22-24; Amos 6:7). This understanding creates a dichotomy between the exiles and the group that remained in Jerusalem, the latter saw themselves as superior and thus, the authentic "*qahal YHWH*" (cf. 11:15).

This calls to mind the words of William Scott Green: "a society does not simply discover its *others*, it fabricates them by selecting, isolating, and emphasizing an aspect of another people's life and making it symbolize their difference."[87] In addition, Green points out the parody nature of definition by *otherness*, which concentrates on the life of the collective and

[82] Daniel I. Block, *The Book of Ezekiel. Chapters 1-24*. NICOT (Grand Rapids: Wm. B. Eerdmans Publishing Co., 1997), 84. The archives, consisting of some 730 tablets, represent our main source of information on the population of the Nippur region at this time. Knowledge of the ethnic composition of the settlers is derived from the personal names that occur in these business records. For studies of these settlements see M. D. Coogan, "Life in the Diaspora: Jews at Nippur in the Fifth Century," *BA* 37 (1974) 6–12; idem, *West Semitic Personal Names in the Murašû Documents*, HSM 7 (Cambridge, Mass.: Harvard University Press, 1975); R. Zadok, *The Jews in Babylonia during the Chaldean and Achaemenian Periods* (Haifa: University of Haifa, 1979); idem, *On West Semites in Babylonia During the Chaldean and Achaemenian Periods: An Onomastic Study*, rev. ed. (Jerusalem: J. J. and Z. Wanaarta and Tel-Aviv University, 1978).

[83] Block, 84. See also R. Zadok, "The Nippur Region during the Late Assyrian, Chaldean and Achaemenian Periods Chiefly according to Written Sources," *IOS* 8 (1978): 266–332.

[84] Ibid., 84.

[85] Soja, *Third Space: Journeys to Los Angeles*, 79.

[86] Block, 83.

[87] William S. Green, "Otherness Within: Towards a Theory o f Difference in Rabbinic Judaism," in *To See Ourselves as Others See Us*, eds. Jacob Neusner and Ernest S. Frerichs (Chico: Scholars Press, 1985), 49.

stereotypes the group according to one major characteristic.[88] Rom-Shiloni captures this sense with particular reference to the tension that existed between the exilic community and the community that remained in Judah. He says:

> Defining "us" and "them" is thus founded on selection, isolation and emphasis of one major divisive difference. In the conflict between the exiles and those who remained, geographic location — residence in the Land of YHWH versus foreign lands — has come to symbolize the difference, and the theological consequences of this division are examined in relation to the concept of God-People-Land.[89]

"The land has been given as a heritage to us"(cf. Ezek 11:15) points to the special privileges of the community that remained in Jerusalem over the land, as opposed to those of the exilic community that had been exiled from it. This concept of "land" is traceable to the Pentateuchal tradition of "land" from the perspective of promise and fulfillment. For instance the phrase, "the land has been given as a heritage to us"(cf. Ezek 11:15), echoes Exodus 6:2-8, a passage that connects the patriarchs and the exodus generation. The land that was promised to the patriarchs (Abraham, Isaac and Jacob) is here given to the sons of Jacob after their slavery in Egypt. This is probably the tradition the community that remained in Jerusalem alluded to when they claimed divine ownership of the land, and as such, gave a new interpretation to the theme of promise and fulfillment.

The *thirdspace* would be the refiguration of the physical *firstspace* and the mental *secondspace* of the exile. It is intrinsic to the narrative. It is a reconfigured space where the excluded become included, and outsiders become insiders. It is an alternative space to the temple/Jerusalem space, where election and boundaries of purity and holiness, upheld by some Jews, precluded some people from full participation in community. As an alternative space to the temple, it becomes a *locus* of divine presence as attested to by the words of YHWH: "I have been a sanctuary to them (in some measures) in the countries where they have gone" (cf. 11:16). In other words, YHWH has not disenfranchised the exiles. They are not excluded from the presence of the Holy. He will be for them a מִקְדָּשׁ מְעַט (a sanctuary in some measure).

The *thirdspace* of the exile, where Ezekiel saw the visions of God, is best seen in the light of the wilderness experience in Exodus, where Moses has a vision of the Holy, despite the pains and testing of the wilderness experience (cf. Exod 3:1-17; Deut 8:2). From the *thirdspace* perspective, the exile space must not *myopically* be seen to be an unclean space nor the place of punishment, nor as Ezekiel would put it, "a valley of dry bones" (cf. Ezek 37). Rather, it is a place of possibilities, a place where the presence of the divine could be experienced. The temple and the land of Israel, in the consciousness of biblical Israel, carry the notion of separateness and exclusivity, distinctiveness and superiority, sacred as opposed to non-sacred. However,

---

[88] Ibid., 49-50.
[89] Dalit Rom-Shiloni, 6.

the different manifestations of the presence of the divine in the visions of Ezekiel show that divine presence cannot be restricted. Even the so-called *unclean* exile space can become the *thirdspace* of divine presence and activities. In this space, the excluded become included, thereby bridging the dichotomy between the "privileged" remnants and the "faraway" exiles. Thus, Soja's *thirdspace*, unambiguously, shows a perspective of *Igwebuike* theology. It is a space of inclusion and complementarity, a space where all are united as a family of God's children.

The exile as *thirdspace* has another significant purpose in the narrative. It is a space for the מַרְאוֹת אֱלֹהִים ("visions of God"). This seems aimed at challenging and changing the people's mind-set toward the people who are in a location other than the land of Israel, especially the temple's religious leadership who thought it necessary to have a temple or to be in the land of Israel in order to experience the Holy One. These social realities and religious boundaries became an increasing problem that would undermine or restrict access to the divine to a selected "chosen ones." Thus, it is not surprising that Ezek 47:21–23 grants the *gērîm* ("resident aliens") in the new covenant the same status as native Israelites so that they receive an equal share in the inheritance. The new boundaries in the renewed city suggest that the new kingdom will preserve the laws of equity and eliminate discrimination against foreign residents, thereby making the experience of the presence of the divine open to all, not just the prerogative of the twelve tribes of Israel.

Gerhard von Rad rightly observes that one of the striking effects of Ezekiel's theology of divine presence is that of the divine mobility.[90] For him, Ezekiel's innovation was the revival of an older כָּבוֹד tradition that inserted an element of mobility and impermanence into the conception of YHWH's presence.[91] Even in the older tradition, the כָּבוֹד travels with the tabernacle as the tribes journey from place to place in their wilderness wanderings, while in Ezekiel the כָּבוֹד comes to the prophet in exile by the river *Chebar* (Ezek 1-3). It removes itself from the Jerusalem temple (Ezek 8-11) and finally enters the grand temple of Ezekiel's last, glorious vision (Ezek 40-48). This shows, unlike in the older tradition, the self-locomotive ability of the כָּבוֹד.

Thus, the כָּבוֹד theology in Ezekiel, particularly its mobile characteristic, shows contrary to popular opinion,[92] that the divine presence cannot be boxed only within the four corners of the sacred space. This mobile characteristic of the כָּבוֹד is made manifest through the image of the wheels, which emphasizes divine mobility (cf. Ezek 1: 15-21; 10: 9-17). Thus, the movements of the divine from the sacred space to the so-called non-sacred space gives credence to the proposal of Kort on bridging the dichotomy between the sacred and the profane.[93] Also,

---

[90] Cf. Gerhard von Rad, "Deuteronomy's Name Theology and the Priestly Document's *Käbôd* Theology" in Studies in Deuteronomy, ed. G. von Rad (London: SCM, 1953), 37-44.

[91] Ibid., 42-43.

[92] In Priestly tradition, the *kābôd* appears only in sacred space: first at the mountain of God (Exod 24:16, 17; 29:43; 40:34, 35; Lev 9:6, 23), later at the tabernacle (Num 14:10, 21,[8] 22; 16:19; 17:7 [16:42]; 20:6).

[93] Cf. Kort, 34-35

THEMES IN IGWEBUIKE PHILOSOPHY AND THEOLOGY

this further confirms the words of Shiner: "space is a homogenous continuum ... Homogeneity means that every point is of equal value to every other point, that no direction has any privilege over any other, that space is continuous and infinite."[94]

While the temple is the original site of divine presence, the accent on the mobility of the כבוד in the visions of Ezekiel demonstrates that the temple is not the exclusive *locus* of divine presence. God's presence can also be experienced in spaces like the exile. Hence, for Ezekiel, God's presence has no boundaries. The same כבוד YHWH that was *tabernacled* in the temple and departed from the same temple (Ezek 11:22-23) is the divine presence that Ezekiel experienced in exile (cf. Ezek 1:1-28).[95]

It appears that Israel's quest to be like other nations (1 Sam 8:5) probably led them to build a shrine in Jerusalem for their patron deity. But a closer look at 2 Samuel 7:5-7 shows that temple was not a necessity; YHWH only permitted it.[96] However, down through the ages, Israel came to deify this structure built by human hands. The destruction of the temple could have been to shatter Israel's sentimental attachment to the temple as the primary *locus* of divine presence, and extend the possibility to spaces other than the temple. It is important to note here that Ezekiel's experience of the divine in exile is not because the temple was destroyed and the divine was homeless, and as such finds abode amidst the exile. No, "Ezekiel encounters the כבוד YHWH in exile (cf. Ezek 1) while the temple was still standing."[97] Thus, the departure of the כבוד in Ezek 8-11 was not "a consequence of the temple's destruction, but a necessary precondition for that destruction."[98]

Furthermore, the condition for the experience of the presence of the Holy One is not really about location. It is not about the exile or the temple: both possess equal opportunity for the experience of the presence of the divine. In the final analysis, what counts is what Soja calls *praxis*, or, in the words of Kort, human *place-relations*. In other words, what counts is the lived experience of the people, with particular reference to their relation with YHWH. Righteousness and faithfulness to the covenant (with respect to Israel), at any given time, determine one's experience of the divine.

Block rightly observes that "the repeated references to the evils being committed in Jerusalem emphasize that YHWH's abandonment of the temple is provoked by human action."[99] This is evident in the offenses described in Ezek 8:3-18: "the introduction of the idol of jealousy into the court of YHWH's temple, the worship of carved images of every sort, the women weeping

---

[94] Shiner, 427.

[95] Kutsko, 92.

[96] Fredenburg, 358.

[97] Steven S. Tuell, "Divine Presence and Absence in Ezekiel's Prophecy," in *The Book of Ezekiel: Theological and Anthropological Perspectives*, eds. Margaret S. Odell and John T. Strong SBLSS 9(Atlanta: SBL 2000), 102.

[98] Ibid., 102.

[99] Daniel I. Block "Divine Abandonment: Ezekiel's Adaptation of the Ancient Near Eastern Motif," in *The Book of Ezekiel Theological and Anthropological Perspectives*, SBL Symposium Series, (Atlanta: SBL, 2000), 36-37.

the Tammuz,[100]and twenty-five men paying homage to the sun."[101]YHWH accuses the people of social and moral crimes (cf. 8:7) – they have provoked the anger of YHWH by their sins. YHWH reiterates this accusation in Ezek 9:9. The text speaks of a land filled with blood and city filled with perversion. YHWH condemns these evils with the sharpest possible terms: *abominable* (Ezek 8:6a, 9, 13, 15, 17; 9:4), *detestable* (Ezek 8:10) and *wicked* (Ezek 8:9). As a result, YHWH's anger is provoked.[102]

On two occasions, YHWH responds in a manner that makes evident the divine wrath, owing to the unrighteous living of the people. In Ezek 8:18, the Holy One says:

> "Therefore I will act in wrath; my eye will not spare, nor will I have pity; and though they cry in my hearing with a loud voice, I will not listen to them."

Also in Ezek 9:9-10 YHWH declares:

> "The guilt of the house of Israel and Judah is exceedingly great; the land is full of bloodshed and the city full of perversity; for they say, 'YHWH has forsaken the land, and the YHWH does not see.' I also will not have pity, my eye will not spare, their wicked deeds (ways) I will bring upon their heads."

First, these texts show that God's presence leaves the temple in reaction to sinful actions. Second, they indicate that divine presence is not a fixed and exclusive prerogative of the Jerusalem temple. On the contrary, God's presence is free to go when the people refuse to live up to the true tenets of their faith.

Thus said, it is righteous practice and faithfulness to the covenant, in the case of Israel, that guarantees the presence of the divine. Margaret Odell puts it even better in relation to both the Jerusalem community and the exilic community. She holds that "just as location does not ensure salvation for the Jerusalemites, neither does it guarantee salvation for the exiles. What matters is not location but orientation."[103]Those whose hearts continue to turn toward idols and against YHWH will not experience the presence of the divine.

---

[100] Most translations have them "weeping for Tammuz," however, Block suggests that Tammuz denotes a special genre of lament, rather than the deity himself. Since this scene follows immediately after the elders' assertion that YHWH had abandoned the land, it appears that these women have either equated YHWH with Tammuz or they are expressing their grief at their own deity's departure by adopting the Tammuz ritual. In either case, the people were replacing true worship of YHWH with a foreign lamentation. See Ibid., 37; Block, *The Book of Ezekiel. Chapters 1-24.* The New International Commentary on the Old Testament (Grand Rapids, MI : Wm. B. Eerdmans Publishing Co., 1997), 294-96.
[101] Block, "Divine Abandonment,"37.
[102] Ibid., 37.
[103] Margaret S. Odell, *Ezekiel,* (Macon, Georgia: Smyth & Helwys Publishing 2005), 125.

THE IMPLICATION OF THE STUDY TO THE PRACTICE OF RELIGION IN OUR CONTEMPORARY WORLD

Here, I do not claim to give a theological overview of the relationships amongst the world's religions, as that would be claiming too much and is definitely beyond the scope of this study. Instead, I intend to restrict my discussion in this section to the theological relationship that seems to exist among the three Abrahamic religions in our world today. A relationship that seems to pitch one religion as superior to the other, or worst still, declare "war" on others who are non-adherents to a particular religion, seeing them as *infidels*.

Victoria S. Harrison observes that "Judaism, Christianity and Islam provide their adherents with distinctive conceptual frameworks for understanding the world they inhabit; in other words, each of the Abrahamic monotheisms provides its adherents with a worldview."[104] However, despite the vast similarities that exist among these religions, their attitudes toward each other, particularly with respect to their view on God and the way they interpret and practice their respective faith, sometimes tend to create dichotomy, instead of unity and understanding. We live in a world that has been bedeviled with religious conflicts and religious leaders' claims to the exclusivity of truth and a *monopoly* on God. According to Katayoun Kishi, in 2018 "more than a quarter of the world's countries experienced a high incidence of hostilities motivated by religious hatred, mob violence related to religion, terrorism and harassments."[105]

This echoes the religious tension that existed between the exilic group and those that remained in Judah; particularly with respect to which of the two groups is the true *qahal* (assembly) YHWH (cf. Ezek 11:15-16; 33:25-29), as this study has highlighted repeatedly. Religious intolerance has become like a cankerworm that affects the fabric of virtually every religious group. An online report by a 2018 Minority Rights Group indicates that "mass killings and other atrocities are increasing in some countries (Syria, Iraq, Nigeria, India, Myanmar, Pakistan and Bangladesh) all in the name of religion. Hostilities against Muslims and Jews also increased across Europe and the United States."[106] These religions, which are supposed to promote peace, love and harmony by their very nature, have become so frequently connected with intolerance and violence toward one another.[107]

Most times, intolerance and aggression are perpetrated by the dominant religion in a particular location against the minority, or by a religion that perceives itself to be superior and *more pure*, compared to the other. This was exactly the drama that played out in the vision of Ezekiel.

---

[104] Victoria S. Harrison, "Scientific and Religious Worldview: Antagonism, Non-antagonistic Incommensurability and Complementarity," Heythrop Journal 47 (2006): 349–350.

[105] Katayoun Kishi, http://www.pewresearch.org/fact-tank/2018/06/21/key-findings-on-the-global-rise-in-religious-restrictions/

[106] https://minorityrights.org/publications/peoplesunderthreat2018/

[107] See https://minorityrights.org/publications/peoplesunderthreat2018/

The Judahites believed they were superior to the exilic community; and as such, they were the true *qahal* YHWH because they had the temple and the land (Ezek 11:15). However, the movements of the כבוד YHWH from the temple in Jerusalem to the exile dismantle any form of religious *triumphalism*. The divine manifestation in the *thirdspace* of the exile challenges the *status quo* and demonstrates that no group should see itself as superior to the other. As such, just as Soja observes, *thirdspace* seeks to resist the dominant order, be it social or religious ideology, including its predetermined notions of pure and impure, holy and profane, insiders and outsiders.[108] If we see every religion as having equal access to the divine, then this will go a long way toward curbing the religious intolerance that has bedeviled our world today; as a consequence, religious plurality would no longer be a challenge but a blessing to our world. Although each religion differs in its social and religious categories, each, like the exile space and Jerusalem temple, is a setting in which God can reveal Himself and relate with people. This understanding will help strengthen the strides made so far in inter-religious dialogue, especially among the three Abrahamic faiths.

The three faith communities hold a belief in "One God, maker of heaven and earth," especially in worship.[109] Pope Gregory VII echoes this, even though partially, in his letter to King Anzir of Mauritania. The pontiff says that Christians and Muslims not only believe in the same God but also praise and worship Him daily as the creator of all ages and the sovereign of this world. Although they might express this belief in different manner from each other, it is still to the same God.[110]

Michael Walzer has a theological equivalent to this argument. In his book, *Thick and Thin: Moral Argument at Home and Abroad*, he introduces "two different but interrelated kinds of moral argument — a way of talking amongst ourselves, here at home, about the thickness of our own history and culture ... and a way of talking to people abroad, across different cultures, about the thinner life we have in common."[111] Amy Pauw, applying Walzer's argument to Christian relationships with other faith traditions, holds that the intramural theological agreement among Christians will be thick; that is, the richly referential, culturally resonant locked into a locally established symbolic system or network of meanings.[112] Pauw further observes that "theological agreement across religious traditions is by contrast thinner, focused on convergence points."[113] This convergence points are seen to be similar, though expressed in different modes and reflected in different histories.[114] Thus, if not in other ways, at least

---

[108] Soja, *Thirdspace: Journeys to Los Angeles*, 68.

[109] Amy Plantinga Pauw, "The Same God?" in Miroslav Volf (ed), *Do We Worship the Same God?: Jews, Christians, and Muslims in Dialogue*, (Grand Rapids: William B. Eerdmans Publishing Company, 2012), 46.

[110] Gregory VII, *Letter to Anzir, King of Mauritania*, in Jacques Dupuis, The Cristian Faith in the Doctrinal Documents of the Catholic Church, 7th ed. (New York: Alba House, 2001), 418-19.

[111] Michael Walzer, *Thick and Thin: Moral Argument at Home and Abroad* (South Bend: University of Notre Dame Press, 1994), xi.

[112] Pauw, 47; also see Walzer xi.

[113] Pauw, 47.

[114] Walzer, 17.

in worship, the thin agreement around God as creator is rooted within the thick theological traditions of each faith community. Pauw puts it even better. She holds that "this agreement among Jews, Christians, and Muslims that they worship the same God who is creator of heaven and earth is a theological minimum."[115] Consequently, it provides a foundation for these religions to come together. But as Walzer also puts it, by its very thinness, it also justifies them to return to the thickness that is their very own.[116]

This *theological minimum* of Pauw, or what Walzar calls moral *thinness*, could possibly be likened to the divine expression in Ezekiel's second vision of the כָּבוֹד YHWH with respect to the exilic community. There, YHWH says of the exiles: "I have been a מִקְדָּשׁ מְעַט (a sanctuary *to them* in some/small measures) in the countries where they have gone" (cf. 11:16). This shows that despite the existential peculiarities of each community of faith, there exists a *theological minimum*, a *small measure* that can form the basis of our experience of the divine who is the origin of the human race. *Nostra Aetate* puts it even more lucidly; it holds that the human race has in common what draws them to fellowship. First, their origin, for God made the whole human race to live over the face of the earth. Second, their final goal, God. His providence, His manifestations of goodness, His saving design extend to all humanity, until that time when the elect will be united in the Holy City, the city ablaze with the glory of God, where the nations will walk in His light.[117] So everyone has the possibility of connecting with the divine. However, what we do with that possibility determines our actual experience of the presence of the divine.

No one religion has the monopoly on God. The Holy One is accessible to all. In his words: "When you seek me, you will find me. Yes, when you seek me with a sincere heart" (cf. Jer. 29:13). Therefore, this is a clarion call to all religions, be it Christianity, Islam or Judaism, to internalize how it sees itself and others and reevaluate beliefs and practices that create tension along the line of the universal accessibility of the divine to all, so as to foster solidarity and a better understanding among different religions.

SUMMARY AND CONCLUSION

This study has shown that interpreting the exile as *thirdspace* and paying close attention to the movements of the כָּבוֹד YHWH in the visions of Ezekiel, not only echoes *igwebuike* theology, but also helps to bridge the gap between the sacred and the non-sacred spaces. The manifestations of the presence of the divine in both the sacred and non-sacred spaces have opened the door for the possibility of the experience of the divine to all, irrespective of location or religion. The experience of the divine is not about location, nor is it all about religious affiliation. What actually counts is *praxis*— our lived experience, with particular reference to

---

[115] Pauw, 47.

[116] Walzer, 11.

[117] Declaration on The Relation of The Church to Non-Christian Religions *Nostra Aetate* Proclaimed by His Holiness Pope Paul VI on October 28, 1965, no. 1.

our relationship with God. Righteousness and faithfulness to the dictates of the divine at any given time determine one's experience of the divine. What matters is not location but orientation. Those whose hearts continue to turn to evil, as opposed to good, will not experience the presence of the divine. Hence, it does not matter one's religious affiliation, nor does it matter one's location. What matters are *righteousness, justice* and *love* in obedience to the dictates of the divine whom we call God, *Adonai, Allah,* etc. These and other good acts guarantee the experience of the presence of the divine. Sometimes, we may think we possess the fullness of truth, as symbolized in the temple with its sacred adornments or as contained in the *Torah,* the *Holy Bible* or the *Koran.* But the reality of the experience of the divine does not necessarily lie in the one who possesses the truth, for it is not the possession of the truth that matters, it is how prepared we are to walk in the light of the truth that we possess. Only this guarantees the experience of the divine.

SELECTED BIBLIOGRAPHY

Benveniste, Emile. *Le vocabulaire des institutions indo-européennes: Pouvoir, droit, religion.* Paris: Minuit, 1969.

Block, I. Daniel. "Divine Abandonment: Ezekiel's Adaptation of the Ancient Near Eastern Motif." Pages 15-42 in *The Book of Ezekiel Theological and Anthropological Perspectives.* Edited by Margaret S. Odell and John T. Strong. SBLSS. Atlanta: SBL 2000.

Block, I. Daniel. *The Book of Ezekiel 1-24.* NICOT. Grand Rapids: Eerdmans 1997.

De Vries, Pieter. "The Relationship between the Glory of YHWH and the spirit of YHWH in the Book of Ezekiel— Part One." JBPR 5 (2013) 109-127.

Block, I. Daniel. *The Käbôd of YHWH in the Old Testament with Particular Reference to the Book of Ezekiel.* Leiden/Boston: Brill 2016.

Finkelstein, Israel and Thomas Römer, "Comments of the Historical Background of the Jacob Narrative in Genesis." ZAW, 126, no. 3 (2014): 317-338.

Fredenburg, Brandon. *Ezekiel.* NIV Commentary. Joplin, Mo. : College Press Pub. Co., 2002.

Green, S. William. "Otherness Within: Towards a Theory o f Difference in Rabbinic Judaism." Pages 49-69 in *To See Ourselves as Others See Us.* Edited by Neusner Jacob and Frerichs S. Ernest. Chico: Scholars Press, 1985.

Gregory VII, "Letter to Anzir, King of Mauritania." Pages 418-419 in *The Cristian Faith in the Doctrinal Documents of the Catholic Church.* Edited by Dupuis, Jacques. New York: Alba House, 2001.

Harrison, S.Victoria. "Scientific and Religious Worldview: Antagonism, Non-antagonistic Incommensurability and Complementarity." HJ 47 (2006): 349–366.

Kanu I. A. Igwebuike as an Igbo-African Hermeneutic of Globalization. *Igwebuike: An African Journal of Arts and Humanities*, Vol. 2 no. 1 2016:1-6.

Kanu, I. A. *Igwe Bu Ike* as an Igbo-African hermeneutics of national development. *Igbo Studies Review. No. 6*. pp. 59-83. 2018

Kanu, I. A. *Igwebuike* as an African integrative and progressive anthropology. *NAJOP: Nasara Journal of Philosophy*. Vol. 2. No. 1. pp. 151-161. 2018

Kanu, I. A. New Africanism: *Igwebuike* as a philosophical Attribute of Africa in portraying the Image of Life. In Mahmoud Misaeli, Sanni Yaya and Rico Sneller (Eds.). *African Perspectives on Global on Global Development* (pp. 92-103). United Kingdom: Cambridge Scholars Publishing. 2018

Kanu, I. A. Collaboration within the ecology of mission: An African cultural perspective. *The Catholic Voyage: African Journal of Consecrated Life*. Vol. 15. pp. 125-149. 2019

Kanu, I. A. *Igwebuike* research methodology: A new trend for scientific and wholistic investigation. *IGWEBUIKE: An African Journal of Arts and Humanities* (IAAJAH). *5. 4.* pp. *95-105*. 2019

Kanu, I. A. *Igwebuikeconomics*: The Igbo apprenticeship for wealth creation. *IGWEBUIKE: An African Journal of Arts and Humanities* (IAAJAH). *5. 4.* pp. *56-70*. 2019

Kanu, I. A. *Igwebuikecracy*: The Igbo-African participatory cocio-political system of governance. *TOLLE LEGE: An Augustinian Journal of the Philosophy and Theology*. *1. 1.* pp. 34-45. 2018

Kanu, I. A. On the origin and principles of *Igwebuike* philosophy. *International Journal of Religion and Human Relations*. Vol. 11. No. 1. pp. 159-176. 2019

Kanu, I. A. (2019b). An *Igwebuike* approach to the study of African traditional naming ceremony and baptism. *International Journal of Religion and Human Relations*. Vol. 11. No. 1. pp. 25-50.

Kanu, I. A. *Igwebuike* as an Igbo-African philosophy for Christian-Muslim relations in Northern Nigeria. In Mahmoud Misaeli (Ed.). *Spirituality and Global Ethics* (pp. 300-310). United Kingdom: Cambridge Scholars. 2017

Kanu, I. A. *Igwebuike* as an Igbo-African philosophy for the protection of the environment. *Nightingale International Journal of Humanities and Social Sciences.* Vol. 3. No. 4. pp. 28-38. 2017

Kanu, I. A. *Igwebuike* as the hermeneutic of individuality and communality in African ontology. *NAJOP: Nasara Journal of Philosophy.* Vol. 2. No. 1. pp. 162-179. 2017

Kanu, I. A. *Igwebuike* and question of superiority in the scientific community of knowledge. *Igwebuike: An African Journal of Arts and Humanities.* Vol.3 No1. pp. 131-138. 2017

Kanu, I. A. *Igwebuike as a philosophical attribute of Africa in portraying the image of life.* A paper presented at the 2017 Oracle of Wisdom International Conference by the Department of Philosophy, Tansian University, Umunya, Anambra State, 27-29 April. 2017

Kanu, I. A. *Igwebuike* as a complementary approach to the issue of girl-child education. *Nightingale International Journal of Contemporary Education and Research.* Vol. 3. No. 6. pp. 11-17. 2017

Kanu, I. A. *Igwebuike* as a wholistic response to the problem of evil and human suffering. *Igwebuike: An African Journal of Arts and Humanities.* Vol. 3 No 2, March. 2017

Kanu, I. A. *Igwebuike* as an Igbo-African modality of peace and conflict resolution. *Journal of African Traditional Religion and Philosophy Scholars. Vol. 1. No. 1. pp. 31-40.* 2017

Kanu, I. A. *Igwebuike* and the logic (Nka) of African philosophy. *Igwebuike: An African Journal of Arts and Humanities.* 3. 1. pp. 1-13. 2017

Kanu, I. A. *Igwebuike* philosophy and human rights violation in Africa. *IGWEBUIKE: An African Journal of Arts and Humanities.* Vol. 3. No. 7. pp. 117-136. 2017

Kanu, I. A. *Igwebuike* as a hermeneutic of personal autonomy in African ontology. *Journal of African Traditional Religion and Philosophy Scholars. Vol. 2. No. 1. pp. 14-22.* 2017

Kort, A. Wesley. "Sacred/Profane and an Adequate Theory of Human Place-Relations." Pages 32-50 in *Constructions of Space: Theory, Geography, and Narrative* vol. 1. Edited by Jon L. Berquist - Claudia V. Camp, New York. London: T & T Clark 2007.

Kutsko, F. John. *Between Heaven and Earth: Divine Presence and Absence in the Book of Ezekiel.* Winona Lake, Indiana: Eisenbrauns, 2000.

Lied, I. Liv . *The Other Lands of Israel: Imagination of the Land in 2 Baruch.* Leiden. Boston: Brill, 2008.

Malachy Theophilus, "The Role of Rehab in the Conquest Story of Joshua as a Manifestation of Igwebuike Theology: A Narrative Analysis of Joshua 2," in *Igwebuike: An African Journal of Arts and Humanities.* Vol. 5, no. 8 (2019): 72-94.

McBride, S. Dean. "The Deuteronomic Name Theology" (Ph.D diss. Harvard University, 1969).

Nathan, MacDonald. *Divine Presence and Absence in Exilic and Post Exilic Judaism,* Forschungen Zum Alten Testament 61. Edited by Nathan MacDonald and Izaak D. de Hulster. Tubingen: Mohr Siebeck 2013.

Odell, S. Margaret. "The Inversion of Shame and Forgiveness in Ezekiel 16:59–63," *JSOT* 56 (1992): 101-112.

Pauw, Amy Plantinga. "The Same God?" Pages 37-49 in *Do We Worship the Same God?: Jews, Christians, and Muslims in Dialogue.* Edited by Volf. Miroslav. Grand Rapids: William B. Eerdmans Publishing Company, 2012.

Rom-Shiloni, Dalit. "Ezekiel as the voice of the Exiles and Constructor of the Exilic Community," HUCA 76 (2005): 1-45.

Schmidt, Francis. *How the Temple Thinks: Identity and Social Cohesion in Ancient Judaism.* Sheffield: Academic Press, 2001.

Second Vatican Council. *Nostra Aetate* (Declaration on The Relation of The Church to Non-Christian Religions). Proclaimed by His Holiness Pope Paul VI on October 28, 1965. Vatican Web Site. Jan 7, 2020.

Shiner, E. Larry. "Sacred Space, Profane Space, Human Space." JAAR 40, no. 4 (1972): 425-436.

Soja, W. Edward. "Thirdspace: Expanding the Scope of the Geographical Imagination." Pages 13-30 in *Architecturally Speaking: Practice of Art, Architecture and the Everyday.* Edited by Read, Alan. London: Routledge, 2000.

Soja, W. Edward. *Postmodern Geographies: The Research of Space in Critical Social Theory.* London/New York: Verso, 1989.

Soja, W. Edward. *Third Space: Journeys to Los Angeles and Other Real-and-Imagined Places.* Oxford: Blackwell 1996.

Soja, W. Edward. *Postmetropolis: Critical Studies of Cities and Religion*, Oxford: Blackwell 2000.

Strong T. John. "God's *Käbôd* : The Presence of Yahweh in the Book of Ezekiel." Pages 69-95 in *The Book of Ezekiel Theological and Anthropological Perspectives*. Edited by Margaret S. Odell and John T. Strong. SBLSS. Atlanta: SBL 2000.

Tuell, S. Steven. "Divine Presence and Absence in Ezekiel's Prophecy." Pages 976-116 in *The Book of Ezekiel Theological and Anthropological Perspectives*. Edited by Margaret S. Odell and John T. Strong. SBL Symposium Series, Atlanta: SBL 2000.

Von Rad, Gerhard. "Deuteronomy's Name Theology and the Priestly Document's *Käbôd* Theology." Pages 37-44 in *Studies in Deuteronomy*. London: SCM, 1953.

Walzer, Michael. *Thick and Thin: Moral Argument at Home and Abroad*. South Bend: University of Notre Dame Press, 1994.

Zadok, Ran. *The Jews in Babylonia during the Chaldean and Achaemenian Periods*. Haifa: University of Haifa, 1979.

THE LESSONS OF PSALM 133 AND THE PRINCIPLE OF UNITY OF IGWEBUIKE PHILOSOPHY

Naanmiap Baamlong, OSA
Estudio Teologico de Valladolid
Spain
fadabaamlong@yahoo.com

ABSTRACT

Complementarity implies the existence of distinct realities that need to relate and collaborate, resulting in a single reality that is better than each of the individual realities alone. This positive idea of complementarity is at the centre of the Igwebuike philosophy, an African philosophy in which individuating differences must work towards a corporate existence, where the 'I' does not stand as the 'I' but as a 'We', where life and living makes meaning. This calls, therefore, for harmony, togetherness and communality amongst people living together. These positive attributes have proven to be functional amongst not only the African societies, but amongst all humans. Because of the positive effect this philosophy has, it is worth emulating and practising. In view of this, from the theological point of view, this write-up aims to demonstrate how the message on unity and harmony of Psalm 133 can contribute more lessons and values to this principle of complementarity of the Igwebuike philosphy, illustrating, therefore, how theological values can help to improve as well the values already existent in the Igwebiuke philosophy.

Keywords: Psalms, Theology, Igwebuike philosophy, unity, harmony, brotherhood, togetherness, blessing.

INTRODUCTION

Igwebuike philosophy is an Igbo-African thought centered on the worldview of complementarity. It is a worldview in which individuating differences must work towards a corporate existence where the 'I' does not stand as the 'I' but as a 'We', where life and living makes meaning[118]. In a

---

[118] Kanu, I. A. (2017). *Igwebuike* as an Igbo-African philosophy for the protection of the environment. *Nightingale International Journal of Humanities and Social Sciences.* Vol. 3. No. 4. pp. 28-38. Kanu, I. A. (2017). *Igwebuike* as the hermeneutic of individuality and communality in African ontology. *NAJOP: Nasara Journal of Philosophy.* Vol. 2. No. 1. pp. 162-179. Kanu, I. A. (2017a). *Igwebuike* and question of superiority in the scientific community of knowledge. *Igwebuike: An African Journal of Arts and Humanities.* Vol.3 No1. pp.

scenario of this kind, difference does not divide nor does it constitute a threat, but rather unites and gives hope that future existence would have meaning. In a cosmogony of this kind, while the ontology of the person is founded on the particularity of the individual, implying that it is the metaphysics of the particular that founds identity; it is the community that gives meaning to such an existence and grounds such an identity[119]. This philosophy, like most philosophies, began within African thinkers based on thier wonder about their environment[120]. With this philosophy in function, it has four basic principles which are the values and ideas that shape this philosophy. While these principles guide *Igwebuike* philosophy, it also justifies *Igwebuike* philosophy. These principles are: the principle of identity, the principle of contrariety, the principle of hierarchy and the principle of unity[121].

This work will concentrate on this last principle and its aim to see how the message on unity and harmony of Psalm 133 can contribute more lessons and values to this principle of unity[122]. This principle understands every individual reality as part and completion of the whole, and thus there is a unity in the midst of diversity. Thus, 'to be' is to live in solidarity and complementarity; and to live outside the parameters of solidarity and complementarity is to suffer alienation. 'To be' is 'to be with the other' in a community of being. I am because we are, and since we are, therefore I am. This African worldview, therefore, is governed by the principle of complementarity, which seeks the conglomeration, unification, summation

---

131-138. Kanu, I. A. (2017a). *Igwebuike as a philosophical attribute of Africa in portraying the image of life*. A paper presented at the 2017 Oracle of Wisdom International Conference by the Department of Philosophy, Tansian University, Umunya, Anambra State, 27-29 April. Kanu, I. A. (2017b). *Igwebuike as a complementary approach to the issue of girl-child education*. *Nightingale International Journal of Contemporary Education and Research*. Vol. 3. No. 6. pp. 11-17. Kanu, I. A. (2017b). *Igwebuike as a wholistic response to the problem of evil and human suffering*. *Igwebuike: An African Journal of Arts and Humanities*. Vol. 3 No 2, March. Kanu, I. A. (2017e). *Igwebuike as an Igbo-African modality of peace and conflict resolution*. *Journal of African Traditional Religion and Philosophy Scholars*. Vol. 1. No. 1. pp. 31-40. Kanu, I. A. (2017g). *Igwebuike and the logic (Nka) of African philosophy*. *Igwebuike: An African Journal of Arts and Humanities*. 3. 1. pp. 1-13. Kanu, I. A. (2017h). *Igwebuike philosophy and human rights violation in Africa*. *IGWEBUIKE: An African Journal of Arts and Humanities*. Vol. 3. No. 7. pp. 117-136. Kanu, I. A. (2017i). *Igwebuike as a hermeneutic of personal autonomy in African ontology*. *Journal of African Traditional Religion and Philosophy Scholars*. *Vol. 2. No. 1. pp. 14-22.*

[119] Cf. https://www.academia.edu/34910747/SOURCES_OF_IGWEBUIKE_PHILOSOPHY_TOWARDS_A_SOCIO-CULTURAL_FOUNDATION, Kanu, I. A., *Sources of Igwebuike philosophy: towards a socio-cultural foundation,* accessed 12/04/2020.

[120] Igwebuike philosophy began with wonder as African traditional thinkers began to wonder at the very nature of their immediate universe. It began from the understanding of their immediate universe which is not detached from the whole universe. As they wondered about the nature of their immediately universe, it began to shape their thoughts, therefore, establishing a connection between philosophy and the cosmos.

[121] Cf. https://www.ajol.info/index.php/jrhr/article/view/190043, Kanu, A., *On the Origin and Principles of Igwebuike Philosophy*, accessed 24/04/2020.

[122] The principle of unity points to the fact that spite of the contrariety of reality, in spite of the singular identity of each reality, there is something common to everything. Igwebuike presents being as that which possesses a relational character of mutual relations. Cf. https://www.ajol.info/index.php/jrhr/article/view/190043, accesed 24/04/2020.

of fragmented thoughts, opinions and other individualized and fragmented thoughts and ideas[123]. To achieve this task, that is, the posible contribution of the theological values of this Bible chapter to this principle of unity of the *Igwebuike* philosophy, a general analysis of the Psalms will be made, stating its structure and the message it contains, and the theological values and ideas that can be of great value to this *Igwebuike* philosophical position.

ABOUT PSALM 133

Psalm I33[124] is a very short Psalms. It has three verses of about seventy words. The Psalm says the following;

> *"Behold, how good and peasant it is when brothers dwell in unity! It is like the precious oil upon the head, running down upon the beard, upon the beard of Aaron, running down on the collar of his robes! It is like the dew of Hermon, which falls on the mountains of Zion! For there the Lord has commanded the blessing, life for evermore".*

This Psalm is part of the collection of fifteen Psalm (120-134) entitled "song of ascent". They are designated this way because most scholars believe that these they were sung by the Israelites as they went to Jerusalem on the annual pilgrimage, on the occasion of their festivities. It was thrice a year: Easter, Pentecost and Tabernacles. They were probably sung by pilgrims on their way to Jerusalem or as part of a festive celebration. When they finally arrived, there used to be great rejoicing and a beautiful spirit of unity among all the people who had gathered in Jerusalem. And all these Psalms are short, except Psalm 132 and, therefore, it is easy to memorize them. These Psalms deal with things of daily life, for example, place of residence, 120; routine activities, 121; importance of husbands and children, 128; and our Psalm, that is, 133 makes reference to unity and harmony amongst people in the community, which was most likely used by ordinary people on their way to Jerusalem and in Jerusalem[125].

STRUCTURE AND TIME OF COMPOSITION OF THE PSALMS

This Psalm, with only three verses, is too short, and as such, it seems too complicated and dificult to divide into subsections. However, it can be divided into these three parts: verse 1 which introduces the concept of unity and harmony with the imperative *"Behold"*. After this invitation to contemplate the goodness and joy of living together, verses 2-3 compare this union with the anointing oil of the priest and the dew of the Hermon mountain. Two simple

---

[123] *Ibíd.*

[124] This Psalms as produced in this work is gotten from the Revised Standerd Version of the bible, published by the Bible societies in 1901. The version used here is the one produced for Society of St. Paul in 1971.

[125] Cf. *The New Interpreter's Bible commentary* Vol. IV. U.S.A., Abingdon Press 2001, 1176.

and beautiful comparisons (oil and dew) are made describing the kind of unity existing. The first is like oil, and what it indicates here is the best olive oil used to consecrate the heads of the guests at the party; and the second comparison is, like dew of Hermon, known for it freshness. The last part of the Psalm is verse 3bc, which concludes the chapter with a blessing. And that's probably the most important thing. Here, it speaks of the result of such harmonious living, which is God's blessing, the eternal life that flows from the inexhaustible source of life, Yahweh Himself.

This Psalm, although difficult to determine its settings and structure, fits well with the other Psalms of pilgrimage, 120-134. As Kraus states, it is very difficult to determine where its Sitz im Leben lies, but it can be said that it comes from the circle of teachers of wisdom and contemplates a situation of daily life[126]. The Psalm praises fraternity. This is the fraternity that binds verse 1 together. Verses 2-3 emphasize the importance of this fraternal union with the verbs *run* and *fall* which appear three times. The repetition of this verb probably alludes to the need to obtain this blessing of God in verse 3. And it is also characteristic of the Psalms of this group[127].

As we have already indicated, this Psalm belongs to the group of the 15 Psalms called the Psalms of pilgrimage. Therefore, it is certainly a hymn of pilgrimage. It has a sapiencial tone. This Psalm is from the circle of the masters of wisdom. The sapiencial judgment begins with the word "behold (look)" which instantly demands attention and points towards something (cf. Ps 127,3ff). Also, the exclamation "how good" is a characteristic of the sapiencial form (cf. Sir 25,4ff)[128]. It enunciates the value and importance of fraternity and harmony amongst people living together[129].

INTERPRETATION AND MESSAGE OF PSALM 133

The first verse introduces the theme of unity and harmony between brothers. But who are these brothers? Many scholars, in an attempt to answer this question, conclude that it refers to siblings in a broad sense. It has been thought of as the unity of the family, the harmony of the fellow citizens or the unity of the community gathered for worship. This latter interpretation is naturally more attractive because of the sacred insertions it contains and that characterise it. Kraus believes, however, that the right thing to do is to think about the order of family life and family law in Israel and the world of the ancient East, where the family heritage remains in the undivided possession of the male children after the death of the father. And so the brethren have to live and dwell together, such as Abraham and Lot, Jacob and Esau who also lived together. This verse is probably a sapiencial saying, praising members for being responsible and

[126] Cf. Kraus, H. J., *Los salmos*, Vol. II. Salamanca, Ediciones Sígueme 1995, 714.

[127] Cf. Allen, L. C., *Word Bible commentary* Vol. XXI. U.S.A, Word Books Publishers 1983, 214.

[128] Cf. Kraus, H. J. *Los salmos*. Vol. II. Salamanca, Ediciones Sígueme 1995, 715.

[129] Cf. Schökel, L. A. y Carniti, C., *Salmos II*. Navarra, Verbo Divino 1993, 1541.

faithful in their task of seeking good for the family and spreading it (cf. Deut 25,5). According to Allen, it refers to the whole congregation of the entire pilgrims in Jerusalem that gathered for the feast. These people are linked not only by race but in the name of God[130].

Verses 2-3b, with two simple and beautiful comparisons, emphasize the importance of this union, of this coexistence, like the *precious ointment* used for the consecration of priests, pointing to a choice of the best olive oil. This is to show the appreciation of this visible union in worship of God. It praises the harmonious coexistence of the brothers in lands that are of common heritage. It describes in images that radiate the peace and happiness of the brothers who live together in harmony. The oil in the east is mixed with aromatic herbs and serves as care for hair and skin (cf. Mic 6,15); it is poured over the head and then descends to the beard (verse 2a)[131]. Verse 3a reads, *as a dew from Hermon*; it probably alludes to a spiritual significance like in Hosea 14, 5. Accorrding to some scholars, although Hermon's significance is unclear, the reference may be to the amount of dew that is appropriate for a sacred mountain[132]. Mount Hermon is the highest in this area (2814 m. above sea level). Another comment says that the parallel with Hermon's dew is probably mentioned because of its extraordinary and copious wealth, and that imparts life and fertility[133].

Verse 3c, probably the most important, concludes the Psalm; it makes reference to what was said in the first verse about brothers in communion. There in the community of united brothers, the Lord sends his blessing, blessing that is life, life that is lasting. Brotherly love is a blessing that attracts blessings; it is full life that prolongs; it is aroma that spreads; it is dew that permeates. In Kraus' words, "Yahweh himself becomes the saving power and force of a community in which brothers coexist harmoniously"[134].

This Psalm talks about the coexistence of the brothers as something necessary, highlighting the need for it. It is a commendable action that brightens and refreshes life, and is also of tremendous importance. The harmonious coexistence of the brothers attracts the blessings of Yahweh. God's saving power radiates with its light the areas of human life[135]. Saint Augustine, in his commentary on this Psalms, states that this Psalms gave rise to monasteries because, although it refers to believers, in a strict sense, this Psalms does not refer to all Christians. In this sense, it would apply only to Christians who live in unity and harmony. Therefore, it does not refer to all, but to some special ones, from whom, however, it reaches out to others. Augustine says: "these words of the psalter, this sweet sound, this pleasant melody in both the song and the understanding, gave rise to the monasteries"[136].

---

[130] Cf. Allen, 215.

[131] Cf. Kraus, 715.

[132] Cf. Allen, 215.

[133] Cf. Briggs, C. A. y Briggs, E. G., *A critical and exegetical commentary*. Vol. II., Edinburgh, T & T Clark 1907, 476.

[134] Cf. Kraus H. J., *Los salmos*. Vol. II. Salamanca, Ediciones Sígueme 1995, 716.

[135] *Ibíd.*

[136] Cf. Cf. Obras de San Agustín XXII, *Enarraciones sobre los salmos*, Madrid, BAC 1967, 463-465.

There are indications that can be identified with the usage of this Psalms within Christianity. For Christians, the term, 'brother,' is used to designate other fellow believers. Jesus admonishes, do not let yourselves be called my lord, for your master is one, and you are all brothers (Mt 23,8-10). There are also indications in Paul's texts. The apostle condemns lawsuits and discord among the brethren (1 Cor 1,11; 6,5s). Instead, he calls for an experience in the unity and love of God; brotherly love is a gift from God. Saint Augustine says that it is the grace of God that makes this coexistence of the brothers and sisters. It is God Himself who makes possible this coexistence, which is not of human origin or fruit of human effort, but the blessing of God[137]. It would be correct, therefore, to mention in the afirmative that the central message and theme of this Psalms is about unity and harmony amongst people living together. And in relation directly to Christian values, such coexistence in unity attracts naturally the presence of God, the Supreme Being.

PSALM 133 VIS-A-VIS IGWEBUIKE PHILOSOPHY

It can be said in the affirmative that Psalms 133, whose central message is about fraternal living, would rightly contribute many postive lessons to this African philosophy of complementarity. As mentioned above, one of the principles of this *Igwebuike* philospohy is unity. In fact, it is the inner or underlying principle of this African philosophy[138]. This unity stems from the coming together and putting into one place the various and different exiting realities. The principle points to the fact that, inspite of the contrariety of reality, in spite of the singular identity of each reality, there is something common to everything. *Igwebuike* understands every individual reality as part and completion of the whole, and thus there is a unity in the midst of diversity. *Igwebuike* presents being as that which possesses a relational character of mutual relations. Thus, 'to be' is to live in solidarity and complementarity, and to live outside the parameters of solidarity and complementarity is to suffer alienation. 'To be' is 'to be with the other', in a community of beings. "I am because we are and since we are, therefore I am"[139].

The first verse of the Psalms precisa mente speaks about unity and harmony amongst brothers. And like we have seen, this brotherhood that the Psalms speaks about is not only limited to blood ties. The brotherhood, based only on blood affinities, is always restrictive and limited. It is, therefore, obvious that the brotherhood involved here is more inclusive and covers a wide range of persons and individuals. Consequently, it makes reference to a large comunity, the entire comunity. This tie stems from not blood and other similar affinities, but from the name of God. This, of course, without any doubt, fits well for the *Igwebuike* concept of unity. The African culture, by its very nature, is very inclusive. Most African societies are characterized

---

[137] *Id*, 475.

[138] Cf. https://www.ajol.info/index.php/jrhr/article/view/180084, Kanu, I. A., *Sources of Igwebuike philosophy: towards a socio-cultural foundation*, acessed 14/04/2020.

[139] Cf. https://www.ajol.info/index.php/jrhr/article/view/190043, Kanu, I. A., *On the Origin and Principles of Igwebuike,* accesed 24/04/2020.

by and have this conscience and belief of *"I am because we are and since we are, therefore I am"*. And beause of this strong sense of togetherness and unity, everyone in a given comunity considers the next person as a brother. As long as you are a member of a given group, you have some strong relationship with and connection to everyone in the society. No one is considered different or outside of the circle that binds the community. To be identified as an individual, one is first considered as part of the whole group. It is the whole that gives meaning and importance to the individual or a particular reality and aspect.

In this line too, that is, in relation to this sense of unity, harmony, community, complementarity and solidarity among the community of beings, one philopspher speaks of the bond on which this unity, togetherness and complementarity is built as the *Beings forces'*, and this *Beings forces'* of the universe are not a multiple of independent forces placed in juxtaposition from being to being. All creatures are found in relationship according to the law of hierarchy. Nothing moves in this universe of forces without influencing other forces by its movement. The world of forces is held like a spider's web of which no single thread can be caused to vibrate without shaking the whole network[140]. This unity and harmony is a force that binds together the individuals and the various particular realities, making it one and strong.

Another aspect of unity in *Igwebuike* philosophy stresses the advantage that stems from this union of various parts. According to the study of Kanu, *Igwebuike* strongly holds that the whole is greater than the corresponding parts. It is also a view that maintains that by the coming together of the individuals or parts, a viable and sustainable whole will emerge, and by this, the parts will get to the brim purpose of their existence[141]. The coming together of the parts to form one single unit makes the various parts strong and powerful. In line with this, it would be relevant the teaching of the psalmist.

It emphasizes this concept of harmony because to produce fruit there have to be strongly in place understanding and intergretion - a community that is together in harmony; we are all aware that in a house, the brothers may be living together but be in quarrels, with resentments. The psalmist speaks of a concept of harmony. For a better understandinding of harmony, it would be good to imagine such in music. Musically, harmony reminds us, for example, of an orchestra. Those who have had the opportunity to see it in action know that it is a large instrumental ensemble typical of classical music, which combines instruments from different families, including bowed string instruments, such as the violin, viola, cello, and double bass; brass instruments, such as the horn, trumpet, trombone; woodwinds, such as the flute, oboe, clarinet and bassoon; and percussion instruments, such as the timpani, bass drum, triangle, snare drum, cymbals, and mallet percussion instruments, each grouped in sections; but there is a director and a work of art that guide them to make a beautiful melody come out. They are all in harmony. The psalmist used two metaphors to reinforce this harmony.

---

[140] *Ibid.*

[141] *Ibid.*

In the first metaphor, it says that this harmony that occurs when people live together is like good oil; but it is not any kind of oil. For example, it is not an oil that serves to cook, it is the oil that is used to anoint the priest Aaron. In the ancient Christian communities, priests and kings were anointed to be set apart for God's service. The oil with which they were anointed was a Holy oil, set apart for this sacred and religious purpose. It indicates that this community of brothers the psalmists is making reference to is set apart for God, for His purposes.

The other image is that of the dew. It is like the dew of Hermon descending upon the mountains of Zion. Scholars say that if one spends the night in that mountainous región of Zion, the next morning one is completely soaked. This dew serves to bring freshness and to nourish the arid and dry soil in the Judean region. In the same line, living together in harmony breeds nourishment and freshness to the entire society. The community must be united not only for its own benefit or for its own order or security. The community must manifest its unity, because a fragmented (or divided) community does not have much to say to a fragmented world. The psalmist, therefore, calls for harmony. This virtue and quality of life is something compulsory for such a community, a community where God exists. Such a community must be the role model to others. It is like when Jesus Christ warns His disciples, you are the salt of the earth, but if it becomes tasteless, what will it be salted with? It's nothing but to be trampled by men (Mt 5,13)[142].

In his work, an aspect stressed by Kanu in line with this principle of unity is the one that touches the theme of anthropology. This idea is developed by Mibiti. Mbiti, in his work on African religion and philosophy, speaks of African ontology in terms of unity, solidarity and complementarity. The anthropocentric ontology is a complete unity or solidarity which nothing can break up or destroy. To destroy or remove one of these categories is to destroy the whole existence, including the destruction of the creator, which is impossible. One mode of existence presupposes all the others, and a balance must be maintained so that these modes neither drift too far apart from one another nor get too close to one another[143]. This idea is much more related to the central message of the Psalms. Unity breeds the presence and blessings of God. Once God is involved, nothing stands against His powers and sovereignty. Therefore, just like Mbiti speaks of the imposiblity of destroying the creator, Psalms 133 mentions clearly that once this harmony and unity is in place, it is imposible to speak of the absence of the blessings of God.

Verse 3 of the Psalm contains a very important message. It makes allusion to what was stressed in the first verse about brothers living together in a community. This coesxitence in harmony always comes with great benefits. It is always a blessing. Blessing that is life, life that is lasting. Brotherly love is a blessing that attracts blessings; it is full life that prolongs; it is aroma that

---

[142] Cf. http://razondelcristianismo.blogspot.com/2016/09/hermeneutica-del-salmo-133-samuel.html, Samuel Rodriguez, hermeneútica del Salmo 133, accessed 24/04/2020.

[143] Cf. https://www.ajol.info/index.php/jrhr/article/view/190043, Kanu, I. A., *On the Origin and Principles of Igwebuike*, accesed 24/04/2020.

spreads; it is dew that permeates. God himself becomes the saving power and force of a community in which brothers coexist harmoniously[144]. The result of this kind of coexistence is this blessing that comes from the Supreme Being Himself. Its result is very practical; it is something that is felt by everybody.

One might ask what is this God's blessing? The Psalm mentions life everlasting which, without doubt, is a blessing and gift from the Lord. However, when we read and reflect on the Scripture, it can be seen that God's blessings are so great, and one can not finish listing and counting them. Brothers, sisters, family, food, shelter, home, happiness, etc., aid in tribulation. And above all, eternal life! It would not be out of place to state that if one attempts to visualize eternal life, one cannot see nor grasps very clearly its significance. Therefore, to grasp the significance it has, it would be good to sit and imagine a great party where you can meet everyone who enjoys spending time with you, with all those who make you feel full and happy and those who make you see the beauty of life. This is most likely how etertnal life would be, and that is why the psalmist mentions that the Lord sends eternal life.

This idea of benefits that come from this community living can be related to the opinión of Edeh, in his reflection about unity, and in this case he mentions a specific cultural society in Nigeria - the Igbos. In his reflection on Igbo metaphysic, he emphasizes the closeness of reality through which reality attains its fulfillment in existence. Accordingly, the Igbo way of life emphasizes 'closeness' but not closed-ness'. There is a closeness in living because each person 'belongs to' others and, in turn, 'is belonged to' by others. By adopting this life of 'closeness' or 'belongingness', an Igbo becomes immersed in the culture's spiritual substance, love; and by love, he acquires a fulfillment as a person beyond mere individuality[145]. This clearly calls, therefore, for unity and collaboration which Psalm 133 stresses: life in a community and a life of unity and together, and not an individualistic or egoistic type of living.

CONCLUSION

Having seen the relationship between the Psalms and philosophy, one can see how theological values can help to improve the values already existent in the *Igwebiuke* philosophy. The Psalm examined begins with an invitation to "behold", to see something important. In this paper, what is presented is a call on *Igwebuike* thought and belief; of the fact that, in theology, it can get many values too to add to the one it has and is still developing. The greatest of this value, however, is not far from the central idea of the *Igwebiuke* pilosophy. This is the value of complementarity[146]. It is, therefore, very positive and encouraging for people to

---

[144] Cf. Kraus H. J., *Los salmos*, Vol. II. Salamanca, Ediciones Sígueme 1995, 716.

[145] Cf. https://www.ajol.info/index.php/jrhr/article/view/190043, Kanu, I. A., *On the Origin and Principles of Igwebuike*, accesed 24/04/2020.

[146] Kanu, I. A. (2018). *Igwebuike* as an African integrative and progressive anthropology. *NAJOP: Nasara Journal of Philosophy*. Vol. 2. No. 1. pp. 151-161. Kanu, I. A. (2018). New Africanism: *Igwebuike* as a philosophical

seek community, not institutions, not organizations. It invites all to embrace the gospel of brotherly living to make the word *"brother"* real in every aspect. Everyone has creative ideas. Some have the ability to approach new people, others to share knowledge, others to make food, ornaments, ideas, etc. It is pertinent that we work for communities that evoke: "Behold how good and how delicious it is to dwell as brothers together in harmony". Everyone has something to offer, and when all is put in one place, everything will work perfectly, because the community now makes everybody strong.

BIBLIOGRAPHY

Allen, L. C. (1983). *Word Bible commentary* Vol. XXI. U.S.A, Word Books Publishers

Briggs, C. A. & Briggs, E. G. (1907). *A critical and exegetical commentary.* Vol. II., Edinburgh, T & T Clark

Kanu, I. A. (2016). Igwebuike as a trend in African philosophy. Igwebuike: An African Journal of Arts and Humanities. Vol.2. No. 1 [97-101].

Kanu, A. I. (2017). Igwebuike as an Igbo-African ethic of reciprocity. Igwebuike: An African Journal of Arts and Humanities. A Publication of Tansian University, Department of Philosophy and Religious Studies. Vol. 3 No 2.[155-160].

Kanu, I. A. (2014). *Igwebuikology* as an Igbo-African philosophy for Catholic-Pentecostal relations. *Jos Studies. 22. pp.*87-98.

Kanu, I. A. (2015b). *Igwebuike as an ontological precondition for African ethics.* International Conference of the Society for Research and Academic Excellence. University of Nigeria, Nsukka. 14th -16th September.

Attribute of Africa in portraying the Image of Life. In Mahmoud Misaeli, Sanni Yaya and Rico Sneller (Eds.). *African Perspectives on Global on Global Development* (pp. 92-103). United Kingdom: Cambridge Scholars Publishing. Kanu, I. A. (2019). Collaboration within the ecology of mission: An African cultural perspective. *The Catholic Voyage: African Journal of Consecrated Life.* Vol. 15. pp. 125-149. Kanu, I. A. (2019). *Igwebuike* research methodology: A new trend for scientific and wholistic investigation. *IGWEBUIKE: An African Journal of Arts and Humanities* (IAAJAH). *5. 4.* pp. *95-105.* Kanu, I. A. (2019). *Igwebuikeconomics*: The Igbo apprenticeship for wealth creation. *IGWEBUIKE: An African Journal of Arts and Humanities* (IAAJAH). *5. 4.* pp. *56-70.* Kanu, I. A. (2019). *Igwebuikecracy*: The Igbo-African participatory cocio-political system of governance. *TOLLE LEGE: An Augustinian Journal of the Philosophy and Theology. 1. 1.* pp. 34-45. Kanu, I. A. (2019). On the origin and principles of *Igwebuike* philosophy. *International Journal of Religion and Human Relations.* Vol. 11. No. 1. pp. 159-176. Kanu, I. A. (2019b). An *Igwebuike* approach to the study of African traditional naming ceremony and baptism. *International Journal of Religion and Human Relations.* Vol. 11. No. 1. pp. 25-50. Kanu, I. A. (2017). *Igwebuike* as an Igbo-African philosophy for Christian-Muslim relations in Northern Nigeria. In Mahmoud Misaeli (Ed.). *Spirituality and Global Ethics* (pp. 300-310). United Kingdom: Cambridge Scholars.

Kanu, I. A. (2015c). *Igwebuike as an Igbo-African philosophy of education.* A paper presented at the International Conference on Law, Education and Humanities. 25th -26th November 2015 University of Paris, France.

Kanu, I. A. (2016a). *Igwebuike* as an Igbo-African hermeneutics of globalisation. *IGWEBUIKE: An African Journal of Arts and Humanities,* Vol. 2 No.1. pp. 61-66.

Kanu, I. A. (2016a). *Igwebuike* as the consummate foundation of African Bioethical principles. *An African journal of Arts and Humanities* Vol.2 No1 June, pp.23-40.

Kanu, I. A. (2016b) *Igwebuike* as an expressive modality of being in African ontology. *Journal of Environmental and Construction Management. 6. 3.* pp.12-21.

Kanu, I. A. (2017). *Igwebuike* as an Igbo-African philosophy for Christian-Muslim relations in Northern Nigeria. In Mahmoud Misaeli (Ed.). *Spirituality and Global Ethics* (pp. 300-310). United Kingdom: Cambridge Scholars.

Kanu, I. A. (2017). *Igwebuike* as an Igbo-African philosophy for the protection of the environment. *Nightingale International Journal of Humanities and Social Sciences.* Vol. 3. No. 4. pp. 28-38.

Kanu, I. A. (2017). *Igwebuike* as the hermeneutic of individuality and communality in African ontology. *NAJOP: Nasara Journal of Philosophy.* Vol. 2. No. 1. pp. 162-179.

Kanu, I. A. (2017a). *Igwebuike* and question of superiority in the scientific community of knowledge. *Igwebuike: An African Journal of Arts and Humanities.* Vol.3 No1. pp. 131-138.

Kanu, I. A. (2017a). *Igwebuike as a philosophical attribute of Africa in portraying the image of life.* A paper presented at the 2017 Oracle of Wisdom International Conference by the Department of Philosophy, Tansian University, Umunya, Anambra State, 27-29 April.

Kanu, I. A. (2017b). *Igwebuike* as a complementary approach to the issue of girl-child education. *Nightingale International Journal of Contemporary Education and Research.* Vol. 3. No. 6. pp. 11-17.

Kanu, I. A. (2017b). *Igwebuike* as a wholistic response to the problem of evil and human suffering. *Igwebuike: An African Journal of Arts and Humanities.* Vol. 3 No 2, March.

Kanu, I. A. (2017e). *Igwebuike* as an Igbo-African modality of peace and conflict resolution. *Journal of African Traditional Religion and Philosophy Scholars. Vol. 1. No. 1. pp. 31-40.*

Kanu, I. A. (2017g). *Igwebuike* and the logic (Nka) of African philosophy. *Igwebuike: An African Journal of Arts and Humanities*. 3. 1. pp. 1-13.

Kanu, I. A. (2017h). *Igwebuike* philosophy and human rights violation in Africa. *IGWEBUIKE: An African Journal of Arts and Humanities*. Vol. 3. No. 7. pp. 117-136.

Kanu, I. A. (2017i). *Igwebuike* as a hermeneutic of personal autonomy in African ontology. *Journal of African Traditional Religion and Philosophy Scholars*. Vol. 2. No. 1. pp. 14-22.

Kanu, I. A. (2018). *Igwe Bu Ike* as an Igbo-African hermeneutics of national development. *Igbo Studies Review*. No. 6. pp. 59-83.

Kanu, I. A. (2018). *Igwebuike* as an African integrative and progressive anthropology. *NAJOP: Nasara Journal of Philosophy*. Vol. 2. No. 1. pp. 151-161.

Kanu, I. A. (2018). New Africanism: *Igwebuike* as a philosophical Attribute of Africa in portraying the Image of Life. In Mahmoud Misaeli, Sanni Yaya and Rico Sneller (Eds.). *African Perspectives on Global on Global Development* (pp. 92-103). United Kingdom: Cambridge Scholars Publishing.

Kanu, I. A. (2019). *Igwebuike* research methodology: A new trend for scientific and wholistic investigation. *IGWEBUIKE: An African Journal of Arts and Humanities* (IAAJAH). *5. 4. pp. 95-105.*

Kanu, I. A. (2019). *Igwebuikeconomics*: The Igbo apprenticeship for wealth creation. *IGWEBUIKE: An African Journal of Arts and Humanities* (IAAJAH). *5. 4. pp. 56-70.*

Kanu, I. A. (2019). *Igwebuikecracy*: The Igbo-African participatory cocio-political system of governance. *TOLLE LEGE: An Augustinian Journal of the Philosophy and Theology. 1. 1.* pp. 34-45.

Kraus, H. J. (1995). *Los salmos*, Vol. II. Salamanca, Ediciones Sígueme

Obras de San Agustín XXII, *Enarraciones sobre los salmos*, Madrid, BAC 1967

Schökel, L. A. & Carniti, C. (1993). *Salmos II*. Navarra, Verbo Divino

IGWEBUIKE ONTOLOGY AND THE ISSUE OF RELIGIO-POLITICAL CRISIS IN NIGERIA

Maduekwe Pius Chukwuebuka
Augustinian Institute
Makurdi, Benue State
payopapaz2711@yahoo.com

ABSTRACT

The relationship that does exist between politics and religion is intimate. More so, the relationship is complex because of the intricacies inherent in the politicization of religion. With emphasis on Nigeria today, there are two dominant religious groups in Nigeria, Islam and Christianity. Islam and Christianity are not recognized here to the trivialization of the position of traditional religion. The integration of politics and religion in Nigerian political history is believed to be one major problem behind the current religious violence and political instability troubling the country. This research is aimed at looking into the chaos that has been caused by religion in Nigeria's socio-political system and has employed the Igwebuike Philosophy with the view of addressing the issues of conflict between the two major religions in Nigeria. Igwebuike principle of solidarity and complementarity will be adopted for this purpose. For the purpose of this thesis, the hermeneutic and phenomenological methods of inquiry will be employed. This thesis, therefore, exposes the misplacement of values by the Nigerian people as they tend to place religion and politics as a single entity, rather than practicing them independently. Nonetheless, religion and politics are complimentary and can be practiced without steps.

INTRODUCTION

The human person, from researches, is said to be a being that needs the presence of the other to foster its own existence; thus, it is not a totally independent being, despite his religion, social or political class. Virtually in all societies of the world, religion has become a key index that carpenters the socio-economic, cultural and political structures, either for good or for bad.

Nigeria, just like any other multi-cultural society, has a number of religious movements and practices, such as: Islam, Christianity and indigenous religion. Before the arrival of the colonial masters into Nigeria, our ancestors were staunch adherents of the African traditional religion

(ATR). The ATR was a system of belief and worship that was totally devoid of acrimony, hate and conflicts.

For administrative convenience, Fredrick Lugard brought forth the thought merging northern and southern protectorates. In 1914, an entity called Nigeria emerged, bringing about 250 ethnic groups together into one political and administrative entity. Today, ironically, the merger became a bane of peace, progress and stability of the Nigerian nation. Although Nigeria has witnessed some pockets of religious conflicts over the years, it assumed an alarming proportion when Nigeria assumed democratic ideals in 1999.

As a multi-ethnic and religious entity, Christians and Muslims (the two major religions in Nigeria) in Nigeria have over the years tried to outwit each other in terms of belief, adherence, structure and growth vis-à-vis the Nigerian nation. Consequently, a dimension of fanaticism was introduced into the religious practice. Unfortunately, the so-called religions have become a source of strife, anarchy and bloodletting in Nigeria in recent times. Today, there is a sharp deviation from the core values of religion, occasioned by the alarming nature of religious crisis in Nigeria, leading to destruction of lives and property. Rather than entrench peace, unity and stability, religion has somewhat threatened the whole essence of Nigeria's nationhood.

Very often, the woes of Nigeria are blamed on the events of "slave trade", "colonialism" and "missionary methods" that were not contextual. Today, it is very clear that the very enemies of Nigeria are Nigerians. The rate at which Nigerians destroy one another morally, intellectually, socially, politically and physically in the present world cannot be compared to the accusation we heap on the Western world. The various crises in Nigeria today need fellow Nigerians to be the light of the world and salt of the earth. This calls for a sense of complementarity and inter-personal dialogue, in which the human person can be a reconciled reconciler. In other words, the human person needs a renewal of heart and change of attitude. It must be remembered that as Nigerians "the sky is wide enough for everyone to fly". This will assists us to develop our gifts and actualize our latent potentials to be the light of the world and salt of the earth.

Thus, the researcher places *Igwebuike* ontology, an Igbo-African philosophy of humanity towards the other or integrative humanism viz-a-viz the issues of religio-political crises as a possible attempt to promote complementarity and enhance a more peaceful co-existence.

STATEMENT OF THE PROBLEM

In the Nigerian society, three types of religion are prominent: Christianity, Islam and African traditional religion. The first two are imported religions; and the last is home grown. Both Christianity and Islam are universal while African traditional religion is particular to Africa. Impliedly, African traditional religion has no body of teaching which is regarded as valid forever (at all times) as it has no universal mission, so proselytization does not exist; hence,

African traditional religion cannot be a divisive force. So, traditional religion does not cause havoc in our society; the problem is in the relationships of Islamic and Christian religions.

The problems are at various levels: conceptualization, worldview, beliefs and perceptions, among others. At the level of conceptualization and articulation, both religions, Islam and Christianity, differ; their philosophies are poles apart as their founders are both in the largeness of heart cum intelligence and articulation of concepts. Christianity is not a parallel concept to Islam, nor is Christianization a parallel concept to Islamization. Each is in a world of its own. While Christianization concerns itself with conversion of willing persons, Islamization concerns itself with conversion of persons both in the spheres of religion and politics with the use of force. At this level, it is clear that Islamic religion is not concerned with human acts as such, for these are acts performed with the aid of knowledge, freedom, voluntariness and intention.

Our problems also are ranging from cosmological exclusivism, lack of leadership, ignorance to corruption, and so on. Man is both a political and religious animal; hence, a total separation of religion from politics is not advocated for, but the politicization of religion should be guarded against in order to avoid emotional outbursts, which have escalated problems by the ensued violence and destruction which claimed lives and property. Irrational latitude to either religion in politics or vice versa remains an issue of concern in the Nigerian state.

This study has its importance lying on the very fact that the contemporary Nigerian society is in no doubt faced with so much religious differences which produce hatred and intolerance. Over the years, religious crises have been a reoccurring decimal and every effort to promote unity, peace and progress in a multi-ethnic and religious society like Nigeria has defied all known solutions. This research is aimed at providing a philosophical platform for peaceful co-existence, rational fraternal cooperation and complementarity between Nigerian Muslims and Christians for a better and more standard political system with a practice of true federalism and democracy and in all to have a greater Nigeria.

The researcher has employed practical, descriptive, expository, historical, dialectic and philosophical approaches in this study. The study has also made use of more secondary sources and a bit of primary sources, as well as the hermeneutic and phenomenological methods.

THE ETYMOLOGY AND MEANING OF *IGWEBUIKE*

Etymologically, the Igbo ontological maxim, *Igwebuike,* is a compound word which is rooted in three Igbo words: *Igwe, Bu* and *Ike.* These words can also be used in a sentence form, by putting them together, although as independent words, thus making up a complete sentence. *Igwe* which means "number or population" is a noun. *Bu* which means "is" is a verb. *Ike* which means "strength or power" is also a noun. Put together, *Igwebuike* comes to mean literally:

"number is strength or number is power." As an Igbo-African philosophy, it rests on two primary principles: solidarity and complementarity. It argues that 'to be' is to live in solidarity and complementarity, and to live outside the parameters of solidarity and complementarity is to suffer alienation. 'To be' is 'to be with the other', in a community of beings (Kanu "African Traditional Religion", 67).

Igwebuike as an ideology has a long history. It was first employed by the Igbo traditional philosophers as "a theory based on an illustrative statement to teach that when human beings come together in solidarity and complementarity, they are powerful or can constitute an insurmountable force, and more so, to express their world of relationship, harmony, continuality and complementarity. At this level, no task is beyond collective capability" (Kanu, *Igwebuike* and the Unity of the African Philosophical Experience" web).

As earlier stipulated, *Igwebuike* factually emanates from a unitary composition, since it emphasizes strength in togetherness or population; just as in the *Ujaama* of Julius Nyerere, it upholds communal living and fraternal cooperation. Furthermore, Kanu postulates that it rests on the philosophy of solidarity and complementarity; thus, to be is to live in solidarity and complementarity, and to live outside the parameters of solidarity and complementarity is to suffer alienation. *Igwebuike* is based on the African cosmology. Iroegbu, thus, affirms this as he opines that it is characterized by a common origin, common worldview, common language, shared culture, shared race, colour and habits, common historical experience and a common destiny (8). *Igwebuike* is the underlining principle of African philosophy and religion. It is the unity of the African philosophical experience. It is, in fact, the fundamental category of African philosophy and religion. It is the substratum of African traditional values, philosophy and religion. Mbiti has classically *proverbialized* the community, determining the role of the individual when he write; 'I am because we are and since we are, therefore I am' (108).

As averred by Kanu, it is attainable that *Igwebuike* philosophy is one that strongly invites the African people to a life of a holistic unism as it goes as far as expressing a sense of belonging to the African, and when the reverse is the case, it presents the African to be alienated from the rest of humanity. Also, when human beings come together in solidarity and complementarity, they are powerful or can constitute an insurmountable force or strength, and at this level, no task is beyond their collective capability. *Igwebuike*, therefore, understands the human person as possessing a relational character, and also as one who is inter-subjective and must necessarily relate with the other in order to make a meaningful existence.

KANU IKECHUKWU ANTHONY: THE PROPONENT OF *IGWEBUIKE* PHILOSOPHY

Kanu Ikechukwu Anthony, the proponent of the Igwebuike philosophy, is an Augustinian Friar and is currently the Rector of Villanova Polytechnic, *Imesi Ile*, Osun state, Nigeria. He was born 20th November, 1981 at *Nkwerre*. He is of Igbo extraction from Arondizuogu, Ideato

North Local Government Area, Imo State Nigeria. Though having his origin from the Eastern part of Nigeria, Kanu had both his nursery/primary and secondary school education in the north in *Jimeta*-Yola, Adamawa State, from the following schools: Command Children Nursery and Primary school, Demonstration Primary School, Army Day Secondary School and St. Peter's Minor Seminary, from 1984-1986, 1987-1992, 1993-1994 and 1995-1999 respectively. After his secondary school education, Kanu, in responding to his call to the religious life, joined the Order of St. Augustine, where his vocation was nurtured. Thus, Kanu proceeded to St. Thomas Aquinas and St. Augustine's Major Seminaries from 2001-2004 and 2005-2009, where he obtained Bachelor of Arts Degree in Philosophy and Bachelor of Arts Degree in Religious Studies respectively. After the completion of his formation to the priesthood and religious life, in 2009 he was ordained a Catholic priest.

Kanu, after his ordination, proceeded to further his studies. He obtained Master's degrees in Philosophy (Metaphysics); Religion and Human Relations from University of *Nsukka*, Enugu state and *Nnamdi Azikiwe* University *Awka*, Anambra state from 2010-2015 and 2010-2012 respectively. In 2012, he continued in the same *Nnamdi Azikiwe* University for his Doctorate degree programme in Religion and Human relations, which he obtained in 2015.

Kanu is a man of great responsibilities and engagements. Apart from his religious and pastoral commitments, he served as the Dean of Students at the International Bio-Research Institute, Ugwogo Nike, Enugu State and lectures in three other institutions, which include: St. Augustine's Major Seminary, Jos; Augustinian Institute of Philosophy, *Makurdi* and *Veritas* University Abuja. He is also a member of various academic societies, like: Igbo Studies Association (I.S.A) USA, Nigerian Philosophical Association (NPA), International Society for African Philosophy Studies (ISAPS), Association of African Traditional Religion and Philosophy Scholars (AATREPS), just to mention but a few. He is also a member of decision making boards like Governing Board, International Bio-Research Institute (IBI), Ugwogo Nike, Enugu State; APURIMAC ONLUS (NGO), Jos-Plateau Sstate; Board of Trustees, Association of African Traditional Religion and Philosophy Scholars (AATREPS), and a host of others (Tumba,69-71).

In his bid to contribute immensely to the pool of knowledge, Kanu has written omnivorously, making impact in various spheres of life through his works, especially in the areas of African Philosophy and African Traditional Religion (ATR) studies in which he has made an indelible impression through his ground-breaking *Igwebuike* philosophy and other written works, prominent among which include: African Philosophy: An Ontologico-Existential Hermeneutic Approach to Classical and Contemporary Issues and A Hermeneutic Approach to African Traditional Religion, Theology and Philosophy. Kanu, so far, has written 20 books, published 116 articles in national and international peer-reviewed journals, 120 papers presented at different conferences. This is no doubt an indication that Kanu is truly a genius and his contributions in creating awareness and imparting positive knowledge cannot be overemphasized. Kanu is also the founder and Editor-in-Chief of *Igwebuike*: An African

Journal of Arts and Humanities, and *Igwebuikepedia*: An Internet Encyclopedia of African Philosophy (Tyogema, 34).

Kanu, being the proponent of *Igwebuike* philosophy, has made great impact in philosophy through its instrumentality. Through *Igwebuike, Kanu* has proposed a new way of looking at reality, using the lens of solidarity and complementarity. His works on *Igwebuike*, among many, include, *Igwebuike* and African Ethics, *Igwebuike* and the Unity of African Philosophy, *Igwebuike* as the Consummate Foundation of African Bioethical Principle, *Igwebuike* as an Igbo-African Philosophy of Education, *Igwebuike* as an Igbo-African Hermeneutic of Globalization, *Igwebuikecracy*: The Igbo-African Participatory Socio-Political System of Governance, *Igwebuike* as the Expressive Modality of Being in Igbo Ontology. Pertinent issues that cloud our contemporary world have been addressed by Kanu using *Igwebuike*. Also, through *Igwebuike*, Kanu has made vital contributions in the areas of metaphysics, ethics, epistemology and political philosophy; thus, elevating it to the status of an academic discipline and worthy of being employed for research in various areas of inquiry for positive impacts on the society (Tyogema, 34).

THE SOURCES OF *IGWEBUIKE* PHILOSOPHY

The Igbo African philosophy, *Igwebuike*, which has its tentacles on the manner of being with the worldview of complementarity, massages the ego of individuals and posits to them a model of living in a society with a common goal of togetherness; that is, the "I thou" relationship is the *kpim* of *Igwebuike* philosophy.

Igwebuike philosophy is based on the Igbo-African worldview of complementarity, that is, the manner of being in African ontology. It is a worldview in which individuating differences must work towards a corporate existence, where the "I" does not stand as the "I" but as a "We," where life and living makes meaning. In a scenario of this kind, difference does not divide nor does it constitute a threat, but unites and gives hope that future existence would have meaning. In a cosmogony of this kind, while the ontology of the person is founded on the particular that founds identity, it is the community that gives meaning to such an existence and grounds such an identity. What are the sources of *Igwebuike* philosophy? It focuses on the raw materials from which *Igwebuike* philosophy is gotten. A cursory glance at the African socio-cultural background reveals that the sources of *Igwebuike* philosophy include the works of professional African philosophers, African proverbs, African folktales, African symbols, African names and African songs (Kanu, Sources of *Igwebuike* Philosophy, 2).

Africans, like other people in the world, are shaped by their culture and they contribute in the shaping and transmission of this culture. The African, therefore, is a *homo culturalis*. By African culture, it is meant those things which go to the refining and developing of the African's diverse mental and psychological endowments.

Also, names among the African people are not just an identification tag for differentiating "A" from "B," but carry with them meanings that are rich and profound. There are times when such names are monumental, in the sense that they tell a history of an event that has occurred. For instance, the Igbo name *Onwudinjo,* which means "death is bad," is usually given to a child to tell the story of maybe the death of the mother at the birth of the child or the death of an important relation at the time of the birth of the child. There are times when such names that are prophetic, like *Ogadimma,* which means "it will be good" could be given to a child to speak of the anticipation of a bright future (Kanu, 4).

African proverbs occupy a very important place in Africa's economy of communication. They have been described variously by the Igbo as vegetable for eating speech; the palm oil with which words are eaten. They are so important that the Zulu of South Africa would say that without proverbs, language would be but a skeleton without flesh, a body without a soul. They carry within them the wisdom and experience of the African people, usually of several ages gathered and summed up in one expression; example, *Aka nri kwo aka ekpe, aka ekpe akwo aka nri*: if the right hand washes the left hand, the left hand would wash the right hand, and others. A glance at the work of contemporary African philosophers reveals that the web that holds their perspective together is the philosophy of complementarity. Although perspectives continue to change and differ, they continue to be united by the idea of harmony (Kanu, 7).

THE PRINCIPLES OF *IGWEBUIKE* PHILOSOPHY

Principally, every school of thought has its source, role and principles that set aright and flaunt the uniqueness of that particular thought. The origin is undeniably the end of a reaction to a given circumstance that is either real or conceptual.

Thus, it responds to the often posited questions such as; "What is the origin of *Igwebuike* philosophy?" How did it begin as a pattern of thought in African ontology? Is it a philosophy that is exclusive to the Igbo or Africa? And in responding to these questions, Kanu, in his work on the origin and principles of *Igwebuike* philosophy, avers that:

> *Igwebuike* is an Igbo word *Igwe* (number), *Bu* (Is), *Ike* (strength), literally meaning that there is strength in unity- however, philosophically pointing to the complementary nature of reality. It confronts discontinuity and the compartmentalization of reality. *Igwebuike* is not a philosophy that is limited to the Igbo world, it is a universal philosophy that is the incarnation and confirmation of the universal relevance of solidarity and complementarity. Although, a philosophy captured in an Igbo word, it has a universal taste and obvious in universal experience. *Igwebuike* emphasis on the complementary nature of reality was at the heart of the discovery of the Ionian philosophers who observed that there was permanence in the midst of change, and also

that there was unity in the midst of the plurality of reality. In their wonder, they concluded that there must be a primary element that would explain the unity in diversity and permanence in change. In this, they acknowledged the complementarity of the diverse departments of reality (Kanu, 159).

The principles of *Igwebuike* philosophy refers to the values or frameworks that shapes *Igwebuike* philosophy. These principles are the values or frameworks on which the philosophy stands. While these principles guide *Igwebuike* philosophy, they also justify *the* philosophy. These principles include: the principle of identity, the principle of contrariety, the principle of hierarchy and the principle of unity (Kanu, 165)

THE PRINCIPLE OF IDENTITY

This principle, as posited by Kanu, is the first principle of *Igwebuike* philosophy and it holds that every being is determined in itself, one with itself and divided from others. It further expresses the uniqueness and individuality of every being, just as qualities of matter, referred to in traditional metaphysics as accidents, such as size, colour, shape, distinguish one being from the other. In other words, the particularity and peculiarity of a being puts an end to the error of generalization and chaos.

THE PRINCIPLE OF HIERARCHY

This principle expresses the levels or degrees of forces in each reality. In the hierarchy of forces, those with a greater force come first, with God at the apex as the source of all force. In Igbo-African ontology, reality can be subsumed under the following categories, according to the hierarchy of their force: Spirit. Spirit as a force has categories of forces. It includes God, the divinities and spirits. God is at the apex of the *Muo* category as the source of all force. Tempels, quoted in the Journal of Religion and Human Relations states, "Above all force is God, it is he who has force, power, in himself. He gives existence, power of survival and of increase, to other forces" (177), and on this hierarchy goes to the next level occupied by the human person who plays a role so vital on this ladder as man is distinct and possesses will and intelligence as he shares in the all-encompassing nature of God the Supreme Being; thus, the human being is the center of the universe as he supersedes the next on the ladder which are things. Things are referred to as happening, an event, an occurrence. It can also be affixed to any adjective to mean specific things". For instance, *ife obuna* (anything), *ife ebube* (thing of wonder), *ife ojoo* (bad thing), *ife oma* (good thing). *Ife* as a force cannot act for itself, and thus can only become active when a greater force like God, divinities, spirits and man act on them. They have no will of their own and thus depend on the will of a greater force. The next in the hierarchy is space (*ebe*). Space talks about place. It is the relation of distance between any two bodies or points. It responds to the question of where. The next is time. Time responds to questions such as: when did you see *Emeka*? When did you pick-up *Nnamdi*? When was the sacrifice offered? The last on the hierarchy is modality, manner or style. Modality of being does emphasize on the manner of being (Kanu, Being and the Categories of Being…). Thus, in relation to *Igwebuike*, the degree of forces determines the level or degree of complementarity or connectedness between beings (Kanu, 179).

THE PRINCIPLE OF CONTRARIETY

Here, the principle speaks of otherness of realties. Otherness points to the state of being different, shifting emphasis from Descartes' philosophical concerns with the other which was struck in abstraction to a concrete other that is located in social and cultural institutions. The question of the otherness of reality has continued to emerge in the various epochs of the history of philosophy, fascinating philosophy and giving rise to questions such as: What does it mean to be other than the self? How do I and must I relate to the other? (Ibid, 176-177).

The word contrariety is from the word contrary. Aristotle defines contrariety thus: "For contrariety is a kind of difference, and difference is a kind of otherness". Aristotle writes that:

> The term contrary is applied to those attributes differing in genius, which cannot belong at the same time to the same subject, to the most different of the things in the same genius, to the most different of the attributes in the same recipient subject, to the most different of things that fall under the same faculty, to the things whose difference is greatest either absolutely or in genius or in species. The other things that are called contrary are so called, some because they possess of the above kind, some because they are receptive of such, some because they are productive of or susceptible to such, or are producing or suffering them, or are losses or acquisitions, or possessions of privations of such (Ibid 763)

THE PRINCIPLE OF UNITY

That which is common to all, that is, in spite of the varieties and dynamism of realities, is what *Igwebuike* identifies as being part of the completion of the whole, and there exists amidst all things which is unity, the unifying principle.

Igwebuike strongly holds that the whole is greater than the corresponding parts. It is also a view that maintains that by the coming together of the individuals or parts, a viable and sustainable whole will emerge, and by this, the parts will get to the brim purpose of their existence. This sense of unity, harmony, community, complementarity and solidarity among the community of beings finds expression in the philosophy of Tempels. 'Beings forces' of the universe are not a multiple of independent forces placed in juxtaposition from being to being. All creatures are found in relationship, according to the law of hierarchy. Nothing moves in this universe of forces without influencing other forces by its movement. The world of forces is held like a spider's web of which no single thread can be caused to vibrate without shaking the whole network (Kanu, 176).

In response to the fundamental questions that have arisen as a result of the wider reading of *Igwebuike* philosophy, this work has been written to address the issue of the origin of *Igwebuike* philosophy.

IGWEBUIKE AND COMPLEMENTARITY

Igwebuike

Igwebuike is an indigenous philosophy of the modality of being for the realization of being. Simply puts, mode of being is relational in nature. It is from the word, *igwebuike*, which is a combination of three words. Thus, it can be understood as a word or sentence: as a word, it is written thus, *Igwebuike*, and a sentence, it is in this form: *igwe bu ike*, with the component words enjoying some independence in terms of space. *Igwe* is a noun which means 'number' or 'population.' *Bu* is a verb, which means 'is.' *Ike* is another verb, which means 'strength' or 'power.' Put together 'number is strength' or 'number is power'. Also, when human beings come together in solidarity and complementarity, they are powerful or can constitute an insurmountable force or strength, and at this level, no task is beyond their collective capability (Kanu, 30).

Complementarity

Complementarity is the characteristic of being or state of being. As a dimension of *Igwebuike* philosophy, it can be seen in the light of disposition for, the positive will to, and the practice of living and working together, crowned by performed mutual assistance: spontaneous or organized, among the members of a group who are brought together either naturally or professionally (Jude et al, 300).

The African practice of solidarity is witnessed on both the economic, social and religious spheres. The traditional Nigerian was his brother's keeper, especially at the communal level. In fact, he was and still is often in solidarity to a fault. In the employment and social distribution spheres, he first considers his clansperson or tribesman before a foreigner, irrespective of qualification or fitness for the job (Jude et al, 301).

A brother's misfortune was a common misfortune. A living example is the practice by which once there is a free accident in which a person's house is burnt, immediately and spontaneously, the whole community gathers to work and rebuild the damaged house fully. This is not only spontaneous; it is also gratis. Could there be a better expression of African concern, care and comforting for a fellow human being? (Ibid).

A brother's success was equally a common success, celebrated as such. "We have made it in you" is echoed. The foundation of solidarity was on the natural and common ties of origin, blood, culture, language, conviviality and worldview that characterize each community (Ibid).

"Complementarism is a philosophy that seeks to consider things in the significance of their singularity and not in the exclusiveness of their otherness in view of the joy that gives completion to all missing links of reality" (Asouzu, 39). *Igwebuike* philosophy argues that existence is not only meaningful, but also possible only in a community and thus, to live outside of complementarity and solidarity is to live outside; it is to suffer alienation (Kanayo et al, 243).

Igwebuike Anthropology

As averred by Kanu in his work on "*Igwebuike* as an African Integrative and Progressive Anthropology," the concept of the human person cultivated by various indigenous African peoples is a core value in each individual socio-cultural context, and more so, a determinant of thought and relationships within the socio-cultural milieu. This is based on the fact the human person is at the centre of the African universe. Mbiti quoted by Kanu, therefore, asserts that "Man is at the very centre of existence and African people see everything else in its relation to this central position of man. It is as if God exists for the sake of man" (*Igwebuike* as an Integrative and Progressive Anthropology, 2). Corroborating Mbiti, Metuh avers that "Everything else in African worldview seems to get its bearing and significance from the position, meaning and end of man" (qtd in Kanu, *Igwebuike* as an Integrative and Progressive Anthropology, 2). The ideas of God, divinities, ancestors, rituals, sacrifices, etc., are only useful to the extent that they serve the needs of the human person. Contrary to the mechanistic concept of the human person, the human person in the African worldview has a purpose and mission to fulfil; he comes into the world as a force amidst forces and interacting with forces. Good status, good health and prosperity are signs of the wellbeing of a person's life-force, and man struggles to preserve it through an appropriate relationship with the spiritual forces around him. The goal of every human person is to achieve his destiny imprinted on his palm by his creator. He is not just an individual person, but one born into a community whose survival and purpose are linked with others. Thus, the human person is first a member of a clan, a kindred or a community (Kanu, 2).

Nonetheless, there have been researches carried out with respect to the African personality and these have been done tilting towards the reflections on symbols and patterned behaviours associated with one level of personality or the other, like the *Chi*, which in Igbo is the symbol of a person's guiding spirit; the *Ofo*, the symbol of a man's individuation; the *Ikenga* and

Odu Enyi, symbols of a person's personal achievement. Although the exposure of African traditional values to Western culture and influence has brought about a lot of alterations in African perspectives, this piece studies the concept of personhood in traditional African ontology with the purpose of establishing the nexus between ancient African traditional society and the present conceptual package. In studying the traditional African concept of personhood, it would be engaged from the dimensions of African personhood as a coherent pluralism and its dialectically progressive character (Ibid, 3).

Igwebuike and the Ethic of Reciprocity

The term 'reciprocity' can mean a situation or relationship in which two people or a group agree to do something similar for each other, to allow each other have the same right (Mariam–Webster Dictionary).

Thus, the ethic of reciprocity is and can be likened to the 'Golden Rule', which states; do to others what you want done to you. Hence, this ethic of reciprocity is across religio-cultural ethical principle that is found in virtually every religious and cultural background (Kanu, 1). It is derived from human feelings and behaviour; it is also relatively simple to articulate and understand, and yet addresses an enormous range of human behaviour. Thus, the ethic of reciprocity stands alone as a legion in its own right and in the form of a general rule.

The point of connection between *Igwebuike* and the ethic of reciprocity is very easily noticeable. While the ethic of reciprocity teaches that you do unto others as you would want done unto you, and the philosophy of *Igwebuike* provides a philosophical foundation for such a perspective - in relation to a fellow human person, more fundamentally, the other is perceived as a part of the self. If the other is a part of the self, one with this understanding would treat the other as one would like to be treated. The philosophy of *Igwebuike* is not just a philosophical foundation for the ethic of reciprocity, but it is the ethic of reciprocity. It presents the ethic of reciprocity not just as a moral principle, but as a duty that one owes to himself or herself - everyone owes himself or herself of treating the other in a way that one would like to be treated (Kanu, 15)

The ethic of reciprocity as stated by Kanu, generally, is imperfect, just as there is hardly a perfect moral law. It has been criticized because it makes the assumption that everyone has the same tastes and opinions and wants to be treated the same way in every situation, and seems to be an injunction to impose one's own way on the other. However, the ethic of reciprocity is a general moral principle, not a hard and fast rule to be applied to every facet of life. Treating other people as we would wish to be treated ourselves does not mean making the assumption that others feel exactly as we do about everything. The treatment we all want is the recognition that we are individuals, each with our own opinions and feelings and for these opinions and feelings to be accorded respect and consideration. This work is not concerned with the shortcomings of the ethic of reciprocity, but has argued that at the heart of *Igwebuike,* as an ethic of reciprocity, is not the idea of treating everyone uniformly; it is rather recognition that everyone, independent of human differences, deserves to be treated with respect and love (Kanu, 7).

The point of connection between *Igwebuike* and the ethic of reciprocity is very easily noticeable. While the ethic of reciprocity teaches that you do unto others as you would want done unto you, and the philosophy of *Igwebuike* provides a philosophical foundation for such a perspective; in relation to a fellow human person, more fundamentally, the other is perceived as a part of the self. If the other is a part of the self, one with this understanding would treat the other as one would like to be treated. The philosophy of *Igwebuike* is not just a philosophical foundation for the ethic of reciprocity, but it is the ethic of reciprocity. It presents the ethic of reciprocity not just as a moral principle, but as a duty that one owes to himself or herself - everyone owes himself or herself of treating the other in a way that one would like to be treated (Kanu 15).

RELIGION AND POLITICS IN NIGERIA VIS-A-VIS IGWEBUIKE ONTOLOGY

Religion: An Overview

Religion etymologically is as old as man itself, but has variously been conceived in the variants of those who attempt a definition of the concept. Religion is a collection of cultural systems, belief systems, and worldview that establishes symbols that relate humanity to spirituality and, sometimes, the moral values. Many a time, the word religion has been interchangeably used as faith or belief system. However, the growth of religion has assumed various forms in different environments or cultures. In some climes, emphasis is placed on belief system as it concerns the religion, while in other environments emphasis is largely placed on religious practice (Clifford, 26).

Religion, from the beginning, has played a very important role in shaping the socio-political thoughts of many nations. In fact, most nations of the world were patterned and influenced by the sacred nature of government. Religion supported and regulated the loyalty that existed between the state and the people. The idea of divine right of kings, which derived its origin from the theocratic concept of governance, vested absolute power and authority in the king or monarch who was seen as a direct representative of God. The monarch was superior and answerable only to God. Ancient history is replete with examples of this idea. For example, in Christianity, the Pope was seen for centuries as the Vicar of Christ on earth, and by virtue of his divine right had the ultimate authority over the Church, and indirectly over the state (Akpanikan, 65). Thus, religion represents a strong social force in the politics of the state, given its capacity for effective political mobilization. Thus, Fox and Sander give six major reasons why this is so. They are;

1. The restriction of religious activities is often difficult for state regimes;
2. Religious organizations often enjoy good patronage in the media;

3. Religious organizations have the capability to easily unite differential social groupings in the society;
4. Religious organizations have the 'ready-made' platform for political meetings;
5. Religious organizations are often strong in weak states;
6. Religious organizations have strong international links and enjoy global solidarity (567-568).

There are also variants of theories that explain the origin of religion. This brings to the fore the statement of Greg M. Epstein, a Humanist Chaplain at Harvard University, who believes that all the world's major religions were founded on the principle that divine beings or forces can promise a level of justice in a supernatural realm that cannot be perceived in this natural one (Epstein, 109). Thus, many of the world's great religions appear to have begun as revitalization movements of some sort, as the vision of a charismatic prophet forces the imaginations of people seeking a more comprehensive answer to their problems than they feel is provided by everyday beliefs. Charismatic individuals have emerged at many times and places in the world. It seems that the key to long-term success and many movements come and go with little long-term effect;has relatively little to do with the prophets, who appear with surprising regularity, but more to do with the development of a group of supporters who are able to institutionalize the movement (Monaghan, 126).

Nigeria is apparently divided between Islam and Christianity, between the North and South respectively. It is glaringly evident that there is a widespread belief, albeit suppressed for political reasons, in traditional religious practices; thus, statistics from world religious survey indicates that 50.4% of Nigeria's population are Muslims; 50.8%, Christians (15% Protestants; 13.7%, Catholics; and 19.6%, other Christians), and followers of other religious faiths were 1.4%, BBC News (2007). In the core Northern Nigeria, they are largely Muslim faithful. In the middle belt, there are good number of both Muslims and Christians. In the Yoruba land (Western Nigeria), there is even distribution of the population between the Christian and Muslim faiths. However, the South-East is predominantly Christians, with great beliefs in the Christianreligious practices, Anglicanism, Methodists, Catholicism, and very few have trado-beliefs. But the region of Niger Delta is mainly Christian-dominated (Nkechi, 18).

A good proportion of Muslims in Nigeria are Sunni, but a fair share of Shia and Sufi also exist, alongside a minority of *Ahmadiya*. Conversely, Christians in this clime are split evenly between Protestantism and Roman Catholicism. The major churches in Nigeria are;

1. Anglican Church
2. Redeemed Christian church of God
3. Nigerian Baptist Convention
4. Assemblies of God Church
5. The Synagogues Church of all Nations
6. The Catholic Church

The Yoruba people are largely Anglicans, while the Igbos are predominantly Catholics. However, there are many adherents of Irunmole spirituality which believes that everyone has divine destiny of becoming Orisha ('Ori', spiritual head); 'sha' is chosen: to be with Olodumare ('Oni odu', the god source of all energy; 'ma re' enlightens). Aside the major Islamic and Christian faiths in Nigeria, other minority spiritual and religions groupings in Nigeria are;

1. Hinduism
2. Judaism
3. The Bahai Faith
4. Chrislam (syncretic merging of Christianity and Islam.

Also, this country has gradually become the hub for the Grail Movement and the Hare Krishnas (Nkechi, 19).

RELIGION AND POLITICS IN NIGERIA

Religion is a set of beliefs concerning the causes, nature and purpose of the universe, especially when considered as the creation of a superhuman agency or agencies, usually involving devotional and ritual observances, and often containing a moral code governing the conduct of human affairs (Dictionary.com). On the other hand, politics is the art or science of government that is concerned with guiding or influencing policy(Mariam Webster).

As a multi-ethnic, multi-religious country, Nigeria's broad religious geography reflects the historical exposure of its northern communities to Islam through the trans-Saharan trade and the success of Christian missionary enterprise in many of its southern parts. However, while historical alliances and shared ethnicity are closely associated with the adoption of these two world religions, religious and ethno-regional identity are cross-cutting, often reinforcing each other. Thus, while Islam had been entrenched in the pre-colonial Hausa cities for centuries, many other northern groups converted to Islam in the wake of the nineteenth century Islamic jihad under *Uthman dan Fodio* (1754-1817), during which the greater part of northern and central Nigeria was incorporated into a new Caliphate, albeit with the exception of the existing, and much older, Islamic kingdom of Borno, which remains the most important rival to Sokoto's claims to represent all of northern Nigeria. Other Muslim groups with a tradition independent of the *Uthmanian* Caliphate include the Yoruba of south-western Nigeria, where people initially converted to Islam as a result of links to Malian trading communities, and Nigeria's middle belt, where large-scale conversion to Islam has continued throughout the postcolonial period (Insa et al, 10).

Nigerian Christianity dates back to the abolition of the trans-Atlantic slave trade in the early nineteenth century, which was followed by the emergence of a literate African elite, consisting of liberated and returned slaves as well as local converts, in coastal cities such as Lagos. Because

Christianity is much younger than Islam in the local context, it is not associated with pre-colonial relations of power. And because its growth in Nigeria was accompanied by the spread of mission education, Nigeria's professional elite was, for a long time, dominated by Christians. Like Islam, Nigerian Christianity is heterogeneous. Roman Catholicism has long been the religion of the Igbo-speaking south-east, although Nigerian-founded Pentecostal churches have made strong inroads into this area over the twenty years prior to this study. In other parts of the country's south, Protestant denominations –including Pentecostal groups – are dominant in the Christian community, but the Yoruba-speaking south-west isj almost equally divided between Christianity and Islam. Moreover, there are important Christian groups in the north, which include both Hausa converts and smaller local groups determined to assert their difference from the Hausa-speaking majority or from relations of power associated with the Caliphate. Moreover, just as there are Muslim migrants from northern Nigeria in many southern cities, there are Christian communities of migrants, or descendants of migrants, from the south in almost all northern Nigerian cities (Insa et al, 10).

Apart from Christianity and Islam, Nigerians also belong to a range of other religious groups. The largest of these comprises followers of traditional religious practice, here referred to as African Traditional Religion (ATR), with the proviso that local belief systems and practices differ widely, and that their subsumption in one term mainly reflects the fact that these practices do not (yet) hold the status of world religions. However, many African Traditional Religious groups share the conviction that the worldly and the sacred are closely interwoven, and that all human relations, including those involving the state and its representatives, reflect both secular and spiritual forces. It is believed that insight into these forces can be gained through divination and revelation, and that they can be influenced through sacrifice, prayer and incantation. Because traditional practices have influenced Christians and Muslims and vice versa, debates about their validity form an important and ongoing part of inter- and intra-religious struggles in Nigeria (Amherd and Nolte, 27). Beyond the engagement with local traditions, Christianity and Islam have expressed a high degree of political competitiveness with each other, at least since the 1970s.

Nigeria's colonial and postcolonial rulers have managed the differences associated with different religious constituencies, especially Islam and Christianity, in various ways. For most of the colonial period, almost all parts of northern Nigeria, the areas belonging to the Uthmanian Caliphate and the kingdom of Borno, were under indirect rule, that is, administered through the structures of the Caliphate, albeit under British guidance. While secular concerns guided important aspects of the local administration, it was thus officially presided over by traditional authorities sanctioned by tradition and Islam, and Islam also constituted the basis for local government. Sharia courts, which had existed before colonial rule, were integrated into the colonial state, and most people turned to sharia law for the mediation and resolution of personal conflicts. Only in the run-up to independence in 1960 were criminal laws codified into secular law. The colonial state's reliance on the structures of the Caliphate in turn affected religious and educational politics in northern Nigeria. In many parts of the north, missionary activity was forbidden, preventing the emergence of an educated elite prepared to challenge either the Emirs or local Muslim traditions. As a result, when the colonial presence was dismantled, the established urban (trading) elite and the local aristocracy emerged as the tenants of northern Nigerian politics. While Islam was deeply entrenched in the traditional sphere of the Nigerian state, Christianity was, especially in the south, mainly associated with modernization. As most missions provided schooling, and later even college training, Christianity was closely associated with the spread of education. The rapid growth of literacy contributed to the emergence of a mostly urban intermediary class of educated men and women who worked as catechists, clerks and teachers. This group soon took up and transformed the local elite's struggles for self-assertion. Directly confronted with racial division in the colonial administration, banking practices and even the mission churches, literate southern Nigerians eventually formed the core of Nigeria's anti-colonial movement. Criticizing both the colonial state and the traditional rulers through which the state had ruled, members of this educated elite considered themselves rather than the representatives of older elite and especially the aristocracy, the natural heirs and rulers of the colonial state after independence (Insa et al, 11).

Religion, for Roseline, is a complex phenomenon; thus, the social functions it performs are quite diverse. Some religious functions are manifest - immediately observable, and some are latent – not immediately discernible. It should be recognized that if an activity helps the integrative performance of an organization, then we call it functional. Roles like support for tolerance, peaceful cooperation and love are promoted through ministerial and lay practice (4).

Schaefer & Lamn identify some democratic utilities of religion which include the integration of human societies composed of individuals and social groups with diverse interests and aspirations. In their view, religious bond transcends these personal and divisive forces. Another important function identified by the two authors is the ability of religion to legitimize the existing social order (273-275).

With reference to the first function of restraining and containing government conduct, religious associations in Nigeria have repeatedly and stridently denounced bad governmental policies or actions that infringe on the interests of the religious community in particular, and/or the welfare of the citizenry in general. Thus, religious associations have joined independence groups in civil society in criticizing the dubious and circuitous nature of the military's democratization project and government's management of the religious disturbances that have convulsed several Northern states. On the stimulation of political participation and civic identification, Nigeria's religious organizations have played an important role in encouraging and mobilizing their members towards active participation in and identification with public affairs and politics. This is done by stimulating a sense of civic identification and participation in their members by urging such members to 'pray and fast' for peace, stability, justice and progress of the nation (Ayorinde, 17).

Thirdly, religion promotes democratic values and norms. This is done through the promotion and propagation of such democratic norms and values as tolerance, moderation, willingness to compromise, and respect for truth, justice and freedom. Religious leaders in Nigeria have at different times demonstrated this commitment to democracy by urging Nigerians not to waver in their support for democratic institutions (Tukur, 29). More so, religion provides avenues for interest representation. Religious organizations articulate, aggregate and represent distinctive societal interests. The Christian representation and mobilization against Nigeria's membership of the country in the OIC represented only one of the many instances of interest representation by the Christian community since 1986. Religion equally generates cross-cutting interest. The existence of cross-cutting interests implies that competing affiliations could operate to secure social peace and democratic stability, and prevent destructive or protracted social conflict, by inducing individuals and groups to divide their emotions in a single explosive line of affiliation. Finally, religious organizations, like many other ordered shares of associational activity or social intercourse, provide an appropriate environment of the development of leadership skills. This is done by displaying an impressive capacity to manage people and resources in their respective organizations by speaking out courageously and consistently against the excesses solutions to nation's problems. Through this, religious leaders have gained some reputation and legitimacy as effective national leaders of thorough and potential statement. It would, however, be misleading to conclude that religious organizations have been uniformly or consistently supportive of democratic processes and values in Nigeria. On the contrary, they have periodically exhibited disturbing anti-democratic proclivities that have found expression in religious violence and intolerance, in the corruption and manipulation of religious leaders. From the foregoing, some religious activities can be described as dysfunctional because their consequences frustrate the stated goals of the groups. In general, religion is functional or dysfunctional, depending on the extent to which it contributes to the achievement of societal goals (Roseline, 5-6).

CHRISTIANS AND MUSLIM INTOLERANCE; CAUSES

In religious conflicts, it is not clear which aims are to be achieved. Gofwen regards political aims as primary; in his view, religious conflicts form a specific form of conflict between groups which differ ideologically along religious lines within a pluralistic setting, with each striving for political relevance. In a similar vein, Takaya (1992) emphasizes the political import of religions:

i.   Religions are parochial and emotional socializers. They specialize in building one-faith exclusive brotherhood communities;

ii. Religion, at some point, is politics and is the most potent and long lasting political association. Moreover, religious creeds excite and extract the deepest possible emotional and physical loyalties from their adherents when in political competition with people of other faiths (10).

One significant element driving conflicts of this type is the attitude of superiority that religious persuasions as a sociological fact often adopt in their dealings or assessment of others. This attitude tends to exclude others, classifies them as ignorant and doomed and, invariably, creates an atmosphere of hostility. This atmosphere of hostility tends to intensify where opposing religious persuasions see their numerical strengths as political advantage. In such a situation, the leaders think that new religions are threats to the hegemonies enjoyed. Further, where the political, social or economic factors are unfavorable, messianic rhetoric can exacerbate the tensions. Thus, Nwaomah observes conversion campaigns, as in Nigeria, "by opposing religion(s) and fanaticism arising from indoctrination of the adherents, mostly due to parochial education, can also reinforce religious hostilities and thus create a conflict". In other words, what makes religious conflicts special are the unique effects of religious doctrines on the perception of the adversaries, the formation of values, and the central role of feelings and emotions for group identification (101).

Fundamentally, the following factors heighten religious crises in Nigeria.

1. Ethnic antipathy: Inter-religious ill-feeling is often intensified by ethnic hostility in a situation where the adherents of Christianity and Islam are also members of two mutually hostile ethnic groups. There seems to be a general agreement that the *Kafanchan* religious riot was aggravated by the ill-feelings harbored by the original natives of *Kafanchan* against the Local Hausa-Fulani "settlers".

2. Role of the press: Mischievous and irresponsible reportage and comments from certain sections of the press on religious issues actually heighten or promote religious riots or crisis. This prompted to state that press reports on the *Kafanchan* riots were highly exaggerated. Many a time, the statements made by religious leaders on religious issues are quoted out of context. These kinds of press reports and comments inflame passions and promote religious ill-feelings and intolerance.

3. Attitude of religious leaders: Most leaders assume the position of God, and will speak on behalf of the co-religionists. The negative attitude of some religious leaders is most unfortunate, since it is only through them that tolerance and peaceful coexistence between Muslims and Christians can be promoted.

4. Key ideological differences: The religious crisis in Nigeria today has roots in our historical past, with regard to our ethnic heterogeneity, and is further compounded by the irresponsible role of certain sections of the press. Be that as it may, other fundamental ideological differences also promoted religious crisis in Nigeria.

    (a) Not only does Christianity reject Mohammed as a prophet, it believes, very strongly, that the way of Christ is the only way to salvation. Other ways, including the way of the Islam, are "shifting sands". This belief is firm in every Christian that everyone without Christ is a stranger from "the covenants of promise, having no hope and without God in the world" (Ephesians 2:12).

(b) Islam, while recognizing Jesus as one of the prophets of Allah, regards itself as the perfecting of all religions. It admits that Christianity, Judaism and Islam are revealed religions, but to a Muslim, Islam is the final and most perfect of all religions. Jesus Himself is interpreted to have said that there would be another messenger after Him. "I have many things to say unto you, but cannot bear them now. How be it when he, the spirit of truth comes he will guide you in all truth" (John 16:12). The Quran revealed that prophet Mohammed is the spirit of truth about whom Jesus had foretold (Quran 61:6). The two positions actually conflict their faiths and beliefs, hence the grave differences between the religions.

(c) The Quran rejects the concept of trinity when it says: "O people of the Book, exceed not the limit in your religion, and say not of God anything but the truth. Verily, the Messiah, Jesus, son of Mary, was only a messenger and his word which he sent down to Mary and say not, "they are three…" (Quran 4: 171172).

(d) Another issue of discord between Islam and Christianity and which caused controversy even at the time of Mohammed is that of the crucifixion of Jesus as atonement for the sins of mankind. The Quran says that Jesus was neither killed nor crucified (Quran 26:45-48).

Besides the four fundamental differences between the two religions, another source of intolerance is that both religions are proselytizing – seeking new converts from the adherents of each other. The two religions are, therefore, in a continuous competition for adherents (Momoh, 9-10).

Both religions have been at loggerhead with each other for about three centuries in the medieval period in what is known as crusades. There was a bloody military contact between Islam and Christianity in the medieval period, when both met in Nigeria in the 19th century, and were unable to tolerate one another. And here, the attitude of the adherents of different faiths to the opposite faith stems from political, tribal and nationalistic rather than religious motivations. It behooves us then to look beyond the religious confines whenever there is religious conflict, be it inter or intra (Momoh, 12).

THE EFFECTS OF RELIGIOUS AND POLITICAL CRISIS IN NIGERIA

Nigeria, today, was the creation of the British Colonialists through the amalgamation of the Northern and Southern protectorates in 1914. Prior to this, Nigeria was a heterogeneous and pluralistic society with many autonomous states within the nation, existing independently, hence the multi-cultural and multi-religious nature of the country. The polarization of religion as an instrumentality for administrative convenience in Nigeria began with the colonial administrations. Regrettably, the seed planted 103years (1914-2017) ago has gradually grown into a monster that is becoming impossible to subdue. The historical root of this tragic development is traceable to constitutional regionalism and the divide-and-rule policy of the colonial administration. The policy, rather than unite the heterogeneous nation like Nigeria, promoted political and religious ideologies that encouraged ethnicity and regional biases. Political parties, political participation, appointments, employments and culprits of coups d'état were viewed and handled with ethnic, religious or political biases. Nigeria, as multi-cultural and multi-religious country, has two major religions: Christianity and Islam, each competing and claiming superiority and dominance over the other in number and in might. This claim of superiority, as well as dominance, has served as the foundation for religious intolerance and several socio-political crises that have bedeviled Nigeria since independence in 1960. Religion is not supposed to be a harbinger of violence, but paradoxically, the character of religious beliefs is in most cases puzzling and fascinating to scholars in humanities. The record of human history has shown that most noble acts of love, self-sacrificing and pious services to humanity are often associated with religion; yet, it is also evident that religion has generated more violence and killed more people than any other institutional force in human history. In the words of Lefebure;

> Many of the violent conflicts in the world today involve religious animosities. Indeed, the history of the encounters among the world's religions is filled with distrust and hatred, violence and vengeance. The deepest tragedy of the history of religions is that the very movements that should bring human beings closer to each other and to their ultimate source and goal have time and time again become forces of division. In one conflict after another around the world, religious convictions and interpretations of revelation have been used and abused as justifications for violence and war (7-8).

Olukunle, writing on "Social Uses and Abuses of Religion in Developing Countries" opines that just as Alfred Nobel invented dynamite to help miners in blasting hard rocks to ease their job, even though dynamites have been misused and abused, so is religion. According to him, religion was meant to create a unique link between God and humanity, and amnog human beings. It was to remind man of the existence of the infinite to help in regulating the relationship between men and in promoting peace. However, religion has been used and abused to promote wars, violence and hatred among humans. The argument here is that men can use good things for negative ends, if they desire. Religion is no exception. In this case, one can say that religion which is essentially good and serves a good and positive purpose has been abused by men, hence the constant conflicts, violence and war among religious groups. An inventory of the religious violence and insecurity in Nigeria for the past three or four decades leaves a lot to be desired. One wonders what the founders of these religions would say to their adherents if they were to return today and see the mayhem done in their names. Why would one use "God" to kill or maim another? Why would religion be linked with violence and terrorism? Could it be ignorance on the part of their adherents or lack of hermeneutical understanding of the Holy Books? In an attempt to answer some of these questions, some scholars have alluded to ignorance, prejudice and stereotyping as major factors behind most of the religious violence we experience today in Nigeria. It is on this note that Okon calls for sensitivity in dealing with religious issues when he said:

> In analyzing religious practices, we must be sensitive to ideals that inspire profound conviction in believers, yet at the same time take a balance view of them. We must confront ideas that seek eternal, while recognizing that religious groups also promote quite mundane goals such as acquiring money or followers. We need to recognize the diversity of religious beliefs and modes of conduct, but also probe into the nature of religion as a general phenomenon (2).

Religion, from the beginning, has played a very important role in shaping the socio-political thoughts of many nations. In fact, most nations of the world were patterned and influenced by the sacred nature of government. Religion supported and regulated the loyalty that existed between the state and the people. The idea of divine right of kings, which derived its origin from the theocratic concept of governance, vested absolute power and authority in the king or monarch who was seen as a direct representative of God. The monarch was superior and answerable only to God. Ancient history is replete with examples of this idea. For example, in Christianity, the Pope was seen for centuries as the Vicar of Christ on earth, and by virtue of his divine right had the ultimate authority over the Church, and indirectly over the state. Islam, on the other hand, believed in the concept of divine right of Caliphs (direct descendants and successors of Prophet Muhammad) as the supreme leaders of the Muslim community. Under Muhammad, the Muslim state was theocratic, with Shari 'a as the religious and moral principles of Islam, and the law of the land. The Caliphs were seen as secular and religious leaders. They were not empowered to promulgate dogma, because it was believed that the revelation of the faith had been completed by Muhammad (Dallai, Encarta).

However, as representatives of Allah and direct successors of Muhammad, Caliphs were to enforce Shari 'a as the religious and moral principles of the land. Their powers were not limited to secular issues only but divine, since they were representing Allah. It was on this note that Muhammad advocated that the Muslim community should choose a successor or a Caliph by consensus to lead the theocratic process of leadership to exemplify the earthly kingdom under divine rule. It is also on this note that Islamic states seek to apply in every detail the Islamic laws in any society they find themselves in order to create an Islamic culture, as evident throughout the Middle East. Africans were not left behind in this concept of divine right. In a typical African society, the rulers were also seen as gods or agents of the gods. Traditionally, they were believed to have possessed both divine and secular powers to do and undo as the gods please. They were traditional priests, custodians and Supreme judges in all traditional matters. In African cosmology, there is no clear distinction between the material and the spiritual things. Religion embraces the totality of human endeavours. The social, economic, political and spiritual lives of the people are all embodied in one holistic life. Man, though mortal, can only have meaning in its social order through divine legislation. It is religion that translates our socio-cultural or socio-political order into reality (IOSR Journal of Humanities and Social Science, 66).

According to Okon, religion sacralizes the socio-political values to give it a divine sanction or meaning (33). It is these religious beliefs that bind the people together, regulate their lifestyle, and give meaning to their values, whether social or political. Again, it is this mental picture of African worldview that enables Africans to understand, express, communicate and govern themselves.

Today, even though democracy has replaced the idea of divine right, religion still plays a major role in the socio-political affairs of most nations of the world. In Nigeria, for example, the introduction of democracy as a form of government did not go well with the Northern Muslims because of its attachment to Western civilization. The influence of Western education was speedily penetrating the fabric of some Islamic values and system that did not go well with some Islamic clerics. To counter this, some Islamic sects began to emerge with the aim of reforming their state along the Islamic laws, promoting Islamic education. Their objective was to prevent Western secularization through education. In the article titled "What Accounts for the Rise of Islam," Kofi Johnson states that a case Study of Nigeria and Senegal (IOSR Journal for Humanities and Social Science, 66-67), between the 70s and 80s, many Muslims became frustrated as a result of pressures coming from the secularized world. Many sought to reject the waves of Western cultural imperialism and return to their Islamic roots. The situation became exacerbated due to constant confrontations between the West and the Arab world over the issues of Palestine and Arab nationalism. These crises reached their crescendo with the Iranian revolution in 1979 (1).

The resultant effects of religious conflicts in Nigeria are enormous. They pervade all the sectors of the economy. Generally, conflicts breed insecurity, discrimination, mutual distrust and slow economic and educational development. This is the case in Nigeria where in addition to the gratuitous killings and maiming of thousands of persons, properties worth billions of naira have been destroyed. Certainly, these huge losses have deprived the nation of needed manpower and services for the growth of its wobbling economy. Religious conflicts in Nigeria have also left their effect on investment options in the crises-ridden areas. The political instability, arising from the insecurity and uncertainty that pervades the region, does not inspire the confidence of foreign investors and thereby deprives the nation of the economic gains. In some instances, the enterprising Southerners who had established thriving businesses in the troubled areas in the North have relocated to other and safer places. Further, religious conflicts in Nigeria have left in their trail a broken society: communities that hitherto co-existed peacefully now treat each other with mistrust and latent or open aggression. Consequently, settlement patterns begin to follow the boundaries of religion in these areas so that adherents can be swiftly mobilized in the event of future riots. The disrupted social harmony is sometimes felt in places far from the crisis scene and thus accounts for the reprisal riots in other parts of Nigeria (Nwaomah, 101-102).

IKECHUKWU ANTHONY KANU

IGWEBUIKE ONTOLOGY VIS-A-VIS THE ISSUES OF RELIGIO-POLITICAL CRISIS IN NIGERIA

Igwebuike philosophy as an ideology encourages solidarity, mutual complementarity, peaceful coexistence, unity, progress and the pursuit of common good. Likewise, it discourages and stands against vices and activities like war or crisis, killing, mutual distrust, unhealthy competition and rivalry. It points to the fact that there is no human being or group of humans that are self-subsistent or independent. Rather, every human necessarily needs the other's complement. *Igwebuike* philosophy argues that when human beings come together in solidarity and complementarity, they are powerful and can constitute an insurmountable force, and more so, to express their world of relationship, harmony, continuality and complementarity. At this level, no task is beyond collective capability (Kanu *"Igwebuike* and the Unity..." web). Thus, while Christians regard religion as a personal faith and view the Church's involvement in or use of political activism as a serious aberration, Muslims reject any attempt to relegate religion to private sphere, viewing it as a violation of Islam principle. For Muslims, Islam is a complete way of life, and there can be no separation between private and public, spiritual and temporal, religion and politics. For this reason, they make every effort, whether through peace or violence, to lay claim of the public space from which Christians tend to retreat. Hence, the slow non-partisanship of Christians in socio-political activism compared to their Muslim counterparts.

Amid the multiplicity of religious practices in Nigeria, there is a possibility of having a nation peacefully coexisting, so long as there is a mutual understanding among religions, and also drawing the line that demarcates religion from politics; that is, certain qualities and goals ought to be the basis of the political system, and not introducing the idea of religion. The appointing or electing of a president, governor, minister or whatsoever political post as the case may be should be done with no attention to religious belief or practice of the candidate, so long as the candidate in question is to come into power and face squarely his political ambition and not lording his/her belief on the nation. And on this note the *Igwebuike* ontology can be adopted in the politics of the nation, a philosophical thought that is devoid of religious or cultural sentiment, but rather upholds complementarity and peaceful coexistence. Be a candidate from the eastern, northern, southern or western part of Nigeria, it does not matter, but that the candidate proposes a vision to be actualized for the common good of the nation.

National political development is about the ability of a nation to improve the lives of its citizens through various measures of improvement, with no emphasis on the religious background of the citizens. From the *Igwebuike* perspective, this ability to improve the lives of citizens must be comprehensive, all-round and balanced. It includes all aspects of the life of an individual and the nation. It is, therefore, holistic in approach, as it aims at full-growth and expansion of our industries, agriculture, education, social, religious and cultural institutions.

Furthermore, captured in the Journal of Moral Education in Africa, Volume 2, Kanu states, in his work on *Igwebuike as an Igbo-African Philosophy for Christian-Muslim Relations in Northern Nigeria,* that;

Religion is a unique phenomenon in the Nigerian society. Although it is one of the few factors that has succeeded in bringing together a good number of Nigerians under one umbrella, irrespective of ethnic considerations, Christianity and Islam in Nigeria have been associated with conflicts and violence which has dealt a terrible blow on the nation's unity and brought untold hardships on the people. Religion has been politicized, manipulated and militarized by unscrupulous people to fan the embers of rivalry, antagonism and ethnic discrimination. One lesson that is evident in the incessant quarrel between Christians and Muslims in Nigeria is that both religions have come to stay. Although both religions have misunderstood themselves by dwelling more on their differences, there is the need for dialogue, which does not deny the significant differences between the two religions. So much energy has been dissipated on violence instead of using it for solving the problems of human suffering and other socio-economic and political challenges that face us in the eye. After several years of interventions, *Igwebuike* is proposed in this work as an indigenous philosophy to help the adherents of both religions to focus on the things that unite them, that is, the importance of dialogue to our common existence. *Igwebuike* is a model that is built on the traditional categories of the Nigerian-African. It refocuses attention on the fact that Muslims and Christians in Nigeria have so many things in common as believers and as human beings: the adherents of both religions live in the same world, in the same Nigeria beset by the same socio-economic and political problems. To fight one another is to engage in a futile enterprise and more so, worsen their conditions. Both religions constitute parts of the intricate web of reality and relationships in the ontological order. Their differences are for complementarity and not conflict (40).

Igwebuike, undoubtedly, has its anchor firmly holding the principle of solidarity and complementarity; thus, to be in existence is to live in utmost solidarity and complementarity, as it does paint the ideal picture of man living in relation and in loving harmony with his neighbour. In other words, living outside this circumference of solidarity and mutual love and complementarity is to suffer alienation, as 'to be' is to be in communion with the other in a community of being. That one is a Christian and the other a Muslim or Traditionalist should not be the basis of existence, rather, the unity in their diversity of brotherhood is to be fostered as it ought to, with no prejudice, segregation, marginalization and sentiment.

RECOMMENDATIONS

Having been exposed to the issues of religio-political crisis in Nigeria and the menace the nation is facing, it is thoughtful to give away negative energies by doing away with political and religious sentiments, biases and extremism, and as such embrace the ideals of politics and religion to foster complementarity, as posited in *Igwebuike* ontology; and to this, the writer recommends that for a more peaceful Nigeria, the following should be employed:

i.   Freedom to practice any religion, so long as it does not infringe on the fundamental human right of another;
ii. There should be a line that delineates politics and religion, that is, non-politicization of religion.
iii. Candidates for political positions should promote peace and harmony.
iv. Religious or ethnic background should not be a basis for politics.
v.   Every candidate should be known for competence and delivery.
vi. A sense of self-governance, peace and unity should be inculcated in every citizen from an early stage.
vii. Political appointments should be devoid of ethnicity or religion but on accountability and qualification.
viii. Exercising of political franchise should be free and fair.

SUMMARY AND CONCLUSION

This research work has looked into the menace of religion and politics in Nigeria and the woes facing the Nigeria political system. In Nigeria, the improper placement and practice of religion have indeed infringed the ideal of politics, thereby disorganizing the nation's politics and also to a large extent has become an avenue for hate, mistrust and marginalization amongst the Nigerian people. This also has led to insecurity, loss of life and property, crashing of the national economy and ethnic and religious clashes. The issues of religio-political crisis has sent scores to their graves, displaced several people from their political and social position, subjecting many to inhuman conditions.

Several reasons are said to have been the cause of the crisis in Nigeria, amongst this causes include: political and power tussle, tribalism, religious extremism and ethnic factor, amidst other causes. Nonetheless, the idea is to lay a pedestal that would hold and promote national peace and brotherhood. Thus, Igwe*buike* philosophy, as an ideology, promotes solidarity and mutual complementarity and is placed side by side with the issues of religio-political crisis. It beckons on the Nigerian people to embrace national unity to foster a healthy political system and religious harmony.

Igwebuike philosophy evidently puts to all that no nation can progress in the absence of peace. It is impossible that a nation experiences growth, progress and development amid prejudice and bias; that is, in uniting, every hand must be on deck, each contributing his quota in commitment and love, and gradually the progress would play out. Living for one another beckons on everyone to embrace the I-Thou relation, upholding that which unifies each person, rather than that that which differs amongst us.

A nation that lacks religion is bound to lack conscience, compassion and progress. Thus, there is need to support unreservedly the free practice of religion in Nigeria, be it Christianity, Islam or African Traditional Religion. No religion in Nigeria should be ranked superior or subordinate to the other, and none should be state-sanctioned or enforced. Notwithstanding, we must be willing to do away with the fuss caused by religion and politics and making religion a tool of our national partisan politics because of the intricacies involved, but uphold humanity amidst complementarity and solidarity.

WORKS CITED

Gabriel Tumba. *The Philosopher and Society: A Portrait of Professor Kanu Ikechukwu Anthony, O.S.A.* Amamihe Journal of Applied Philosophy Vol. 14 No. 1, 2016.

Iroegbu Pantaleon. *Metaphysics: The Kpim of Philosophy.* Owerri: International Universities Press, 1995.

Kanu I. A. *A Hermeneutic Approach to African Traditional Religion, Theology and Philosophy.* Jos: Augustinian Publications, 2015.

Kanu I. A. "Igwebuike and African Ethics." *Igwebuikepedia Internet Encyclopedia of African Philosophy.*(Eds.) Kanu Anthony and Jerome Okonkwo. Augustinian Institute. Igwebuikepedia.Web. Accessed Jan., 2020.

Kanu I. A. "Igwebuike and the Unity of African Philosophy." *Igwebuikepedia Internet Encyclopedia of African Philosophy.*(Eds.)Kanu Anthony and Jerome Okonkwo. Augustinian Institute. Igwebuikepedia.Web. Accessed 16 Jan., 2020.

Kanu I. A. "Igwebuike as an Igbo-African Philosophy for Christian-Muslim Relations in Northern Nigeria." *Igwebuike: An African Journal of Arts and Humanities* vol.2 No.2. 24488-9210, June 2016.

Kanu I. A. "Igwebuike, Personal Identity and Alterity." *IgwebuikepediaInternet Encyclopedia of African Philosophy.* Kanu Anthony and Jerome Okonkwo (Editors). Augustinian Institute.Igwebuikepedia.Web. Accessed 17th Jan., 2020.

Kanu I. A. "Igwebuikology as an Igbo-African Philosophy for Catholic-Pentecostal Relations." *Jos Studies* vol.22. 978-2023-36-1, 2014.

Kanu, I. A. (2017). *Igwebuike* as an Igbo-African philosophy for the protection of the environment. *Nightingale International Journal of Humanities and Social Sciences.* Vol. 3. No. 4. pp. 28-38.

Kanu, I. A. (2017). *Igwebuike* as the hermeneutic of individuality and communality in African ontology. *NAJOP: Nasara Journal of Philosophy.* Vol. 2. No. 1. pp. 162-179.

Kanu, I. A. (2017a). *Igwebuike* and question of superiority in the scientific community of knowledge. *Igwebuike: An African Journal of Arts and Humanities.* Vol.3 No1. pp. 131-138.

Kanu, I. A. (2017a). *Igwebuike as a philosophical attribute of Africa in portraying the image of life.* A paper presented at the 2017 Oracle of Wisdom International Conference by the Department of Philosophy, Tansian University, Umunya, Anambra State, 27-29 April.

Kanu, I. A. (2017b). *Igwebuike* as a complementary approach to the issue of girl-child education. *Nightingale International Journal of Contemporary Education and Research.* Vol. 3. No. 6. pp. 11-17.

Kanu, I. A. (2017b). *Igwebuike* as a wholistic response to the problem of evil and human suffering. *Igwebuike: An African Journal of Arts and Humanities.* Vol. 3 No 2, March.

Kanu, I. A. (2017e). *Igwebuike* as an Igbo-African modality of peace and conflict resolution. *Journal of African Traditional Religion and Philosophy Scholars. Vol. 1. No. 1. pp. 31-40.*

Kanu, I. A. (2017g). *Igwebuike* and the logic (Nka) of African philosophy. *Igwebuike: An African Journal of Arts and Humanities.* 3. 1. pp. 1-13.

Kanu, I. A. (2017h). *Igwebuike* philosophy and human rights violation in Africa. *IGWEBUIKE: An African Journal of Arts and Humanities.* Vol. 3. No. 7. pp. 117-136.

Kanu, I. A. (2017i). *Igwebuike* as a hermeneutic of personal autonomy in African ontology. *Journal of African Traditional Religion and Philosophy Scholars. Vol. 2. No. 1. pp. 14-22.*

Kanu I. A. "Igwebuike as an Igbo-African Ethic of Reciprocity." An African Journal of Arts and Humanities Vol. 3 No 2, March 2017.

Lawhead F. William. *The Voyage of Discovery: A Historical Introduction to Philosophy.* USA: Wadsworth/Thomson Learning. 2002.

Luther M. King Jr. *Strength to Love.* Benin City: Religious Broadcasting, 2013.

Mbiti J.S. *African Religions and Philosophy.* London: Heinemann, 1969.

THE INTER-PERSONALIST IDEOLOGY OF IGWEBUIKE AND THE WORKINGS OF NEURONS: AN INTERPERSONALITIC-NEUROSCIENTIFIC INQUIRY

Dozie Iwuh, OSA
Department of Philosophy
Augustinian Institute Makurdi
Benue State
registered501@gmail.com

ABSTRACT

The human brain research has always been an interesting field of study, understanding how it coordinates itself, receiving and giving out information, encoding, decoding and even encrypting signs. It is a delicate organ in the human body, whose work is so important that if compromised, the human person will be considered as lacking in that quality that makes him human, namely his rational consciousness. In contemporary times, brain research and study has been termed as neuroscience (having many subfields under it, namely, neurophilosophy, molecular neuroscience, cognitive, behavioral, computational neuroscience, etc. Neuroscience studies the nervous system, combining fields, such a physiology, anatomy, molecular biology, developmental biology, cytology, mathematical modeling, computer science, genetics, medicine, philosophy and psychology, to give credence to its study of neurons and the neural circuits). The importance of the human brain stems from the reality of what specifically defines the human, namely, his rationality. I had earlier termed this as a rational consciousness. This is because the human being is rational and is conscious of the fact that he is rational. More to this, he is conscious and is conscious of the fact that he is conscious. This is principally what separates us from the genus of the animal. There is a certain kind of consciousness that resides in brutes, and indeed every living creature, that is non-animal like. For instance, some plants, like the Humulus Lupulus, have a tendency to move when touched, a phenomena that is known as thigmotropism. Other plants, like the Venus Flytrap, are conscious whenever an insect wanders into their wide open jaws. They thus close up and ingest the insect. Such instances we may term as a response to stimulus, anchored by Mother Nature, but such response is yet reminiscent of a sort of consciousness. In all that has been said, the human consciousness is by far the most intriguing. What makes this so? A study into the brain and how consciousness arises from the working of the brain has revealed that there are small molecular cells at work in the brain, known as neurons. It is being speculated (this implies that it has not been holistically accepted in the entirety) in some neuroscientific quarters that it is these neurons that are the chief source of the consciousness in man. That is to say that these cells are the ones behind man's conscious awareness. Since the dawn of the discovery of the neurons in the late 1800s, the investigation into the brain has skyrocketed and more insights into the workings and modalities of operation of the brain have been unveiled. The workings of neurons have proven to be insightful and broken grounds in the medical/scientific/philosophical field. Nonetheless, what lesson can be garnered by the workings of the neurons in the light of the interpersonalism that is the heart of the Igwebuike philosophy? The Igwebuike philosophy portrays the sense of an interpersonalistic rapport between individuals. Having its root in the Igbo culture of south-eastern Nigeria, this ideology carries with it two vital principles, namely: solidarity and complementarity. Yet, can this ideology be understood further by looking at how the neurons in the brain work, complementing each other? Can the solidarity of the neurons and its network, leading to a well orchestrated brain operation and indeed a very well organized human functioning, be used to throw some light on how this solidarity, as espoused by Igwebuike, can lead to better interpersonal affinity and empathy, thus resulting in a better understanding of one another? We do not seek to consider a certain neuroscientific field; we aim at showing how effective Igwebuike is, not only to the Igbo society, but to the world at large, via looking at the workings of the neurons of the brain.

Keywords: Neurons, Neuroscience, Solidarity, Complementarity, Igwebuike, Brain, Interpersonalism.

NEURONS AND THEIR FUNCTIONING

This is a late nineteenth century Greek term which refers to highly specialized "nerve cells". A neuron exhibits a highly complex repertoire of specialized membranous structures, embedded ion channels, second messengers, genetic and epigenetic elements and unique complements of various proteins such as the receptors. Neurons are excitable cells (i.e., able to conduct electrical impulses of action potentials), which form elaborate networks through axons and dendrites. This ensemble is responsible for integrating, processing and transmitting information, and forms the basis for e.g., coordinated muscle movements and brain functions, including learning and memory formation.[147] Neurons have four morphologically defined regions: the cell body, dendrites, axon, and presynaptic terminals. A bipolar *neuron* receives signals from the dendritic system; these signals are integrated at a specific location in the cell body and then sent out by means of the axon to the presynaptic terminals. There are neurons which have more than one set of dendritic systems, or more than one axon, thus enabling them to perform simultaneously multiple tasks; they are called *multipolar neurons*.[148] A neuron is

---

[147] M. D. Binder, N. Hirokawa, U. Windhorst (Eds.), *Encyclopedia of Neuroscience*, Springer-Verlag GmbH, Berlin Heidelberg, Germany, 2009, 2751.

[148] A. Borisyuk et al, eds., *Tutorials in Mathematical Biosciences I. Mathematical Neuroscience*, Springer-Verlag Berlin Heidelberg, Germany 2005, 1. Neurons may be classified into

an electrically excitable cell that processes and transmits information by electro-chemical signalling. Unlike other cells, neurons never divide, nor do they die off to be replaced by new ones. By the same token, they usually cannot be replaced after being lost, although there are a few exceptions. The average human brain has about 100 billion neurons (or nerve cells) and many more neuroglia which serve to support and protect the neurons.[149] Each neuron may be connected to up to 10,000 other neurons, passing signals to one another via as many as 1,000 trillion synaptic connections, equivalent by some estimates to a computer with a 1 trillion bit per second processor. Estimates of the human brain's memory capacity vary wildly from 1 to 1,000 terabytes. Information transmission within the brain, such as takes place during the processes of memory encoding and retrieval, is achieved using a combination of chemicals and electricity.[150] The neuron, as seen in Fig 1.1, is made up of a cell body called the soma, branched projections called dendrites and an axon, which is the long, slim nerve fibre that transmits information to muscles, glands and other neurons. Signals are received at the dendrite, processed in the nucleus of the soma and transmitted away from the soma along the axon.

Bipolar: similar to retinal cells, two processes extend from the body of bipolar neurons.

Unipolar: there are two dorsal root ganglion axons for each unipolar cell. One axon stretches out in the direction of the spinal cord and the other in the direction of the skin or muscles.

Multipolar: these neurons contain many processes that branch out from the cell body. However, here the neurons each only have one axon (e.g. spinal motor neurons).

Pseudo-unipolar neurons, a variant of bipolar neurons that sense pressure, touch and pain, have no true dendrites. Instead, a single axon emerges from the cell body and heads in two opposite directions, one end heading for the skin, joints and muscle and the other end traveling to the spinal cord.

Anaxonic: An anaxonic neuron is a neuron where the axon cannot be differentiated from the dendrites. Some sources mention that such neurons have no axons and only dendrites. They are found in the brain and retina, which act as non-spiking interneurons.

Pseudounipolar: A pseudounipolar neuron is a kind of sensory neuron in the peripheral nervous system. This neuron contains an axon that has split into two branches. These neurons have sensory receptors on skin, joints, muscles, and other parts of the body. The area of the axon that is closest to the receptor is the trigger zone for the neuron. The signal is conducted through the axon to the dorsal root ganglion's cell body, then through the axon and ending at the sensory nuclei in the dorsal column-medial lemniscus pathway of the spinal cord.

Another very basic method for the classification of neurons is by identifying which way they transmit information:

Efferent neurons (motor neurons): these direct information away from the brain towards muscles and glands.

Afferent neurons (sensory neurons): these transmit information to the central nervous system from sensory receptors.

Interneurons: found in the central nervous system, these pass information between motor neurons and sensory neurons.

[149] 90% of the brain cells are glial cells, which primarily protect brain by absorbing possible chemicals which might endanger the body's operations. These specified cells are a key component of the nervous system as they represent the vehicles that carry the messages from one part of the body to the other.

[150] J. Zhang, *Basic Neural Units of the Brain: Neurons, Synapses and Action Potential*, in IFM LAB TUTORIAL SERIES No. 5, 2019, https://arxiv.org/pdf/1906.01703.pdf, 1-38.

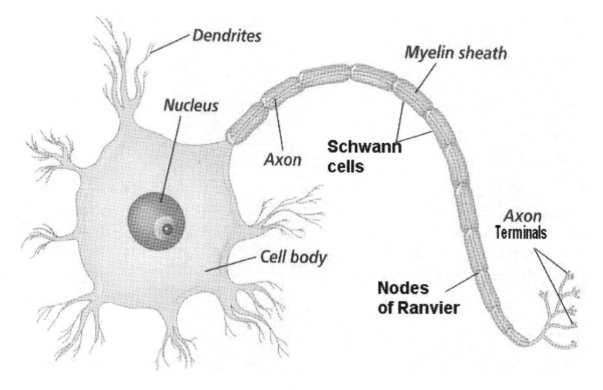

Fig 1.1

Parts of a Neuron include:

1. Soma: The soma is the body of the neuron. As it contains the nucleus, most protein synthesis occurs here. The nucleus can range from 3 to 18 micrometers in diameter.

2. Dendrites: The dendrites of a neuron are cellular extensions with many branches. This overall shape and structure is referred to metaphorically as a dendritic tree. This is where the majority of input to the neuron occurs via the dendritic spine.

3. Axon: The axon is a finer, cable-like projection that can extend tens, hundreds, or even tens of thousands of times the diameter of the soma in length. The axon primarily carries nerve signals away from the soma, and carries some types of information back to it. Many neurons have only one axon, but this axon may - and usually will -undergo extensive branching, enabling communication with many target cells.

4. Axon Hillock: The part of the axon where it emerges from the soma is called the axon hillock. Besides being an anatomical structure, the axon hillock also has the greatest density of voltage-dependent sodium channels. This makes it the most easily excited part of the neuron and the spike initiation zone for the axon. In electrophysiological terms, it has the most negative threshold potential. While the axon and axon hillock are generally involved in information outow, this region can also receive input from other neurons.

5. Myelin: Myelin is a lipid-rich substance formed in the central nervous system by neuroglia called oligodendrocytes, and in the peripheral nervous system by Schwann

cells. Myelin insulates nerve cell axons to increase the speed at which information travels from one nerve cell body to another or, for example, from a nerve cell body to a muscle. The myelinated axon can be likened to an electrical wire with insulating material (myelin) around it.

6. Node of Ranvier: Unlike the plastic covering on an electrical wire, myelin does not form a single long sheath over the entire length of the axon. Rather, each myelin sheath insulates the axon over a single section and, in general, each axon comprises multiple long myelinated sections separated from each other by short gaps called Nodes of Ranvier.

7. Axon Terminal: The axon terminal is found at the end of the axon farthest from the soma and contains synapses. Synaptic boutons are specialized structures where neurotransmitter chemicals are released to communicate with target neurons.[151]

Every neuron maintains a voltage gradient across its membrane, due to metabolicallydriven differences in ions of sodium, potassium, chloride and calcium within the cell, each of which has a different charge. If the voltage changes significantly, an electrochemical pulse called an action potential (or nerve impulse) is generated. This electrical activity can be measured and displayed as a wave form called brain wave or brain rhythm. This pulse travels rapidly along the cell's axon, and is transferred across a specialized connection known as a synapse to a neighboring neuron, which receives it through its feathery dendrites. A synapse is a complex membrane junction or gap (the actual gap, also known as the synaptic cleft, is of the order of 20 nanometres, or 20 millionths of a millimetre) used to transmit signals between cells, and this transfer is, therefore, known as a synaptic connection. Although axon-dendrite synaptic connections are the norm, other variations (e.g. dendrite-dendrite, axon-axon, dendrite-axon) are also possible. A typical neuron fires 5 - 50 times every second.[152] Each individual neuron can form thousands of links with other neurons in this way, giving a typical brain well over 100 trillion synapses (up to 1,000 trillion, by some estimates). Functionally related neurons connect to each other to form neural networks (also known as neural nets or assemblies). The connections between neurons are not static, though, they change over time. The more signals sent between two neurons, the stronger the connection grows (technically, the amplitude of the post-synaptic neuron's response increases), and so, with each new experience and each remembered event or fact, the brain slightly re-wires its physical structure.[153]

HOW NEURONS COMMUNICATE WITH ONE ANOTHER

From the foregoing, we have learnt that neurons are connected to one another through synapses, and these are sites where signals (electric) are transmitted in the form of chemical messengers. Each neuron in the body is *interlinked* to another and is capable of carrying

---

[151] Ibid

[152] Ibid

[153] Ibid

varied complex computations. According to R. Jahn, "each neuron has an antenna zone comprising the cell body and its extensions (dendrites). It is here that it receives signals from other neurons".[154] This is the place that communication occurs. The signals are then computed and forwarded by a cable, "the axon, in the form of electrical impulses. In the emitter region, the axon branches to form contact sites known as synapses, where the signals are transmitted to other neurons. At the synapse, electrical impulses arriving from the axon are converted into chemical signals. The information then flows in one direction,[155] that is to say that one cell (neuron) talks, and another listens. In the communication of neurons, the dendrites of the first neuron receive information from, for instance, a sensory receptor on the finger detecting pain from a hot object. The message, in the electrochemical form, is transmitted up to the brain by a chain of neurons to be assessed by the many neurons in the brain. Then this information is carried to the dendrites of the first neuron, then to its body and nucleus where the information is interpreted. Next, the message is passed on by charges in the neuron onto the axon which is at *resting potential,*[156] but soon its charge is altered by positive and negative ions to bring it to an *action potential* state.[157] When this electrical signal reaches the end of the axon, a neurotransmitter[158] is deployed, and this restarts the process (this communication by neurons is one way and this transfer of messages can be visualized by Fig 1.2).[159] What is being said here is that neurons communicate to one another, by making use of special chemical, known as neurotransmitters. Neurotransmitters are the one that send messages from one neuron to another.[160] Each neurotransmitter binds only to its specific receptor, just as a key fits

---

[154] R. Jahn, *How Neurons Talk to Each Other,* in Neuroscience News, 24th September, 2016, https://neurosciencenews.com/neurons-synapses-neuroscience-5119/ Retrieved 7th May, 2020.

[155] Ibid.

[156] Resting potential is the membrane potential (electric charge) in a neuron that is not currently transmitting a signal.

[157] Action Potential is a brief depolarization (reduction in the magnitude of the charge) along the neuron's axon: action potentials are all-or-nothing (they do not have degrees of magnitude). The starting state is called resting potential which is when the cell is negatively charged inside and positively charged outside. This balance is altered by elements that move through the membrane such as: Sodium (NA^+), Potassium (K^+), Calcium (Ca^{2+}) and Chlorine (Cl^-).When the chemical distribution is changed, such as when Sodium moves into the axon as NA^+ channels open - making it positively charged inside the axon - it is called the action potential. When this occurs, the neurotransmitter is released. During this whole process the electrochemical signals are transmitted between neurons via junctions called synapses and these are located and the end of the axon terminal and before the dendrites of the subsequent neuron. However, once a neuron has fired the impulse to the next neuron, it cannot fire again for a 1000th of a second - this is called the absolute refractory period. However, if a neuron obtains a stimulus much stronger than its usual threshold then it can fire again and this is referred to as the relative refractory period. (V. Whiteley, *Describe the structure of the nervous system. How do neurons communicate*)

[158] These are chemical messengers that communicate between adjacent neurons; release of neurotransmitters from one neuron will either help depolarize ir hyperpolarize (increase the magnitude of the charge) the adjacent neuron, making an action potential either more or less likely to occur in the next neuron.

[159] V. Whiteley, *Describe the structure of the nervous system. How do neurons communicate,* in the Research Gate Online Journal, https://www.researchgate.net/publication/301888628, Retrieved 7th May, 2020.

[160] M. Ludwig, *How Your Brain Cells Talk to Each Other* in Frontiers for Young Minds, 5:39, 26th July, 2017, https://kids.frontiersin.org/article/10.3389/frym.2017.00039, Retrieved 7th May, 2020.

only a particular lock (fig 1.3).[161] Depending on the neurotransmitter, it either excites the other neuron or inhibits (that is to say that neurotransmitters are either excitatory or inhibitory), making it either more likely or less likely to fire an action potential of its own.[162] It should be noted that all these happen with very high precision and are repeated again and again, at very fast speed, going up to 100m/s. This kind of communication between neurons is called wired communication.[163]

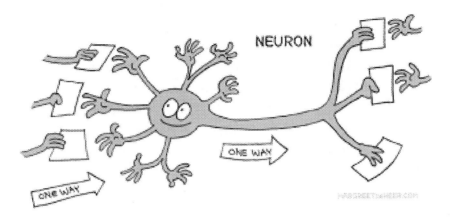

Fig 1.2

According to Gazzaniga et al

> Neurons receive, evaluate, and transmit information. These processes are referred to as *neuronal signaling*. Information that is received by the neuron at its input synapses passes through the cell body and then, via the axon, to output synapses on the axon terminals. At these output synapses, information

---

[161] A neurotransmitter is *a chemical that relays signals across the synapses between neurons*. Neurotransmitters travel across the synaptic space between the terminal button of one neuron and the dendrites of other neurons, where they bind to the dendrites in the neighbouring neurons. Furthermore, different terminal buttons release different neurotransmitters, and different dendrites are particularly sensitive to different neurotransmitters. The dendrites will admit the neurotransmitters only if they are the right shape to fit in the receptor sites on the receiving neuron. (J. Walinga-C. Stangor, Introduction to Psychology 1st Canadian Edition, BCCampus Vicotria B.C., Canada, 2014, 129-131, Retrieved from https://opentextbc.ca/introductiontopsychology/)

[162] Talking about neurotransmitters, they appear in two main forms: excitatory or inhibitory. An example of an excitatory neurotransmitter is **Nitric Oxide**, which induces the excitatory postsynaptic potential which makes the impulse continue to be transmitted along the neurons. An inhibitory neurotransmitter could be serotonin and this works in the reverse way to induce an inhibitory postsynaptic potential which will stop the transmission of the impulse and hence end the communication between neurons. (V. Whiteley, *Describe the structure of the nervous system. How do neurons communicate*). An excitatory transmitter promotes the generation of an electrical signal called an action potential in the receiving neuron, while an inhibitory transmitter prevents it. Whether a neurotransmitter is excitatory or inhibitory depends on the receptor it binds to.

[163] Ibid.

is transferred across synapses from one neuron to the next neuron; or to non-neuronal cells such as those in muscles or glands; or to other targets, such as blood vessels. Within a neuron, information moves from input synapses to output synapses through changes in the electrical state of the neuron caused by the flow of electrical currents within the neuron and across its neuronal membrane. Between neurons, information transfer across synapses is typically mediated chemically by neurotransmitters (signaling molecules); these synapses are called chemical synapses. At electrical synapses, however, signals between neurons travel via transsynaptic electrical currents. Regarding information flow, neurons are referred to as either presynaptic or postsynaptic in relation to any particular synapse. *Most neurons are both presynaptic and postsynaptic:* They are presynaptic when their axon's output synapses make connections onto other neurons or targets, and they are postsynaptic when other neurons make a connection at input synapses onto their dendrites or elsewhere on the receiving neuron.[164]

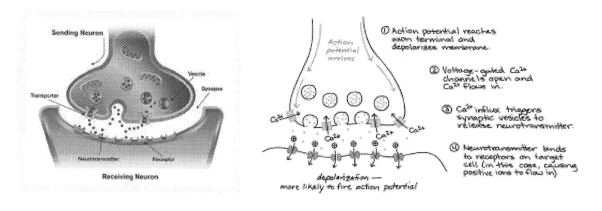

Fig 1.3

IN SUM:

What should be noted here is that the nervous system works using an electrochemical process: which is that the electrical charge moves through the neuron, and it is the chemicals that are employed to transmit the information between the neurons. It is by means of the chemicals that these electric current is transmitted from one neuron to another, however, within the neuron, it is the electric current that moves. This implies that the electric current is the message that is being communicated, but the chemicals are there to ensure that such message is transmitted from one neuron to another. These chemicals are aroused when the electric signals reach the terminal buttons. These chemicals are referred to as neurotransmitters which occasion a communication of these electric current between neurons spaced out by synapses. The electric

---

[164] M.S. Gazzaniga, R.B. Ivry, G.R. Mangun, *Cognitive Neuroscience. The Biology of the Mind,* W. W. Norton & Company, New York, 2019, 28.

current moving through the neuron is due to changes in the electrical charge of the axon. The axon would normally remain in its resting potential (where the interior of the neuron contains a greater number of negative charged ions than its exterior. This further means that at its ground state, the neuron is negatively charged. It only becomes positively charged, when there is a message being transmitted through it). When the segment of the axon that is closest to the cell body is stimulated by the electrical signals from the dendrites and if this electric signal is strong enough that it passes a certain level or threshold, the cell membrane in this first segment opens its gates, allowing positively charged sodium ions (Na^+) that resided in the outside to flow inside. This change that occurs in the neuron when a nerve impulse (a message) is transmitted is known as the Action Potential (once this action potential occurs, the internals of the neuron becomes more positively charged than the exteriors, because the number of positively charged ions exceeds that of the negative ions. As the message passes one section of the axon, the positive charge drops, and that segment of the axon returns back to its high number of negative charged ions, also known as the resting potential. It should be noted that this message that is transmitted in each segment of the axon moves in a set of small jumps.[165] The movement of this message is done in an all or nothing manner, that is to say that either the neuron fires completely or it does not fire at all. For the neuron to fire completely, it has to move fast, very fast. The speed of the message is what prioritizes the message and not its strength. As the message passes from one neuron to another repeatedly, the mode of communication between the two is strengthened, such that if a message is relayed again, the synaptic gap separating the two neurons becomes more acquainted with one another, that the message is easily passed on from the two "friendly" neurons (this is the means by which people form habits or become addicts). That is to say that communication becomes more fluid and less hectic between the acquainted neurons.

IGWEBUIKE AS AN INTERPERSONALISTIC PHILOSOPHY

Before we venture into the interpersonalistic philosophy of *Igwebuike*[166], we better separate the two words, inter- and personalism. Let us start off with the latter, personalism. It derives from the Latin word, 'Persona', which means person or personality. It is a trend in philosophy which acknowledges the person as the prime creative reality, having the highest spiritual

---

[165] J. Walinga-C. Stangor, Introduction to Psychology 1st Canadian Edition, BCCampus Vicotria B.C., Canada, 2014, 129-131, Retrieved from https://opentextbc.ca/introductiontopsychology/

[166] Kanu, I. A. (2019). *Igwebuikeconomics*: The Igbo apprenticeship for wealth creation. *IGWEBUIKE: An African Journal of Arts and Humanities* (IAAJAH). *5. 4.* pp. *56-70.* Kanu, I. A. (2019). *Igwebuikecracy*: The Igbo-African participatory cocio-political system of governance. *TOLLE LEGE: An Augustinian Journal of the Philosophy and Theology. 1. 1.* pp. 34-45. Kanu, I. A. (2019). On the origin and principles of *Igwebuike* philosophy. *International Journal of Religion and Human Relations.* Vol. 11. No. 1. pp. 159-176. Kanu, I. A. (2019b). An *Igwebuike* approach to the study of African traditional naming ceremony and baptism. *International Journal of Religion and Human Relations.* Vol. 11. No. 1. pp. 25-50. Kanu, I. A. (2017). *Igwebuike* as an Igbo-African philosophy for Christian-Muslim relations in Northern Nigeria. In Mahmoud Misaeli (Ed.). *Spirituality and Global Ethics* (pp. 300-310). United Kingdom: Cambridge Scholars.

value. It views the world as a manifestation of the supreme person. It differentiates between the concepts of the "individual" and the "person". **A** human being is an individual as a member of society, as a part defined in correlation with the whole. As a person, one can affirm oneself in freewill and in an eternal source-God. The decision of a person presupposes an intention, a choice, a moral evaluation and an affirmation of personal freedom.[167]

Personalism would consider the persona as an individual being which is realized through conscious ownership and independent disposal of an own self. The concept of person, which was unknown to the Greek philosophy, developed under the influence of Jewish-Christian thinking as late as in the patristic era and then it gradually found its place in philosophy.[168] According to E. Mounier, personalism is a philosophy; it is not merely an attitude. It is a philosophy but not a system.[169] The personalistic philosophy pays tribute to the person as the center of all that concerns reality. Arising from the term "person", it maintains that a person is one who is consciously aware of his acts, doing it in an awareness that arises from his free will. Personalists consider personhood as the fundamental notion, one which gives meaning to all of reality and constitutes its supreme value. Personhood carries with it an inviolable dignity that merits unconditional respect.

The term, 'Inter-,' as a prefix is used to form words from the outside, in contrast to the prefix, 'Intra-'. Interpersonalism translates to a person-to-person conscious interaction, one that is willfully mediated and orchestrated for the sake of the other person. It is a philosophy that embraces and brings under its wings the existential, ontological reality of the person, while not handling lightly the individuality of the person, but giving it more credence. The interpersonalistic nature of the *Igwebuike* is mirrored by the Zulu proverb: *Umuntu Ngumuntu Ngabantu* (I am because you are; you are because we are). In Africa, we say that a person is a person because of other people. Our conception of being is held in common. We agree with our ancestors in believing that our humanness is not an individual quality but something that is of necessity shared.[170] According to R.J. Khoza,

In metaphysical terms, Ubuntu is first and foremost a statement of being- the "I am" in all of us. It declares that each of us, in our separate lives, draws existence from the collective and we are only persons through other persons. This is a meta-statement because it makes a fundamental assertion about the nature of our existence which is not reducible to anything else. I am because others are. The reach of this statement is enormous. Its repercussions flow through all subsequent statements about who and what we are; ontologically how should we see the world; epistemologically what our knowledge amounts to; logically what is reasonable;

---

[167] T. Zaverzhenets, *The Personalism of Emmanuel Mounier*, in Mozaik 1, 2003, 20.

[168] P. Dancak, Personalism. The philosophical Movement for Human Development in Advances in Social Science, Education, Social Sciences And Humanities Research, Vol.124, 2017, 51-55.

[169] E. Mounier, Personalism, Routledge & Kegan Paul Ltd, London, 1950, Vii.

[170] Dr R.J. Khoza, *The Ubuntu Philosophy as a Conceptual Framework for Interpersonal Relationships and Leadership*, An address given to Nedbank Group Technology Leaders on the 15th of September 2012,

ethically how we should act for the good of all; politically how decisions should be made; aesthetically how beauty can be collectively perceived.[171]

The *Igwebuike* interpersonalistic ideology holds on to two basic tenets of solidarity and complementarity[172]. *Igwebuike* is very much like the Ubuntu philosophy in this regard.[173] It argues that 'to be' is to live in solidarity and complementarity, and to live outside the parameters of solidarity and complementarity is to suffer alienation. 'To be' is 'to be with the other', in a community of beings. This is based on the African philosophy of community, which is the underlying principle and unity of African Traditional Religious and philosophical experience.[174] B.I. Ekwulu emphasizes this concept of complementarity as he notes:

If the other is my part or a piece of me, it means that I need him for me to be complete, for me to be what I really am. The other completes rather than diminishes me. His language and culture make my own stand out and at the same time, they enrich and complement my own. In the presence of his language and culture, the riches and poverty of my language and culture become clear and I see that his own and my own when put together form a richer whole when compared to any of them in isolation.[175]

What B.I. Ekwulu notes is the crux of that which pertains to the *Igwebuike* ideology, namely that: I am personally linked to the other person, who is also personally linked to me. This interpersonal linkage does not in any way reduce or tamper with the reality of the person's individuality. It rather emphasizes it. A.I Kanu buttresses this point:

The principle of identity is the first principle of Igwebuike philosophy. It states that every being is determined in itself, is one with itself and is consistent in itself. Thus, every being is one with itself and divided from others. The qualities of matter, referred to in traditional metaphysics as accidents, such as size, colour, shape, etc., distinguish one being from the other. If reality does

---

[171] Ibid.

[172] Kanu, I. A. (2018). *Igwebuike* as an African integrative and progressive anthropology. *NAJOP: Nasara Journal of Philosophy*. Vol. 2. No. 1. pp. 151-161. Kanu, I. A. (2018). New Africanism: *Igwebuike* as a philosophical Attribute of Africa in portraying the Image of Life. In Mahmoud Misaeli, Sanni Yaya and Rico Sneller (Eds.). *African Perspectives on Global on Global Development* (pp. 92-103). United Kingdom: Cambridge Scholars Publishing. Kanu, I. A. (2019). Collaboration within the ecology of mission: An African cultural perspective. *The Catholic Voyage: African Journal of Consecrated Life*. Vol. 15. pp. 125-149. Kanu, I. A. (2019). *Igwebuike* research methodology: A new trend for scientific and wholistic investigation. *IGWEBUIKE: An African Journal of Arts and Humanities* (IAAJAH). *5. 4.* pp. *95-105.*

[173] D. Iwuh OSA, *Action Understanding Is Not Entirely Neutral It Is Existential, It Is Igwebuike* in Igwebuike: An African Journal of Arts and Humanities Vol. 5 No 6, September 2019, 51-70.

[174] A. I. Kanu, *Igwebuike As A Trend In African Philosophy*, in Igwebuike An African Journal of Arts and Humanities Vol. 2 No 1, March 2016, 108-113.

[175] B.I. Ekwulu, Igbo concept of Ibe (the other) as a philosophical solution to the ethnic conflicts in African countries in B. I. Ekwulu (Ed.), philosophical reflections on African issues, Enugu Publications, Delta, 2010, 183-192.

not have an identity, then everything would be everything, giving birth to one thing since nothing can be differentiated from the other. In this case, there would be no subject and object relationship.[176]

The interpersonalism of *Igwebuike* is inherent in its principles of solidarity and complementarity, but is seen further in the underlining principle of "sharedness". A.I. Kanu notes:

The Igbo would… refer to the 'other person' as *ibe m* which means 'my piece' or *mmadu ibe m* (my fellow human being). This is the concept also employed in reference to relationships and reciprocity: love one another (*hunu ibe unu n'anya*), help one another (*nyere nu ibe unu aka*), respect one another (*sopuru nu ibe unu*), etc. Since the 'other' refers to my own piece, it would, therefore, mean that to love the other is to love oneself, to help the other is to help oneself and to respect the other is to respect oneself.[177]

According to this philosophy, each person may have his own individual paths to thread, it yet does not negate the fact that we all share in one supreme desire, which is *wellbeing*. This *wellbeing* that is sought after by all and sundry can only be attained by banding together to working for this common desire. It demands from persons commitment, alignment and, above all, communication. The interpersonalism that *Igwebuike* breeds is one that situates the human person as the center of all that happens in the world. This is because it is the human person that makes sense of what is happening around him, based on the conscious awareness that he has. Interpersonalism says that the human person is not a solitary being, he is not solipsistic, he is interrelational, he is part of a bigger family of persons, who complement one another. The interpersonalism of *Igwebuike* bespeaks of the human person who is characterized by a common origin, common world-view, common language, shared culture, shared race, colour and habits, common historical experience and a common destiny.[178]

[176] A.I. Kanu, *On The Origins and Principles of Igwebuike Philosophy*, Journal of Religion and Human Relations, Volume 11 No. 1, 2019, 159-176.

[177] A.I. Kanu, Igwebuike As An Igbo-African Ethic Of Reciprocity, in Igwebuike. An African Journal of Arts and Humanities Vol. 3 No 2, March 2017, 153-160.

[178] Kanu, I. A. (2017b). *Igwebuike* as a wholistic response to the problem of evil and human suffering. *Igwebuike: An African Journal of Arts and Humanities.* Vol. 3 No 2, March. Kanu, I. A. (2017e). *Igwebuike* as an Igbo-African modality of peace and conflict resolution. *Journal of African Traditional Religion and Philosophy Scholars.* Vol. 1. No. 1. pp. 31-40. Kanu, I. A. (2017g). *Igwebuike* and the logic (Nka) of African philosophy. *Igwebuike: An African Journal of Arts and Humanities.* 3. 1. pp. 1-13. Kanu, I. A. (2017h). *Igwebuike* philosophy and human rights violation in Africa. *IGWEBUIKE: An African Journal of Arts and Humanities.* Vol. 3. No. 7. pp. 117-136. Kanu, I. A. (2017i). *Igwebuike* as a hermeneutic of personal autonomy in African ontology. *Journal of African Traditional Religion and Philosophy Scholars. Vol. 2. No. 1. pp. 14-22.*

SYNTHESIS BETWEEN THE INTERPERSONALISTIC *IGWEBUIKE* AND NEURON COMMUNICATION

Let us think of the brain as a forest of dense proportions, one in which different kinds of trees grow near, around and on top of one another, their branches and roots intertwining. Indeed, as all trees share one basic structure, that is roots, trunk, branches, etc., but do not look exactly alike, all neurons in the brain are variations on a common structural basis. That is to say that even if the neurons have one and the same structure, they are not alike (although scientific research is still ongoing as to this aspect). Irrespective of the fact that neurons are not all alike, yet this does not hinder communication; that is to say that they still transmit electrochemical messages with one another. Each neuron is linked to the other, not standing on its own, and does not operate on its own. It rather operates in tandem with other neurons to produce optimal result.

As it is witnessed, there are times when there is break in communication amongst neurons, for instance, a stroke is just one example of a condition when communication between nerve cells breaks down. Micro-failures in brain functioning also occur in conditions such as depression and dementia. In most cases, the lost capacity will return after a while. However, consequential damage will often remain so that the functional capability can only be restored through lengthy treatment. This treatment will involve relearning all that one has previously learnt, for instance, motor activities, as in the case of a patient with a stroke. This is because significant alterations occur in neural cells while the communication pathways are blocked.

Neuron networks reconnect during such periods of inactivity and become hypersensitive. If we imagine that normal communication pathways are motorways, when they are blocked, a form of traffic chaos occurs in the brain, whereby information is re-routed in a disorganized form along what can be called side streets and minor routes. Additional synapses are generated everywhere and begin operating. When the signal is reinstated, the previously coordinated information routes no longer exist and, as in the case of a child, the appropriate functions need to be learned from scratch. Since they are receiving no normal signals during the phase of brain malfunction, the nerve cells also become more sensitive in an attempt to find the missing input. Once the signals return, this means they may overreact.[179] This implies that the basic functioning route that the neuron takes in its communication pathway ought not to be hindered, lest the human person risks losing one of the vital functions that pertain to his being. For this communication pathway to be fostered continually, there is the need of a link that connects the two neurons. This link is known as neurotransmitters, as already noted. Without the neurotransmitters, the possibility of connecting one neuron to another would be impossible. There is, in essence, an *interneuronal* relationship that exists in the brain amongst neurons.

---

[179] University of Erlangen-Nuremberg, *What happens when nerve cells stop working? Total breakdown in the brain*, in Science Daily, 27 September 2017, <www.sciencedaily.com/releases/2017/09/170927093300.htm>.

Much like the neurons in the brain, the human being is entirely the same, structure wise, but no two persons are the same. Our individuality is contained in the fact of our being persons. "Individual," as an English word, is derived from two Latin words, namely, in- and –dividus, which translates literally to "not divisible". In the light of the non-divisibility of the person, Boethius defines the person as *naturae rationalis individualis substantia*.[180] According to Norris Clark, commenting on the thought of St Thomas Aquinas:

> …to be a person it is not enough merely to possess a complete individual intellectual nature which all admitted was an essential requisite, according to the classical definition of Boethius: a person is "an individual substance of a rational nature." To be a person in its own right such a nature would have to possess or "own" its own act of existence (*esse*). Thus the human nature of Christ, though a complete human *nature*, just like ours, was not a human *person*, because it was owned by a Divine Person (the Son or Word of God), in what is technically called the Hypostatic (i.e., personal) Union of God and man. Hence, it is the nature's own proportionate act of existence, actualizing it as an existent, which formally constitutes that nature a person. The person is the concrete whole resulting from this union, expressed by the term "I." Ordinary language indicates quite clearly the distinction by two distinct questions: "*who am I?*" (person) and "*what am I?*" (nature). Thus for St. Thomas the person could be defined as "an intellectual nature possessing its own act of existence, so that it can be the self-conscious, responsible source of its own actions." In a word, in perhaps the briefest and still one of the best descriptions of person ever given, a person is a being that is *dominus sui*, that is, master of itself, or *self-possessing* (in the order of knowledge by self-consciousness; in the order of will and action by self-determination or freewill).[181]

Communication between human persons has to be willfully orchestrated; this actually implies that without the full participation of the will, then, interpersonal relationship would not be possible. We should think of the human will as the neurotransmitters that enable communication between the neurons; the will, thus, is what enables one person to engage in an interrelational rapport with the other person. Each single neuron serves a primary purpose in the grand scale of all that refers to coordination and functioning; this is what makes important the interneuronal relationship that is seen in the human brain. Each human person also serves a primary purpose in the grand scheme of all that is (reality). Thus, an interpersonal rapport is central to the human person. *Igwebuike* ideology, which stands in support of this interpersonal

---

[180] *Substantia* (substance) is used to exclude accidents; *Individua*, that is *individum in se*, Boethius considers it synonymous to singularies (singular); *Rationalis naturae*, meaning that the person is predicated only of intellectual being. L. Geddes, Person, in the Catholic Encyclopedia, Robert Appleton Company, New York, 1911, http://www.newadvent.org/cathen/11726a.htm, retrieved 10th May, 2020.

[181] N. Clark, *Person and Being. Aquinas Lectures*, Marquette University Press, Milwaukee, 1993, 26-28.

affinity amongst persons, gives the latter more credence in noting that there is also the ethic of reciprocity inherent in this ideology. According to A.I. Kanu,

> The philosophy of Igwebuike is not just a philosophical foundation for the ethic of reciprocity, but it is the ethic of reciprocity. It presents the ethic of reciprocity not just as a moral principle, but as a duty that one owns to himself or herself- everyone owns himself or herself of treating the other in a way that one would like to be treated. This is because Igwebuike sees a very strong relationship between every reality- an intricate web. To treat the other- that which is different from the self in a way that accords with honour is to treat oneself in a way that is honourable. However, to treat the other in a way that is dishonourable to dishonor oneself, because everything we do to the other has a way of getting back at us. Thus, in Igwebuike, the ethic of reciprocity is not just a moral principle, but a moral obligation one must have towards the other. In fact, from the above understanding, it is not just a moral obligation one owns the other, but an obligation to oneself.[182]

An interpersonal bond amongst persons, in the light of *Igwebuike*, should arise willfully, based on an understanding that every individual is a part of a grand scheme, greater than his/her selfish inclinations or trends. Such a bond is strengthened by continued interrelational acts, aimed at the "sharing of the" good (*Igwebuike* bespeaks of sharing). It is acknowledged that there can be no strengthening of bond, if there is no bond to start with. As such, a willfully initiated relation, based on an understanding of the position of the human person in the greater scale of humanity, is key in the fostering this bond. This is the philosophy of *Igwebuike*[183].

CONCLUSION

It is impossible to situate the relationship of the human person on the determined relationship of neurons in the brain; true. But this is where the will of the human person comes in. As much as the neurotransmitters enable relations between neurons amidst the synaptic gap

---

[182] A.I. Kanu, *Igwebuike As An Igbo-African Ethic Of Reciprocity*, in Igwebuike: An African Journal of Arts and Humanities Vol. 3 No 2, March 2017, 153-160.

[183] Kanu, I. A. (2017). *Igwebuike* as an Igbo-African philosophy for the protection of the environment. *Nightingale International Journal of Humanities and Social Sciences*. Vol. 3. No. 4. pp. 28-38. Kanu, I. A. (2017). *Igwebuike* as the hermeneutic of individuality and communality in African ontology. *NAJOP: Nasara Journal of Philosophy*. Vol. 2. No. 1. pp. 162-179. Kanu, I. A. (2017a). *Igwebuike* and question of superiority in the scientific community of knowledge. *Igwebuike: An African Journal of Arts and Humanities.*Vol.3 No1. pp. 131-138. Kanu, I. A. (2017a). *Igwebuike as a philosophical attribute of Africa in portraying the image of life*. A paper presented at the 2017 Oracle of Wisdom International Conference by the Department of Philosophy, Tansian University, Umunya, Anambra State, 27-29 April. Kanu, I. A. (2017b). *Igwebuike* as a complementary approach to the issue of girl-child education. *Nightingale International Journal of Contemporary Education and Research*. Vol. 3. No. 6. pp. 11-17.

that is present between them, the will enables such relations between human persons. Yet, the will should be motivated by one truth, being that: life is a shared reality, one that presupposes a tailormade-cloth, measured, cut and sewn to fit into the curves, contours, shape and size, peculiarities and particularities of a being. Thus, every being has a missing part and is, at the same time, a missing part.

BIBLIOGRAPHY

A. Borisyuk et al, eds., *Tutorials in Mathematical Biosciences I. Mathematical Neuroscience*, Springer-Verlag Berlin Heidelberg, Germany 2005.

B.I. Ekwulu, Igbo concept of Ibe (the other) as a philosophical solution to the ethnic conflicts in African countries in B. I. Ekwulu (Ed.), philosophical reflections on African issues, Enugu Publications, Delta, 2010.

E. Mounier, Personalism, Routledge & Kegan Paul Ltd, London, 1950.

D. Iwuh OSA, *Action Understanding Is Not Entirely Neutral It Is Existential, It Is Igwebuike* in Igwebuike: An African Journal of Arts and Humanities Vol. 5 No 6, September 2019.

Dr R.J. Khoza, *The Ubuntu Philosophy as a Conceptual Framework for Interpersonal Relationships and Leadership*, An address given to Nedbank Group Technology Leaders on the 15th of September 2012.

J. Walinga-C. Stangor, Introduction to Psychology 1st Canadian Edition, BCCampus Vicotria B.C., Canada, 2014.

J. Zhang, *Basic Neural Units of the Brain: Neurons, Synapses and Action Potential*, in IFM LAB TUTORIAL SERIES No. 5, 2019.

I. A. Kanu. Igwebuike as an Igbo-African Hermeneutic of Globalization. *Igwebuike: An African Journal of Arts and Humanities*, Vol. 2 no. 1 2016:1-6.

I. A. Kanu. *Igwe Bu Ike* as an Igbo-African hermeneutics of national development. *Igbo Studies Review. No. 6.* pp. 59-83. 2018

I. A. Kanu. *Igwebuike* as an African integrative and progressive anthropology. *NAJOP: Nasara Journal of Philosophy.* Vol. 2. No. 1. pp. 151-161. 2018

I. A. Kanu. New Africanism: *Igwebuike* as a philosophical Attribute of Africa in portraying the Image of Life. In Mahmoud Misaeli, Sanni Yaya and Rico Sneller (Eds.). *African*

Perspectives on Global on Global Development (pp. 92-103). United Kingdom: Cambridge Scholars Publishing. 2018

I. A. Kanu. Collaboration within the ecology of mission: An African cultural perspective. *The Catholic Voyage: African Journal of Consecrated Life*. Vol. 15. pp. 125-149. 2019

I. A. Kanu. *Igwebuike* research methodology: A new trend for scientific and wholistic investigation. *IGWEBUIKE: An African Journal of Arts and Humanities* (IAAJAH). *5. 4.* pp. *95-105.* 2019

I. A. Kanu. *Igwebuikeconomics*: The Igbo apprenticeship for wealth creation. *IGWEBUIKE: An African Journal of Arts and Humanities* (IAAJAH). *5. 4.* pp. *56-70.* 2019

I. A. Kanu. *Igwebuikecracy*: The Igbo-African participatory cocio-political system of governance. *TOLLE LEGE: An Augustinian Journal of the Philosophy and Theology. 1. 1.* pp. 34-45. 2018

I. A. Kanu. On the origin and principles of *Igwebuike* philosophy. *International Journal of Religion and Human Relations*. Vol. 11. No. 1. pp. 159-176. 2019

I. A. Kanu. (2019b). An *Igwebuike* approach to the study of African traditional naming ceremony and baptism. *International Journal of Religion and Human Relations*. Vol. 11. No. 1. pp. 25-50.

I. A. Kanu. *Igwebuike* as an Igbo-African philosophy for Christian-Muslim relations in Northern Nigeria. In Mahmoud Misaeli (Ed.). *Spirituality and Global Ethics* (pp. 300-310). United Kingdom: Cambridge Scholars. 2017

I. A. Kanu. *Igwebuike* as an Igbo-African philosophy for the protection of the environment. *Nightingale International Journal of Humanities and Social Sciences*. Vol. 3. No. 4. pp. 28-38. 2017

I. A. Kanu. *Igwebuike* as the hermeneutic of individuality and communality in African ontology. *NAJOP: Nasara Journal of Philosophy*. Vol. 2. No. 1. pp. 162-179. 2017

I. A. Kanu. *Igwebuike* and question of superiority in the scientific community of knowledge. *Igwebuike: An African Journal of Arts and Humanities*.Vol.3 No1. pp. 131-138. 2017

I. A. Kanu. *Igwebuike as a philosophical attribute of Africa in portraying the image of life.* A paper presented at the 2017 Oracle of Wisdom International Conference by the Department of Philosophy, Tansian University, Umunya, Anambra State, 27-29 April. 2017

I. A. Kanu. *Igwebuike* as a complementary approach to the issue of girl-child education. *Nightingale International Journal of Contemporary Education and Research.* Vol. 3. No. 6. pp. 11-17. 2017

I. A. Kanu. *Igwebuike* as a wholistic response to the problem of evil and human suffering. *Igwebuike: An African Journal of Arts and Humanities.* Vol. 3 No 2, March. 2017

I. A. Kanu. *Igwebuike* as an Igbo-African modality of peace and conflict resolution. *Journal of African Traditional Religion and Philosophy Scholars. Vol. 1. No. 1. pp. 31-40.* 2017

I. A. Kanu. *Igwebuike* and the logic (Nka) of African philosophy. *Igwebuike: An African Journal of Arts and Humanities.* 3. 1. pp. 1-13. 2017

I. A. Kanu. *Igwebuike* philosophy and human rights violation in Africa. *IGWEBUIKE: An African Journal of Arts and Humanities.* Vol. 3. No. 7. pp. 117-136. 2017

I. A. Kanu. *Igwebuike* as a hermeneutic of personal autonomy in African ontology. *Journal of African Traditional Religion and Philosophy Scholars. Vol. 2. No. 1. pp. 14-22.* 2017

I. A. Kanu, *Igwebuike As A Trend In African Philosophy*, in Igwebuike An African Journal of Arts and Humanities Vol. 2 No 1, March 2016.

I. A. Kanu, *On The Origins and Principles of Igwebuike Philosophy*, Journal of Religion and Human Relations, Volume 11 No. 1, 2019.

I. A. Kanu, *Igwebuike As An Igbo-African Ethic Of Reciprocity*, in Igwebuike: An African Journal of Arts and Humanities Vol. 3 No 2, March 2017.

L. Geddes, Person, in the Catholic Encyclopedia, Robert Appleton Company, New York, 1911, http://www.newadvent.org/cathen/11726a.htm, retrieved 10th May, 2020.

M. Ludwig, *How Your Brain Cells Talk to Each Other* in Frontiers for Young Minds, 5:39, 26th July, 2017.

M.D. Binder, N. Hirokawa, U. Windhorst (Eds.), *Encyclopedia of Neuroscience*, Springer-Verlag GmbH, Berlin Heidelberg, Germany, 2009.

M.S. Gazzaniga, R.B. Ivry, G.R. Mangun, *Cognitive Neuroscience. The Biology of the Mind*, W. W. Norton & Company, New York, 2019.

N. Clark, *Person and Being. Aquinas Lectures*, Marquette University Press, Milwaukee, 1993.

P. Dancak, Personalism. The philosophical Movement for Human Development in Advances in Social Science, Education, Social Sciences And Humanities Research, Vol.124, 2017.

R. Jahn, *How Neurons Talk to Each Other*, in Neuroscience News, 24th September, 2016, https://neurosciencenews.com/neurons-synapses-neuroscience-5119/ Retrieved 7th May, 2020.

T. Zaverzhenets, *The Personalism of Emmanuel Mounier*, in Mozaik 1, 2003.

University of Erlangen-Nuremberg, *What happens when nerve cells stop working? Total breakdown in the brain*, in Science Daily, 27 September 2017.

V. Whiteley, *Describe the structure of the nervous system. How do neurons communicate*, in the Research Gate Online Journal.

IGWEBUIKE PHILOSOPHY AND SOLIDARITY DURING THE ERA OF COVID-19 PANDEMIC

Mary Winifred Gloria Eche, DMMM, PhD
Saint Thomas Aquinas Major Seminary
Makurdi, Benue State
winieoge@yahoo.com

ABSTRACT

Igwebuike is an Igbo word which means strength in number. Solidarity, on the other hand, is a bond of unity or agreement between individuals who are united around a common goal. As the saying goes "united we stand, divided we fall". As it is today, Covid-19 is a pandemic that has traumatized people, and isolated them from their loved ones, brought untold hardship to many people, taken away the lives of many and is still killing many people today. Therefore, using the principle of Igwebuike and solidarity with oneself, family, neighbour, state, country, world, etc., we would go a long way to save the world. The analytical method is used in this work and the aim of this paper is to portray how the Igwebuike principle can go a long way to salvaging the situation at hand.

Keywords: Igwebuike, Philosophy, Solidarity, COVID-19 Pandemic, Principle

INTRODUCTION

Oxford Advanced Learner's Dictionary describes pandemic as "a disease that spreads over a whole country or the whole world." It is a global outbreak of disease. It happens whenever a new virus emerges to infect people and its spread is sustained. Its long period of spread is caused by the fact that there is "little or no pre-existing immunity against the new virus."[184] This Covid-19 outbreak was "characterized as pandemic on March 11 by the WHO external icon." [185] It is also rapidly spreading from person to person. The National Center for Disease Control in Nigeria (NCDC) maintains that this is the first pandemic known to be caused by a new coronavirus, even though "in the past century, there have been four pandemics caused

---

[184] Centers for Disease Control and Prevention (2019). Coronavirus Disease 2019, (COVID-19). Available at https//www.cdc.gov/coronavirus2019-ncov/index.html

[185] Centers for Disease Control and Prevention (2019).

by the emergence of new influenza viruses. As a result, most research and guidance around pandemics is specific to influenza, but the same premises can be applied to the current COVID-19 pandemic."[186] It also explains the nature of such pandemics thus,

> Pandemics of respiratory disease follow a certain progression outlined in a Pandemic intervals Framework. Pandemics begin with an investigation phase, followed by recognition, initiation, and acceleration phases. The peak of illnesses occurs at the end of the acceleration phase, which is followed by a deceleration phase, during which there is a decrease in illnesses. Different countries can be in different phases of the pandemic at any point in time and different parts of the same country can also be in different phases of a pandemic.[187]

The World Health Organization (WHO) has also affirmed that this Coronavirus disease (COVID-19) is an infectious one caused by a newly discovered coronavirus as mentioned above. Coronaviruses are a large family of viruses that are common in people and many different species of animals, including camels, cattle, cats and bats. It mostly spreads through droplets of saliva or discharge from the nose when an infected person coughs or sneezes. It is a respiratory disease, which can affect anyone but in different ways. However, people with pre-existing health conditions or problems and older people are more at risk of developing complications, or even death, should they catch the virus. Most infected people will develop mild to moderate symptoms and recover without requiring special treatment. The most common symptoms include fever, tiredness and dry cough. While other symptoms include shortness of breath, aches and pains, sore throat, and very few people will report diarrhoea, nausea or a runny nose. [188]

BRIEF ANALYSIS OF COVID-19

Even though little has been said about the Coronavirus pandemic in the introduction, it is also good to elaborate more on this virus by tracing its origin and spread in order to widen our knowledge. According to Shereen, Coronaviruses belong to the *Coronaviridae* family in the Nidovirales order.[189] Viruses, and the diseases they cause, are often given different names. In fact, majority of persons know the name of a disease without having the knowledge of the virus that causes the disease. For example, HIV is the virus that causes AIDS. "Viruses are named based on their genetic structure to facilitate the development of diagnostic tests, vaccines and

---

[186] Centers for Disease Control and Prevention (2019).

[187] Centers for Disease Control and Prevention (2019).

[188] World Health Organization (WHO), 2019. Coronavirus Disease (Covid-19) Outbreak. Available at http://www.who.int/health-topics/coronavirus/emergencies-redirect.

[189] Shereen, M.A., (2019). **"COVID-19 infection: Origin, transmission, and characteristics of human coronaviruses"** in Journal of Advanced Research, vol. 24, p.91.

medicines. Virologists and the wider scientific community do this work, so viruses are named by the International Committee on Taxonomy of Viruses (ICTV)."[190]

Shereen describes this Coronavirus as being in form of crown-like spikes on the outer surface; under the microscope, the viruses look like they are covered with pointed structures that surround them like a crown. Since they are named by their appearance, thus, it was named as a Coronavirus. They are minute in size, like 65–125 mm in diameter, and contain a single-stranded RNA as a nucleic material, its size ranging from 26 to 32kbs in length. There are also other types of Ccoronaviruses found to be in the family. They are alpha (α), beta (β), gamma (γ) and delta (δ) coronavirus. The severe acute respiratory syndrome coronavirus (SARS-CoV), H5N1 influenza A, H1N1 2009 and Middle East respiratory syndrome coronavirus (MERS-CoV) cause acute lung injury (ALI) and acute respiratory distress syndrome (ARDS) which leads to pulmonary failure and result in fatality. These viruses were actually thought to infect only animals, until humans witnessed a severe acute respiratory syndrome (SARS) outbreak caused by SARS-CoV, 2002 in Guangdong, China. A decade later, another pathogenic Coronavirus emerged, known as Middle East respiratory syndrome coronavirus (MERS-CoV). This caused an endemic in Middle Eastern countries. And now, just at the end of 2019, Wuhan, an emerging business hub of China, experienced an outbreak of a novel Coronavirus that killed more than eighteen hundred and infected over seventy thousand individuals within the first fifty days of the epidemic. This Coronavirus has been reported to be a member of the β group of Coronaviruses. This new virus was named as Wuhan Coronavirus or 2019 novel Coronavirus (2019-nCov) by the Chinese researchers. The International Committee on Taxonomy of Viruses (ICTV) named the virus as SARS-CoV-2 and the disease as COVID-19. In the history, SARS-CoV (2003) infected 8098 individuals, with mortality rate of 9%, across 26 countries in the world. On the other hand, the new Corona virus (2019) infected 3,301,219 individuals, with 233,716 deaths across 213 countries, till the date of this writing, that is, 30th of April, 2020. It shows that the transmission rate of SARS-CoV-2 is higher than SARS-CoV, and the reason could be genetic recombination event at S protein in the RBD region of SARS-CoV-2, which may have enhanced its transmission ability.[191]

COVID-19 MODES OF TRANSMISSION

Coronavirus was defined by David[192] as "illness caused by a novel coronavirus now called severe acute respiratory syndrome coronavirus 2 (SARS-CoV-2; formerly called 2019-nCoV.

---

[190] World Health Organization (WHO), 2019

[191] C/f Shereen, M.A., (2019). "COVID-19 infection: Origin, transmission, and characteristics of human coronaviruses" in Journal of Advanced Research, vol. 24, p.91.

[192] **David J Cennimo, MD, FAAP, FACP, AAHIVS** Assistant Professor of Medicine and Pediatrics, Adult and Pediatric Infectious Diseases, Rutgers New Jersey Medical School is a member of the following medical societies: American Academy of HIV Medicine, American Academy of Pediatrics, American College of Physicians, American Medical Association, HIV Medicine Association, Infectious Disease Society of America, Medical Society of New Jersey, Pediatric Infectious Diseases Society.

The name was chosen to avoid stigmatizing the virus's origins in terms of populations, geography, or animal associations."[193] The most dangerous part of this virus is its mode of transmission, even though based on the available information through the mass media and other sources of information, one is not clear enough of the transmission routes. Although we currently understand that the respiratory transmission from human to human is the major transmission route, "other ways for transmission, such as gastrointenstinal transmission or aerosol propagation, is not so clear."[194] According to 'africanews,' which is distributed by APO[195] group on behalf of World Health Organization (WHO), the transmission from person to person is through respiratory droplets and contact routes. Droplet transmission occurs when a person is in in close contact (within 1 m) with someone who has respiratory symptoms (e.g. coughing or sneezing,) and is therefore at risk of having his/her mucosae (mouth and nose) or conjunctiva (eyes) exposed to potentially infective respiratory droplets (which are generally considered to be > 5-10 μm in diameter). Droplet transmission may also occur through fomites in the immediate environment around the infected person. Therefore, transmission of the COVID-19 virus can occur by direct contact with infected people and indirect contact with surfaces in the immediate environment or with objects used on the infected person (e.g. stethoscope or thermometer).[196]

BRIEF EXPLANATION OF *IGWEBUIKE* AND SOLIDARITY

Igwebuike, as noted above, means "number is strength... that is, when human beings come together in solidarity and complementarity, they are powerful or can constitute an insurmountable force,"[197] while solidarity is "a bond of unity or agreement between individuals united around a common goal or against a common enemy, such as the unifying principle that

---

[193] David J. Cennimo, (2020). "Coronavirus Disease 2019 (Covid19), Practice Essentials, Background, Route of Transmission", Medscape. Available on https // emedicine .medscape . com/article/2500114-overview. Accessed 04/05/2020.

[194] Qian, X., Ren, R., Wang, Y. *et al.(2020)* "Fighting against the common enemy of COVID-19: a practice of building a community with a shared future for mankind/ *Infectious Disease of Poverty*" Available at https ://idpjournal. Biomedcentral.com/articles/10.1186/s40249-020-00650-1. Accessed on 05/05/2020

[195] Alpha Phi Omega-Omicron(APO) is a national co-educational service fraternity founded on December 16, 1925. It is organized to provide community service, leadership development, and social opportunities for college students. The purpose of the fraternity is to develop Leadership, to promote Friendship, and to provide Service to humanity; and to further the freedom that is our national, educational, and intellectual heritage. Alpha Phi Omega's primary focus is to provide volunteer service within four areas: service to the community, service to the campus, service to the fraternity, and service to the nation and world.C/f. https:// apo.org.uiowa.edu/about-us.

[196] APO, (2020). "Modes of transmission of virus causing COVID-19: implications for IPC precaution recommendations". Africanews. Accessed 05/05/2020.

[197] Eche, Mary Winifred G., (2019). "Igwebuike and the Right of Inheritance of Igbo Women" in IGWEBUIKE: An African Journal of Arts and Humanities Vol. 5 No 7, p. 40. ISSN: 2488-9210(Online)

defines the labor movement; mutual support within a group"[198] etc. Solidarity is that virtue which enables the human family to share fully both the treasures of material and spiritual goods.

The strength attributed to "Igwebuike," that is, with number, is founded on the interdependence, mutual support and reliance on each other in difficult times, or a pursuit of a particular goal. It is this "organic" interdependence of the components parts, that is, "the number, the many" that is called solidarity[199]. The number is, therefore, seen as strength only and only if there is solidarity. In African philosophy and religion, we identify this number and support through the extended family. Africans have an extended family structure. Hence, for the traditional Africans, the family does not stop with the immediate brothers and sisters and parents (nuclear family), but also includes grandparents, uncles, aunts, nephews, nieces, cousins, etc. This accounts for why the African notion of family is extended and wider than the nuclear family.

Family within the African context is usually the major source of the basic necessities of life, health, love and tenderness, food, water, clothing, shelter and sanitation. The extended family ideally provides economic, social and psychological security to all its members. This family system defines social and moral norms and safeguards both material and spiritual customs and traditions as well as provides a variety of role models preparing the way for adulthood.[200] The strength of this extended family is to support one another.

In this pandemic period, for example, the Nigerian government, in compliance with the advice of the WHO, has asked her citizens to stayathome, as a necessary precaution to stop the spread of the virus. It is almost unimaginable, but this is the case, that these people are asked to stay at home without adequate provision of palliatives or means of survival for a people who depend on their daily outdoor work and petty businesses to feed themselves. Though this situation has been very challenging for most Nigerians, the exchange and support mechanism of solidarity in extended families have been the saving grace for many. The strength and unity of the number, "Igwebuike,"[201] have become the source of relief and hope for the suffering

---

[198] The American Heritage Dictionary of the English Language, Fifth Edition (2016). Houghton Mifflin Harcourt Publishing Company.

[199] Kanu, I. A. (2017). *Igwebuike* as the hermeneutic of individuality and communality in African ontology. *NAJOP: Nasara Journal of Philosophy*. Vol. 2. No. 1. pp. 162-179. Kanu, I. A. (2017a). *Igwebuike* and question of superiority in the scientific community of knowledge. *Igwebuike: An African Journal of Arts and Humanities*. Vol.3 No1. pp. 131-138. Kanu, I. A. (2017a). *Igwebuike as a philosophical attribute of Africa in portraying the image of life*. A paper presented at the 2017 Oracle of Wisdom International Conference by the Department of Philosophy, Tansian University, Umunya, Anambra State, 27-29 April. Kanu, I. A. (2017b). *Igwebuike* as a complementary approach to the issue of girl-child education. *Nightingale International Journal of Contemporary Education and Research*. Vol. 3. No. 6. pp. 11-17.

[200] Patricia M. Amos, (2013). "Parenting and Culture – Evidence from Some African Communities". Available at ... Accessed 05/05/2020.

[201] Kanu, I. A. (2017e). *Igwebuike* as an Igbo-African modality of peace and conflict resolution. *Journal of African Traditional Religion and Philosophy Scholars. Vol. 1. No. 1. pp. 31-40.* Kanu, I. A. (2017g). *Igwebuike* and the

"parts" of the family. It is in this sense, that the solidarity and unity of the number, 'Igwebuike,' ultimately become their strength. Hence, this sense of solidarity becomes the bond of love and force of victory over challenges and needs.

Solidarity is, therefore, the acceptance of our social nature and the affirmation of the bonds we share with all our brothers and sisters. Solidarity creates an environment in which mutual service is encouraged. It is also the social conditions in which human rights can be respected and nurtured. The ability to recognize and accept the whole range of corresponding duties and obligations that are embedded in our social nature can occur only in an atmosphere enlivened by solidarity.[202]

THE ROLE OF *IGWEBUIKE* IN THE ERA OF COVID-19

In the midst of the hopelessness that has taken over the whole world, what can the principle of *Igwebuike* offer to the world to assist during this pandemic. Medical personnel and other experts have advised that we take basic precautions such as regular washing of hands with soap, the use of hand sanitizers, keeping of our environments clean, wearing of face masks, maintaining of social distance and most importantly staying at home, etc. We obtain such information through the mass media and social media of different types, such; as television, radio, newspapers, Internet, WhatsApp, Twitter, Telegram, Facebook, etc. But many Nigerians who live in the villages and some that live in the cities have no phones or televisions, or even radios to listen to news, and to have access to such information. More so, many of them are not educated (that is, they have not acquired formal education). Most of them still doubt the existence of Covid-19. Someone from the village called me and said that the sickness is made for rich men and women who travel abroad, and not for poor people like them. I began to explain to him more about the Covid-19.

This is one of the major areas where the principle of *Igwebuike* comes into play. Because of the large size of the extended family, there must be some members that are more enlightened and richer. Such members may, therefore, have access to the social media; in that case, they

---

logic (Nka) of African philosophy. *Igwebuike: An African Journal of Arts and Humanities.* 3. 1. pp. 1-13. Kanu, I. A. (2017h). *Igwebuike* philosophy and human rights violation in Africa. *IGWEBUIKE: An African Journal of Arts and Humanities.* Vol. 3. No. 7. pp. 117-136. Kanu, I. A. (2017i). *Igwebuike* as a hermeneutic of personal autonomy in African ontology. *Journal of African Traditional Religion and Philosophy Scholars.* Vol. 2. No. 1. pp. 14-22. Kanu, I. A. (2018). *Igwebuike* as an African integrative and progressive anthropology. *NAJOP: Nasara Journal of Philosophy.* Vol. 2. No. 1. pp. 151-161. Kanu, I. A. (2018). New Africanism: *Igwebuike* as a philosophical Attribute of Africa in portraying the Image of Life. In Mahmoud Misaeli, Sanni Yaya and Rico Sneller (Eds.). *African Perspectives on Global on Global Development* (pp. 92-103). United Kingdom: Cambridge Scholars Publishing. Kanu, I. A. (2019). Collaboration within the ecology of mission: An African cultural perspective. *The Catholic Voyage: African Journal of Consecrated Life.* Vol. 15. pp. 125-149. Kanu, I. A. (2019). *Igwebuike* research methodology: A new trend for scientific and wholistic investigation. *IGWEBUIKE: An African Journal of Arts and Humanities* (IAAJAH). 5. 4. pp. 95-105.

[202] Rev. Robert A. S., (2010). "Solidarity: The Fundamental Social Virtue", in Religion &Liberty: Vol 11, No.5

should not hesitate to communicate to other less-privileged family members about the dangers of Covid-19, and also encourage them to take the necessary precautions as stipulated by the World Health Organization (WHO) and the NCDC.

Furthermore, the solidarity principle and support mechanism also are forces that encourage the rich or fairly rich members of the family to provide food and other material needs for the less-privileged members of the family. As the case is today, when government is emphasizing that citizens should stay at home, while many Nigerians survive solely on a day-to-day hawking, they have neither savings account nor reservoir; how will they survive, if there is no one to assist them? The principle of *Igwebuike*, manifesting through love of the other, gives life to the hopeless.

Outside the members of the family, the *Igwebuike* principle advocates for universal unity, love and care. This is because, even though the word is an Igbo word, it has a universal relevance. Every language possesses the words 'unity,' 'solidarity,' 'complementarity,' 'love,' etc. Apart from family members supporting their relations, the *Igwebuike* principle invites the rich members of our communities, states and countries to support the poor by donating money, drugs, buildings for isolation centers and provision of medical personnel. Retired medical personnel should volunteer to assist with their wealth of experience, which many have done and many are expected to follow suit. This is the time to help the poor and needy. If this is not done, the poor may contract the virus and transmit it to every member of the community. So the rich need to help them so that they can stay at home. On the hand, the principle of *Igwebuike* requires the poor and needy to obey the instructions that have been given. It is very necessary and obligatory that all residents in the potential risk areas should accept to stay at home. This is an effective way to block the transmission routes.

For example, I met an electrician who went about working for people, and I observed that he had been doing his normal routine work without qualms, as if everything was normal. When I tried to tell him to stay at home, explaining the implications of refusing to stay safe at home, his response was: "Whether corolla kills me or hunger kills me, death is death." He further said that the government did not give them anything to eat and they were asking him to stay at home. I went further to ask him: "What of if this is war, will you not run after your life? Will you be waiting for the government to provide food for you, or do you care to save your life first?" I advised him to see this Covid-19 as a war and do everything possible to save his life. Instead of making empty arguments, people should make effort to stay at home to avoid spreading this virus or to avoid contracting it.

It has been observed through some video clips that some mischievous infected persons do everything possible to make sure that many people suffer along with them, thereby trying to spit on objects, touch them, sneeze without protection etc. *Igwebuike* principle speaks against such attitudes. It encourages protection of one another in love and unity. It confirms the "universal relevance of solidarity and complementarity."[203] This is expressed through proverbs such as: "A person is a person because of other people." "Sticks in a bundle cannot be broken." "When spiders unite, they can tie up a lion." "Behind an able man there are always other able men." "It takes a village to raise a child." "I am because we are, and since we are, therefore, I am." [204]

WAY FORWARD

Based on the *Igwebuike* principle, as individuals we can reduce our chances of being infected or of spreading COVID-19, by taking simple precautions in our mode of living (e. g. washing and sanitizing of hands, social distancing, avoiding of crowded places, staying at home and going out only when necessary, etc.), aware that what affects us affects our families and the entire community. The leaders and those in authority have to do their best to discharge their duties diligently and to find ways of cushioning the effects of the restriction of movement and the economic hardship that have ensued. In disbursing palliatives, all forms of discriminations should be avoided. Also, the security personnel that are guarding our boarders and road checkpoints should be honest in discharging their duties and avoid taking bribes from people who contravene the restriction of movement. Selfishness and greed on their part can lead to the destruction of so many lives. They are on the roads to protect lives not to eliminate.

CONCLUSION

The Covid 19 pandemic has unleashed destruction of lives, suffering and untold hardship upon the world. However, a number of lessons are being learnt. One of such lessons is that love is the greatest force available to us for overcoming obstacles, and indeed, it is the fundamental element that makes life meaningful. According to Einstein; "Love is Light, that enlightens those who give and receive it. Love is gravity, because it makes some people feel attracted to others. Love is power, because it multiplies the best we have, and allows humanity not to be extinguished in their blind selfishness. Love unfolds and reveals".[205]

In this era of the pandemic, people have become more conscious of the fragility of human life and the relevance of family relationship, friendship and solidarity among individuals, states and nations. The need for interdependence, cooperation and solidarity among peoples and nations has become more apparent. These values are at the basis of the *Igwebuike* principle. This paper makes a clarion call to everybody living today to look around and see what help

---

[203] Ikechukwu A. Kanu., (2019) "On the Origin and Principles of Igwebuike Philosophy" Journal of Religion and Human Relations, Vol. 11 No. 1, pg. 160

[204] Ikechukwu A. Kanu., (2019) "On the Origin and Principles of Igwebuike Philosophy" pg. 176

[205] **Einstein A., (1938). "A letter from Albert Einstein to his daughter: on The Universal Force of Love". Available at https://monoset.com/blog/journal/a-letter-from-albert-einstein-to-his-daughter-on-the-universal-force-of-love. Accessed on 06/05/2020**

we can give to our neighbours, someone that is hungry, thirsty, naked and homeless. Let us try and extend a helping hand, no matter how little; in this way, we shall be participating in the fight against Covid 19 and other conditions that endanger human life.

BIBLIOGRAPHY

APO, (2020). "Modes of transmission of virus causing COVID-19: implications for IPC precaution recommendations". Africanews. APO, (2020). "Modes of transmission of virus causing COVID-19: implications for IPC precaution recommendations". Africanews.

Centers for Disease Control and Prevention (2019). Coronavirus Disease 2019, (COVID-19). Available at https//www.cdc.gov/coronavirus2019-ncov/index.html

David J. Cennimo, (2020). "Coronavirus Disease 2019 (Covid19), Practice Essentials, Background, Route of Transmission", Medscape. Available on https // emedicine .medscape. com/ article/2500114-overview.

Eche, Mary Winifred G., (2019). "Igwebuike and the Right of Inheritance of Igbo Women" in IGWEBUIKE: An African Journal of Arts and Humanities Vol. 5 No 7, (p.40) ISSN: 2488-9210 (Online)

Einstein A., (1938). "A letter from Albert Einstein to his daughter: on The Universal Force of Love". Available at https://monoset.com/blog/journal/a-letter-from-albert-einstein-to-his-daughter-on-the-universal-force-of-love.

Kanu, I A. (2019). On the Origin and Principles of Igwebuike Philosophy. *Journal of Religion and Human Relations*, Vol. 11 No. 1. (p.160)

Kanu, I. A. (2014). *Igwebuikology* as an Igbo-African philosophy for Catholic-Pentecostal relations. *Jos Studies. 22. pp.*87-98.

Kanu, I. A. (2015b). *Igwebuike as an ontological precondition for African ethics.* International Conference of the Society for Research and Academic Excellence. University of Nigeria, Nsukka. 14th -16th September.

Kanu, I. A. (2015c). *Igwebuike as an Igbo-African philosophy of education.* A paper presented at the International Conference on Law, Education and Humanities. 25th -26th November 2015 University of Paris, France.

Kanu, I. A. (2016a). *Igwebuike as an Igbo-African hermeneutics of globalisation. IGWEBUIKE: An African Journal of Arts and Humanities,* Vol. 2 No.1. pp. 61-66.

Kanu, I. A. (2016a). *Igwebuike* as the consummate foundation of African Bioethical principles. *An African journal of Arts and Humanities* Vol.2 No1 June, pp.23-40.

Kanu, I. A. (2016b) *Igwebuike* as an expressive modality of being in African ontology. *Journal of Environmental and Construction Management. 6. 3.* pp.12-21.

Kanu, I. A. (2017). *Igwebuike* as an Igbo-African philosophy for Christian-Muslim relations in Northern Nigeria. In Mahmoud Misaeli (Ed.). *Spirituality and Global Ethics* (pp. 300-310). United Kingdom: Cambridge Scholars.

Kanu, I. A. (2017). *Igwebuike* as an Igbo-African philosophy for the protection of the environment. *Nightingale International Journal of Humanities and Social Sciences.* Vol. 3. No. 4. pp. 28-38.

Kanu, I. A. (2017). *Igwebuike* as the hermeneutic of individuality and communality in African ontology. *NAJOP: Nasara Journal of Philosophy.* Vol. 2. No. 1. pp. 162-179.

Kanu, I. A. (2017a). *Igwebuike* and question of superiority in the scientific community of knowledge. *Igwebuike: An African Journal of Arts and Humanities.*Vol.3 No1. pp. 131-138.

Kanu, I. A. (2017a). *Igwebuike as a philosophical attribute of Africa in portraying the image of life.* A paper presented at the 2017 Oracle of Wisdom International Conference by the Department of Philosophy, Tansian University, Umunya, Anambra State, 27-29 April.

Kanu, I. A. (2017b). *Igwebuike* as a complementary approach to the issue of girl-child education. *Nightingale International Journal of Contemporary Education and Research.* Vol. 3. No. 6. pp. 11-17.

Kanu, I. A. (2017b). *Igwebuike* as a wholistic response to the problem of evil and human suffering. *Igwebuike: An African Journal of Arts and Humanities.* Vol. 3 No 2, March.

Kanu, I. A. (2017e). *Igwebuike* as an Igbo-African modality of peace and conflict resolution. *Journal of African Traditional Religion and Philosophy Scholars. Vol. 1. No. 1. pp. 31-40.*

Kanu, I. A. (2017g). *Igwebuike* and the logic (Nka) of African philosophy. *Igwebuike: An African Journal of Arts and Humanities. 3. 1.* pp. 1-13.

Kanu, I. A. (2017h). *Igwebuike* philosophy and human rights violation in Africa. *IGWEBUIKE: An African Journal of Arts and Humanities.* Vol. 3. No. 7. pp. 117-136.

Kanu, I. A. (2017i). *Igwebuike* as a hermeneutic of personal autonomy in African ontology. *Journal of African Traditional Religion and Philosophy Scholars. Vol. 2. No. 1. pp. 14-22.*

218

Kanu, I. A. (2018). *Igwe Bu Ike* as an Igbo-African hermeneutics of national development. *Igbo Studies Review. No. 6.* pp. 59-83.

Kanu, I. A. (2018). *Igwebuike* as an African integrative and progressive anthropology. *NAJOP: Nasara Journal of Philosophy.* Vol. 2. No. 1. pp. 151-161.

Kanu, I. A. (2020). COVID-19 and the Economy: An African Perspective. Published in *Journal of African Studies and Sustainable Development.* Vol. 3. No. 2. pp. 29-36. A publication of the Association for the Promotion of African Studies.

Kanu, I. A. (2020). COVID-19 Pandemic and the Health of African Migrants. *AMAMIHE: Journal of Applied Philosophy.* Vol. 18. No. 2. pp. 56-64.

Kanu, I. A. (2020). Saint Augustine and COVID-19 Pandemic: The Future and Divine Providence. *Tansian University Journal of Arts, Management and Social Sciences. Vol. 7. pp. 151-162.*

Patricia M. Amos, (2013). "Parenting and Culture – Evidence from Some African Communities". Available at http://www.intechopen.com>books>parenting-andculture

Qian, X., Ren, R., Wang, Y. *et al.(2020)* "Fighting against the common enemy of COVID-19: a practice of building a community with a shared future for mankind/ *Infectious Disease of Poverty*" Available at https ://idpjournal. Biomedcentral.com/articles/10.1186/ s40249-020-00650-1

Robert A. S., (2010). "Solidarity: The Fundamental Social Virtue", in Religion &Liberty: Vol 11, No.5

Shereen, M.A., (2019). "COVID-19 infection: Origin, transmission, and characteristics of human coronaviruses" in Journal of Advanced Research, vol. 24

The American Heritage Dictionary of the English Language, Fifth Edition (2016). Houghton Mifflin Harcourt Publishing Company.

World Health Organization (WHO), 2019. Coronavirus Disease (Covid-19) Outbreak. Available at http://www.who.int/health-topics/coronavirus/emergencies-redirect.

ABOUT THE AUTHOR

Ikechukwu Anthony KANU, O.S.A is a Friar of the Order of Saint Augustine, Province of Nigeria. He is Professor of African Philosophy and Religion, Tansian University, and a Tenured Professor of Orthodox Studies at The University of America, San Francisco, USA. The former Rector of Villanova Polytechnic, Imesi Ile, Osun State and currently an Adjunct Professor to the University of Jos, Plateau State, Veritas University Abuja and Saint Albert the Great Major Seminary, Abeokuta. He is the President of the Association for the Promotion of African Studies (APAS) and the Global President of the World Cultural Studies Research Association (WCRA).

Printed in the United States
by Baker & Taylor Publisher Services